T0246397

BEYOND BRITANNIA

Leadership: Lessons from a Life in Diplomacy

SIMON McDONALD

Beyond Britannia

Reshaping UK Foreign Policy

First published in 2023 by
Haus Publishing Ltd
4 Cinnamon Row
London SW11 3TW

Copyright © Simon McDonald, 2023

A CIP catalogue for this book is available from the British
Library

The moral right of the author has been asserted

ISBN 978-1-913368-90-6
eISBN 978-1-913368-91-3

Typeset in Sabon by MacGuru Ltd

Printed in the UK by CPI

www.hauspublishing.com

For Olivia

Contents

Still more majestic shalt thou rise,
More dreadful from each foreign stroke;
As the loud blast that tears the skies
Serves but to root thy native oak.
'Rule, Britannia, rule the waves;
Britons never will be slaves.'

James Thomson, 'Rule, Britannia!' (1740)

Preface

Before despatch to the publisher, I showed the manuscript of my first book to three people. One expressed disappointment; he thought someone who had helped shape British foreign policy for almost four decades would have more to say about the UK's role on the world stage. This is the book George wanted me to write.

At the risk of finding myself obliged to produce a third book to satisfy someone else's view of what I should write about, I must admit some of what this book is not. It is not a blueprint. It is not comprehensive; it does not cover, for example, migration, terrorism, cyber threats, or pandemics. It does not embrace any ideology; rather it advocates a few detailed policy proposals.

Grand strategic thinking is found more often among students of international relations than among foreign policy practitioners. No foreign secretary while I worked for the Foreign Office (1982–2020) had an overarching vision; their speeches set out immediate priorities or their response to the crisis of the day. Most policy thinking was short-term, responding to a developing problem or preparing for a particular meeting; thinking was modest, practical, and collaborative. Politicians in opposition, contemplating the challenges they would like to tackle, are sometimes tempted to set out their vision but, as Robin Cook discovered with his pledge of foreign policy with an 'ethical dimension', such visions tend not to survive first contact with reality.

While writing this book, I realised that my preferences for the UK's foreign policy were personal; few people would agree – and some would disagree – with everything I suggested. Although I believe my ideas make a coherent whole, they do not need to be a package to make sense; they are a menu, aimed at the next British government, a government that will have a mandate for the rest of the 2020s.

I studied history at university; I learned that, no matter what the challenge, understanding its history is key to making progess. I do not believe the UK can have a coherent foreign policy without a keen sense of its history. A 'sense of history' is different from 'sentimentality about history'. Many British commentators and politicians seem burdened by history, either regretful that the UK is not as powerful as it was or pretending that we have preserved more power than is provably the case.

My whole prescription rests on the knowledge that the UK is not as capable as it was: we can no longer impose our will on other countries; we can no longer fight a war on our own; we have less hard power than the US, China, and Russia, the only three countries that could contemplate extended conflict alone. The fact that the conflict which Russia started in Ukraine in 2014 is not going according to its plan is proof that even the small club that can contemplate conflict is better advised not to initiate it. For the UK, decisive hard power is a debilitating memory.

But we do not need to be as potent as we used to be in traditional capabilities to make a difference. We have strengths in newer ways of demonstrating power ('soft power'). We can embrace that change. If we are enthusiastic about that embrace, we can discard the remnants – the expensive, irrelevant-to-the-present-task capabilities – that still tie us to our imperial past. Unlike some, I do not believe that soft power without hard power is no power at all. Rather I believe that attachment to some of the vestiges of hard power prevents the UK from fully developing its soft power.

In all the jobs I did in the Foreign Office, I was aware of constraints, most frustratingly so in the top job. In more junior jobs, you expect constraints. When I was a child, I thought that growing up meant having more control over my life; as an adult I discovered that was a false hope. I learned in the civil service that seniority did not equate to ministers listening most carefully to me before they took decisions.

When we step back to contemplate the bigger picture, we tend not to be satisfied by modesty or pragmatism, but in diplomacy they generally work best. Especially when confronted by a blank piece of paper, policy planners are tempted to throw their weight about. But humility and incrementalism are robust and sensible policy choices. It took me my whole career to learn that railing against constraints is pointless; it is better to incorporate them. What follows tries to incorporate the constraints that limit the UK's plausible ambition in the world, to be honest that the history, geography, and money we have are more important than alternatives we would wistfully prefer.

I start this book with an account of the day when everything changed for British foreign policymakers; I then look back (centuries) to make sense of that moment before looking forward to what a medium-sized power might do next. Unless clearly not the case, 'we' and 'our' refer to the United Kingdom.

I need to thank many people but name only George Busby, Richard Mortier, and Richard Wilson, and I dedicate the book to the most wonderful person of all, Olivia.

PART I

Background

1

Starting Point: 24 June 2016

What the UK does next starts with Boris Johnson. Until Johnson joined the Leave campaign in February 2016, David Cameron was confident of Remain winning the referendum to decide the UK's future relationship with the European Union (EU). In some ways, Johnson is an unlikely champion of Britishness. For a member of the British establishment, his ancestry is unusually exotic. When I was permanent under-secretary (PUS), my Turkish opposite number explained the importance of my new boss' Turkish roots. First, he owed his physical appearance to his Turkish ancestors. Blonde hair and a big frame are characteristic of the inhabitants of Kalfat, a remote village on the high Anatolian plateau, where the family of Johnson's great-grandfather, Ali Kemal, came from. Second, Turkey helped form Johnson's character. Kemal was a journalist and rebel, whose liberal views led to him falling out successively with absolutist Sultan Abdul Hamid II and the Young Turks who overthrew the sultan. During his first banishment from the Ottoman Empire, Kemal met and wooed Winifred Brun in Switzerland; they married in England (home of Brun's mother) in 1903.

After the Young Turk Revolution in 1908, Kemal returned briefly to Constantinople, where he unsuccessfully contested a parliamentary seat for the Liberal Party. The victorious Young Turks accused Kemal and his party of conspiring with

Armenians, the Ottomans' bitterest internal foe, so he fled with his family to England, where Winifred gave birth to their third child, a son called Osman Wilfred Kemal, in Bournemouth in 1909. She died of puerperal fever shortly afterwards.

Kemal returned to the Ottoman Empire, marrying a second time. His English mother-in-law was unhappy that her late daughter's two surviving children were being brought up in such a precarious household. Osman and his sister Celma eventually settled with her. She gave them her maiden name, and Osman became known as Wilfred Johnson (the name by which his grandson Boris knew him). The two children had lived most of their lives in England by the time their father was murdered, aged fifty-three, in 1922.

When one of Elizabeth II's ladies-in-waiting explained to Her Majesty the proximity of Turkey in Boris Johnson's ancestry, the queen remarked that the relationship was as close as hers to Prince George. Indeed. Johnson, too, has a royal German connection – a fact he has referred to humorously in speeches. Wilfred Johnson married Irene Williams, the great-granddaughter of Baron Karl Pfeffel von Kriegelstein and his wife, Karoline von Rottenburg, the illegitimate daughter of Prince Paul of Württemberg. Prince Paul's father was Frederick I, the first king of Württemberg. The fact that Frederick I was immense in every way – 2.12 m tall and over 200 kg in weight – provided his great-great-great-great-great-grandson with amusing, self-deprecating material for speeches two centuries after his death.

I first met Boris Johnson in November 2004, when I was British ambassador to Israel and he was visiting as part of a delegation organised by Conservative Friends of Israel for new MPs and parliamentary candidates; he had been elected for Henley three years earlier. The delegation included George Osborne and Theresa Villiers. Despite the presence of two other future cabinet ministers, Johnson made the biggest impact on his hosts. I asked Yair Lapid – at the time a journalist but later prime minister of Israel – which MP he thought would go furthest in politics. Unhesitatingly he replied, 'Boris!'

Our next encounter was fleeting. Johnson was campaigning for election as mayor of London. One spring morning in 2008, I was walking to the Cabinet Office from Waterloo station when I spotted the candidate in the middle distance on one of the Golden Jubilee Bridges, surrounded by a flock of Central Office types. As we passed, I caught his eye. His look was sheepish. We did not speak but his shrug of the shoulders implied, 'I have to submit to what these bozos demand.'

Our third encounter was three weeks after he changed the UK and its foreign policy possibilities forever.

Before becoming the Leave campaign's mascot and physical embodiment, Johnson didn't disguise his hesitation about choosing sides. He drafted two articles for the *Sunday Telegraph*, each passionately making a diametrically opposed case; by his own account, he veered between them like a man trying to control a shopping trolley before submitting the 'leave' version. Dominic Cummings later adopted the shopping trolley as his emoji of choice to represent Johnson in his tweets.

Since the newspaper published his 'leave' article on 21 February 2016, Johnson has displayed the zeal of a convert. Other leavers embraced him as enthusiastically as early Christians embraced St Paul: the man who could have crushed them led them instead to victory. By the time he resigned as foreign secretary in July 2018, his every act was compatible with his role as the leavers' standard bearer. But I was not convinced by his conversion. I observed that Johnson hated the trappings of the EU, the popinjay presidents and proliferating institutions, its ambition to displace its member states on the global stage, the fact that it was all undeniably continental in ethos and outlook. But he knew almost nothing about the economics of membership; until he came to the Foreign and Commonwealth Office (FCO), he did not know how the single market worked, what a customs union was, or how the EU negotiated.

By the time he resigned from the FCO, his reputation was inextricably bound to Brexit. However nuanced his feelings in 2016, two years later they were adamantine: Brexit was essential to the UK's prosperity and standing on the world stage. What had started as a 50:50 proposition had come to define him. Contemplating the Republicans' programme when they replaced the Democrats as the majority in the House of Representatives in 1953, the long-serving speaker, Sam Rayburn, said that 'any jackass can kick a barn down, but it takes a good carpenter to build one'. Boris Johnson was haunted by the possibility that he was merely a jackass; he needed to prove that he was a good carpenter, building a better future for the UK.

Friday 24 June 2016 was the most dramatic day in my FCO career. My wife Olivia and I were living in Fulham. After midnight, we settled down to watch the BBC's referendum coverage. Jeremy Vine explained that analysts had looked at each constituency and calculated the strength of the leave vote needed in each to suggest a leave victory. Polling during the campaign indicated that cities, Scotland, Northern Ireland, and the South East were more strongly pro-EU; rural areas, Wales, and the North, East, and South West were more pro-Leave.

With the groundwork established, we awaited the first results. The smallest unit – Gibraltar – reported first with a pro-Remain vote of over 90 per cent. I noted that even this thumping majority for Remain was slightly less than BBC modelling had predicted. Newcastle declared first in England. Again, it voted Remain but by a significantly smaller majority than the BBC modelling suggested was needed for an overall Remain victory. A large university city was less persuaded by the benefits of remaining in the UK than the Remain campaign needed if it were to win.

Sunderland declared next. The result came in at 12:16 a.m. According to the BBC's model, Sunderland had to vote Remain for Remain to win overall. It voted Leave. As the returning officer read out the result, Leave campaigners in the hall were jubilant. Margaret Thatcher had persuaded Nissan to build a flagship factory in Sunderland in the 1980s (still the most efficient car production line in the world) because cars made there had direct, duty-free access to the huge European Economic Community (EEC) market. I saw people whose manufacturing jobs were dependent on UK membership of the EU rejoicing at the suddenly realistic prospect of leaving. I looked at Olivia. 'We're going to leave,' I said. 'I'm going to bed.'

I barely slept. I tried to decide what I would say to staff in the morning. I came up with five points. Years later, when I was telling a Cambridge audience about that day, a student asked if I could remember all five; I could not. The two that were discarded when I met directors general (DGs) had disappeared from my memory. After four hours' tossing and turning, I got up. Downstairs, I found Olivia in tears. David Dimbleby was in the middle of declaring that the UK would leave the EU.

My car arrived before 6 a.m. DGs met in my office just after 6:30 a.m. We were joined by directors after about half an hour. They refined three of my points and persuaded me to junk the other two. We decided to hold an all-staff meeting at 2 p.m., when most of the network around the world would be able to tune in. About 400 people would be able to fit into the Locarno Reception Room, the grandest in the FCO, and open phone lines would connect colleagues unable to cram into the room. Before my early morning meeting broke up, the press office heard that the prime minister was expected to make a major announcement in Downing Street at 8:15 a.m. Some stayed to watch the TV in the corner of my private secretaries' office as David Cameron accepted responsibility and resigned. Then DGs left to brief their teams. Later one of them reminded me that, as they filed out, I said something like, 'Our world has just changed. Don't pretend it hasn't.' Then silence descended on SW1. We had no word from Number 10 or the Cabinet Office for the rest of the day.

In the void, I resolved to hold a meeting for colleagues from around Whitehall. I also decided to post regularly on the FCO's intranet. I could feel the bewilderment around the building. Colleagues wanted any scrap of information. I posted a score of messages over the course of the day, simply keeping people up to date with what I was doing. At 10:30 a.m., two dozen senior civil servants gathered in the media suite. They hailed from the Cabinet Office, Home Office, and Ministry of Defence; they came because they had nowhere else to go.

At 11:30 a.m., I went to Buckingham Palace; new ambassadors from Israel and Georgia were presenting their letters of credence, the necessary formality before they could begin their work as their governments' representatives in the UK. In the middle of my busiest day I saw the queen, in a half-hour of calm before I returned to the fray.

The all-staff meeting at 2 p.m. was the tensest of the nineteen I held as PUS. The room was packed, with colleagues peering through the two sets of huge double doors into the Locarno Dining Room. Over 2,000 phone lines were open, allowing colleagues from Washington (9 a.m. local time) to New Delhi (6:30 p.m.) to tune in. Later I heard that people joined from beaches and hotel rooms on holiday. I felt, but did not know for sure, that the audience was in shock, most having voted Remain; I knew that some had voted Leave but had no sense of how many.

In the moment, I decided to share, for the first and last time in my career, how I voted; I told them that I had voted Remain. I knew the Leave campaign assumed that senior civil servants were overwhelmingly remainers, and I would not pretend otherwise. But so what? My personal convictions were irrelevant to the task ahead. Like everyone else in the Locarno Suite and listening in from around the world, I was a diplomat whose task was clear. We were civil servants who worked to deliver the policies of the government of the day within the law. The rules of the referendum were novel; referendums are rare in the UK. And even though formally it had been consultative, both sides had campaigned on the basis that the result would bind Parliament. Although the activist Gina Miller had yet to engage the law firm Mishcon de Reya to challenge the idea that the executive could trigger Article 50 of the Lisbon Treaty (the formal route out) without consulting Parliament, I assumed that the referendum had definitively decided that the UK would leave the EU.

I wanted everyone, including ministers in the incoming government, to know that personal preferences would not affect professional duty. My duty as a civil servant was to protect and promote UK interests as best I could in delivering the policy of the new government. I then set out the three points, as modified by DGs at dawn.

First, I said that the result was final. I noted that commentators were already speculating that the UK might reconsider, that there might be a second referendum to decide whether the exit deal when negotiated was a strong enough basis for departure. I advised everyone to ignore the froth. At some point in the not-too-distant future, the UK would leave the EU.

Second, I said that the forthcoming negotiation would be all-consuming for the whole of the government, and the FCO would be central to the effort. Other important work would have to be put on ice. Colleagues would be diverted to the new task. Until the day we left, Brexit would be our single biggest task.

And, third, I said that the UK would come through this momentous rupture. We had faced tougher challenges in the past. We would be changed – and we would not merely survive but flourish. Looking ahead, the FCO's work would increase; since 1973, UKRep, the UK's permanent representation in Brussels, had housed ever more officials from domestic departments as areas of EU competence grew. That would stop and be reversed. As I told colleagues, 'Foreign just got a whole lot bigger.'

Over the remaining four years of my PUS-ship, the basic messages did not change. I spent less time mourning than some of my permanent-secretary colleagues and their teams. In retrospect, I rationalise this as (a) an acknowledgement that some colleagues were celebrating rather than grieving and (b) a belief that personal feelings should not distract from a professional task. I focused on the future.

My last meeting of the day was with ambassadors of EU member states. They were visibly shocked. With them, I made three different points. First, that they and their capitals should be clear that the civil service's role was to implement the policy of the new government, and that Brexit would be the key policy of the next prime minister. Second, that although our work together would change, it would be just as intense. Collectively, we needed to reach a new modus vivendi that worked for everyone. And, third, that the UK had voted to leave one of more than eighty international organisations of which it was a member. We remained close neighbours and allies through the North Atlantic Treaty Organization (NATO). We would disappear from the Berlaymont building but not from the rest of their professional lives.

At some point in the following fortnight, as we waited for

the Conservative Party to decide who should succeed David Cameron, I met directors again. I launched the idea that motivated me to write this book. Could it be that historians would see 24 June 2016 as a decisive watershed in British history? The rise and fall of a great power takes time. But, looking back, countries suffer acute crises that catalyse long and slow trends already underway. I mentioned Spain in the seventeenth century.

At the end of the sixteenth century, Philip II had ruled one of the largest empires the world had ever seen. He had bemoaned and belittled his heir: 'God, who has given me so many kingdoms, has denied me a son capable of ruling them.'[1] But Philip III was in some ways more successful than his father. In Hugh Trevor-Roper's assessment, 'In the decade after 1610, Philip III seemed "monarch of the world", more powerful in peace than his father had been in war.'[2]

Nevertheless, by the time Philip IV succeeded his father, Spain was undeniably on the slide, piling up debt and losing ground to France, which was emerging from the inactivity Marie de' Medici preferred while steadying the state after the assassination of her husband, Henry IV, in 1610. By the mid-1620s, when Richelieu was First Minister to Marie de' Medici's son, Louis XIII, France was eclipsing Spain. But by any measure the Spanish king remained the second most powerful monarch in Europe. Decline was disguised by occasional successes and enduring magnificence, as recorded in the royal portraits by Rubens and Velázquez. At its peak, the Spanish Empire was not uniformly splendid: the system of collecting taxes was always corrupt and inefficient, and provinces remote from the Iberian Peninsula rebelled frequently.

Decline is compatible with continued power, but sometimes single events trigger a reassessment of how steep the decline really is. That happened in Spain on 17 September 1665, when King Philip IV died aged sixty in Madrid. Like all Habsburgs, he had tried to provide his empire with an heir. But his first marriage had produced only one son, Balthasar, who died just before his seventeenth birthday in 1646. (Only one of his six daughters by Elisabeth of France survived to adulthood: Maria Theresa, who became the first wife of Louis XIV.) His second marriage, to his niece Maria Anna of Austria, produced a daughter, Margaret Theresa, who married the Holy Roman Emperor, Leopold I. Three other children did not live to see their fourth birthdays. But in 1661, Maria Anna gave birth to a son, Charles, who succeeded Philip as King Charles II on 17 September 1665.

It was already clear that, aged four, Charles was unlikely to have a healthy, long life, even if he reached adulthood. Given that only two of his eleven legitimate siblings had survived to adulthood, few people expected him to live long. He was Exhibit A for the perils of in-breeding: stunted, epileptic, Habsburg-jawed, and rickety. His mother became regent, and government continued. But his illegitimate half-brother opposed her rule. As regent, Maria Anna was holding the fort until the king could take over, yet the court had reason to doubt that he would ever be able to. King Charles II embodied the Spanish state; he held territory across Europe and the New World by right of inheritance. A vigorous monarch was necessary for the system to work; Charles's evident weakness had immediate and irreparable consequences for the state.

Spain did not disappear from the world stage. It did not give up its efforts to defend and promote its interests, but it did cease to have agency in the world. It became the target of other rulers' ambitions. Charles's inability to produce an heir fired the imaginations of Europe's other leading powers. His family's policy of intermarriage with other dynasties had left both the Holy Roman Empire and France with aspirations to occupy a throne which from the 1660s they calculated would fall vacant without a direct heir. After Charles's death in 1700, Spain became a field for others to fight over.

The transition had been decades in the making, but it crystallised on one day: the day the four-year-old invalid Charles became king. In that meeting with my colleagues in July 2016, I wondered whether historians might one day view 24 June 2016 for Britain in the same way as they did 17 September 1665 for Spain. My inexact thesis attracted immediate criticism from a future British ambassador at Madrid, but it took up residence in my head. On 24 June 2016, did the UK irreversibly damage its ability to act on the world stage? This book is an extended answer to that question. Before taking a stab at that answer, I consider how we got where we are today and what foreign policy options are available to a country suddenly confronted by a watershed in its history.

2

British History That Matters

Jack Straw was surprised to become foreign secretary in June 2001. Later he told me that it was a job he had always wanted one day, but he had been expecting to become transport secretary after the re-election of Tony Blair's government. After energetic family celebrations, he flew to Luxembourg for a meeting of the EU's Foreign Affairs Council and threw himself into the detail of a dozen policy issues.

Even before arriving in King Charles Street, Straw read a lot of history. His *Desert Island Discs* book was Michael Howard's *The Franco-Prussian War: The German Invasion of France, 1870–1871*. He drew on his wide reading when putting together his ambitions as foreign secretary. Sitting in the vast gilt-and-red-leather office commissioned by Lord Palmerston, he often mused about the nineteenth century; he drew my attention to the story of Don Pacifico.

David Pacifico was born in about 1784 in Gibraltar (or possibly Oran in North Africa). As with all practising Castilian and Aragonese Jews, his ancestors had been expelled from Spain in 1492. They made their way to Tuscany, where they lived for several generations before his grandfather returned to Iberia, settling in Gibraltar. Pacifico lived in Portugal during its civil war (1828–1834), supporting the liberals. When they prevailed, he was rewarded with Portuguese citizenship and a consulship in Morocco.

In 1837, he transferred to Athens, where he served as Portuguese consul-general. For apparently exceeding his instructions, he was sacked in 1842 but remained in the city, a prosperous businessman and prominent member of the Jewish community. According to his own account, he was minding his own business when his house became the focal point of local ire at Easter 1849.

Not unusually, the Greek government of the day was strapped for cash. Hoping to raise a loan, ministers persuaded James Mayer de Rothschild to visit in April 1849. His visit coincided with Orthodox Easter, when locals traditionally burned an effigy of Judas Iscariot. Fearing that the practice might offend a visitor they were hoping to impress, the authorities banned it. Reacting badly, a crowd descended on Pacifico's house, blaming him for the cancellation.

Three days later, Pacifico wrote to Edmund Lyons, British minister at Athens, complaining:

> It is with much grief that I feel myself obliged to communicate to your Excellency a dreadful event which has happened to me, and as an English subject to beg your protection. Last Sunday, Easter-day, at about 12 o'clock, a crowd of people ... presented themselves at the door of my house, which they very soon battered down ... These brigands, in number about 300 or 400, entered my house, and swearing dreadfully, began beating my [family]. After having broken ... every article of furniture, they robbed me of my jewels ... vases, candlesticks, gold and silver ornaments, diamonds, and lastly a box containing money to the amount of 9,800 drachmas, of which 2,300 were my own private property, and 7,500 [of] which had been deposited with me by the Jewish community of Italy ... These barbarians did not even leave me the Consular Portuguese archives, which were torn by

them to pieces. These papers being my security from that nation for the sum of 21,295 l. 1s. 4d. sterling.³

Next month, Lyons informed the Foreign Office that he had applied to the Greek government for compensation for Don David Pacifico, a British subject. Palmerston, foreign secretary at the time, took up the case. By the end of the year, dissatisfied with Greek foot-dragging, Palmerston set out the action he proposed to take in a letter to Lyons's successor as minister:

> I have desired the Admiralty to instruct Sir William Parker to take Athens on his way back from the Dardanelles, and to support you in bringing at last to a satisfactory ending the settlement of our various claims upon the Greek Government. You will, of course, in conjunction with him, persevere in the *suaviter in modo* as long as is consistent with our dignity and honour, and I measure that time by days – perhaps by some very small number of hours. If however, the Greek Government does not strike, Parker must do so ... that is, by taking possession of some Greek property; but the King would probably not much care for our taking hold of any merchant property, and the best thing, therefore, would be to seize hold of his little fleet, if that can be done handily. The next thing would be a blockade of any or all of his ports.⁴

On 22 January 1850, Parker sent word that he had seized the Greek government's entire fleet. The British quarrel with Greece went wider than Don Pacifico's claims, but he became the focus of parliamentary unhappiness with Palmerston's high-handedness. The House of Lords passed a motion rebuking the foreign secretary. In the House of Commons, Palmerston (whose Irish peerage allowed him to sit as an MP) delivered a five-hour speech seeking to vindicate not only his handling of the Don Pacifico affair but his whole conduct of foreign policy:

> As the Roman, in days of old, held himself free from indignity, when he could say *Civis Romanus sum*, so also a British subject, in whatever land he may be, shall feel confident that the watchful eye and the strong arm of England will protect him from injustice and wrong.[5]

In particular, he took issue with the anti-Semitic prejudice that 'because a man is of the Jewish persuasion, he is fair game for any outrage'.[6] Her Majesty's Government persuaded the Commons to support Palmerston's policies. A special commission decided Don Pacifico's compensation; eventually he received 120,000 drachmas and £500.

The story is a textbook example of 'gunboat diplomacy'. Whatever the merits of Don Pacifico's complaints, Palmerston's critics felt that his response was disproportionate, that he wanted to teach King Otto of Greece a wider lesson than the unwisdom of showing a cold shoulder to a cashiered Portuguese consul-general who happened to be born in a British colony. In an earlier parliamentary debate, in 1848, Palmerston coined advice that Jack Straw and every other British foreign secretary I've worked for has quoted: 'We have no eternal allies, and we have no perpetual enemies. Our interests are eternal and perpetual, and those interests it is our duty to follow.'[7]

In the intervening 175 years, it has become harder for the UK to defend those interests alone. Commentators (less often practitioners) often fail to acknowledge the UK's reduced capabilities: Palmerston's spirit lives on. To explain why, I propose ten elements of Britishness, handed down by history, that continue to fuel a Palmerstonian presumption of British exceptionalism:

- early unification – of England in 927, of Great Britain in 1707, and of the United Kingdom in 1801 – providing the basis for stable internal government, ruled by an elite adept at co-opting potential opponents and aware of its imperfections, which are generally addressed by incremental change rather than revolution;
- a unique ability over the last thousand years not merely to repel invaders (consider Russia) but also to prevent would-be invaders from making landfall;
- a presumed superiority over its neighbours, particularly the French, who until recent times had greater heft internationally and a notably larger population;
- equality before the (common) law, dating back to time immemorial (the death of Henry II in 1189) and the Magna Carta in 1215;
- pride in muddling through, combined with inventiveness, preferring empirical to theoretical methods to solve problems, trusting and elevating the amateur above the professional ('keep calm and carry on' rivals 'Dieu et mon droit' as the national motto);
- good manners at all times ('manners makyth man' is the motto of Winchester College, England's oldest public school), preferring modesty to display, and quiet pride in behaving with dignity in defeat;
- a national church which embodies, safeguards, and spreads its confident understanding of Christ's teaching, with an emphasis on helping those less fortunate;
- commercial flair, with Napoleon's purported jibe that 'the English are a nation of shopkeepers' worn as a badge of honour;
- a sense of responsibility to protect liberty, democracy, and human rights, which (in the view of its elite) the British did more than any other nation to develop and

then propagate elsewhere, linked to a willingness to be 'last man standing', defending core beliefs when other countries have given up the fight; and

- a sense of fair play, fostered in team sports, and embracing a preference for the underdog, even when the UK has no dog in the fight.

All ten propositions were seeded long ago in British history, and all ten can be disputed in general and proved wrong in detail. But then no national legend survives close examination; Britons are not unusual in preferring not to delve into disagreeable aspects of their past. Self-image is mostly myth. So, most Britons are ignorant about their history. Shamefaced, I include myself. Travelling the world on government business, I was struck that officials I met invariably knew more about British involvement in their country than I did.

Facts do not change, but we choose which facts to remember. Countries collectively write their own narratives, cherry-picking facts and ascribing motivation in order to fit that overall narrative. National narratives are characterised by grand sweep rather than granular accuracy. What follows is a personal selection of episodes in British history that best illustrate the UK's appreciation of itself, illuminated by the ten propositions.

In common with most countries, the four nations of the UK believe their early history was embattled. Difficult circumstances were temporary; even when protracted, they ended, as witnessed when the country was uniting internally and then expanding internationally. Heroic failure was consistently celebrated, even glorified. But the fact that historically the Scots' main external enemy was the English resonates. Even though the invention of Great Britain could be seen as a reverse takeover, many Scots still resent their southern neighbours.

According to W. C. Sellar and R. J. Yeatman, the first of only two 'Genuine Dates' in British history was 55 BC, when Julius Caesar invaded but failed to hold Britain. The following century, under Claudius, the Romans came back and stayed. Local resistance to foreign occupation is the main thing British schoolchildren learn about the 400-year Roman occupation of southern Britain. Caractacus led the way, but Boadicea is more fondly remembered (the British memorialise strong female leaders). Thomas Thornycroft worked on a statue of Boadicea from the 1850s until his death in 1885; it was cast in bronze in 1902 and placed at the western end of Westminster Bridge opposite the Houses of Parliament.

Britons know only dimly about the invasions by Angles, Saxons, Jutes, and Vikings in the six centuries after the Romans left. The Angles gave England its name, and the Saxons gave England its first hero king, Alfred the Great, an autodidact and lousy cook, who saw the potential of ships to defeat invaders before they made landfall. The Angles and Saxons combined to give the country an alternative adjective that is still used today (mainly when distinguishing the British Isles from anything 'continental').

Danish Vikings interrupted the process of English unification, which had advanced under Alfred. At the start, the Vikings raided and went home. Then they exacted Danegeld, a tax raised as a bribe not to wreak havoc. Finding that they could constantly raise the price, they delayed complete conquest but eventually moved in. The unwisdom of giving in to bullies was a lasting lesson; in 1940, Winston Churchill defined an appeaser as 'one who feeds a crocodile hoping it will eat him last.'

Over time, the Danes became domesticated; posterity treats them as local as much as foreign. Their most famous king, Cnut, still gives schoolchildren a lesson in vainglory. As with many favourite British stories, appearances are deceptive. Look closer and the apparently stupid is in fact profound. In *Our Island Story* (published in 1905 and David Cameron's favourite childhood book), Henrietta Marshall rescues the reputation of King Cnut, when he was still Canute: 'a great king, for he ruled not only over England, but over Denmark, Norway and Sweden'. His nobles miscalculated the power of flattery. Marshall illustrates her point:

> One day, as they were walking upon the seashore, the nobles began, as usual, to tell Canute how powerful he was.
>
> 'All England obeys you,' they said. 'And not only England... Should you desire it, you need but command all the nations of the world and they will kneel down before you as their king and lord. You are King on sea and land. Even the waves obey you.'
>
> Now this was foolish talk. And Canute, who was a wise man, did not like it. He thought he would teach these silly nobles a lesson. So he ordered his servants to bring a chair.
>
> When they had brought it, he made them set it on the shore, close to the waves. The servants did as they were told, and Canute sat down, while the nobles stood around him.
>
> Then Canute spoke to the waves. 'Go back,' he said, 'I am your lord and master, and I command you not to flow over my land. Go back, and do not dare to wet my feet.'
>
> But the sea, of course, neither heard nor obeyed him. The tide was coming in, and the waves rolled nearer and nearer until the king's feet and robe were wet.
>
> Then Canute rose, and turning sternly to his nobles said, 'Do you still tell me that I have power over the waves? Oh! foolish men, do you not know that to God alone belongs such power? He alone rules earth and sky and sea, and we and they alike are His subjects, and must obey Him.'

A key part of the lesson for my primary school teacher was Cnut's wisdom. For a long time, Miss Field explained, Cnut's reputation suffered because people had focused on the fact that he sat enthroned on the beach trying to defy nature rather than on the reason why he made the vain effort. The lesson was that we should look at motives as well as actions: Cnut had been trying to demonstrate to his courtiers the limits of his power; he never had any expectation that he could order the tide to turn. Everyone recalling the story they learned as a child knows that Cnut was not a sap, but whenever he is cited it is always as a pompous ignoramus; it seems that the idea of a stupid leader appeals more than the idea of a wise one.

Brits widely view the invasion of William the Conqueror as the 'last home defeat' (the invitation issued by seven peers to William of Orange to unseat James II disqualifying the landing at Brixham in 1688). Even today, 1066 – the second 'Genuine Date' – is one of the UK's top passcodes for security systems. Having succumbed for a final time nearly 1,000 years ago, the UK has adopted defiance of would-be invaders as its unique selling point.

In a wholly unscientific survey of Brits I know, the two main episodes remembered from school history lessons are the Second World War and the Spanish Armada. In 1588, Philip II of Spain sent a fleet of over 130 ships to invade England. His new commander, the Duke of Medina Sidonia, though successful as a general on land, had no naval experience; worse, he was unlucky. By contrast, the English commanders were as competent as they were fortunate. Under Francis Drake and Charles Howard, the English harried the Spanish the length of the Channel; eight fireships scattered most of the Spanish fleet outside Calais before the English and their Dutch allies inflicted a crushing defeat at the Battle of Gravelines.

Queen Elizabeth I addressed her troops the next day at Tilbury:

Let tyrants fear ... I am come amongst you ... being resolved, in the midst and heat of battle, to live and die amongst you all – to lay down for my God, and for my kingdom, and for my people, my honour and my blood, even in the dust. I know I have the body of a weak and feeble woman; but I have the heart and stomach of a king – and of a King of England too, and think foul scorn that Parma or Spain, or any prince of Europe, should dare to invade the borders of my realm.

In the Second World War, Hitler's armies marched across Europe encountering only ineffective resistance in the final months of 1939 and first months of 1940. After the Nazis' invasion of Norway in April, some in the British government openly speculated that it could be better for the UK to sue for peace. By choosing Churchill rather than Edward Wood, earl of Halifax, to replace Chamberlain, the House of Commons resolved to fight on. After the fall of France in June 1940, the UK was the only European country continuing to fight. In June 1941, Hitler turned on his erstwhile ally, launching Operation Barbarossa against the Soviet Union, the largest invasion in human history. The British had to wait another six months for the US to enter the war, when the Japanese bombed Pearl Harbor. Reflecting on the contrasting contributions of the three main allies, Stalin is often quoted as saying: 'To defeat Nazism, the British gave time, the US gave money, and the Soviets gave blood.'

As well as nurturing a belief in being the doughty underdog able to repel all comers, Britons have taken pleasure in being the nastiest thorn in the side of the French. Stephen Clarke went so far as to call his 2010 bestseller *1000 Years of Annoying the French* (recommended to me by a future British ambassador at Paris). Of those 1000 years, a significant proportion was occupied by the Hundred Years' War, for a more balanced treatment of which I recommend Jonathan Sumption's magnum opus.

For more than 110 years in the fourteenth and fifteenth centuries, the English harried the French. In the 1330s, Edward III began making the case that he was the legitimate king of France, arguing that, after the Capetian dynasty died out in the male line, his claim was strongest as the eldest surviving grandson of Philip IV (his mother, Isabella, was the only one of Philip's children whose sons survived to adulthood). But twenty years earlier the peers of France had invented (or, by their own account, rediscovered) the Salic law, which recognised the claim only of male heirs in the male line. At the time, Philip V, younger brother of the unmourned Louis the Stubborn, wanted to displace his niece; the peers of France preferred a king in apparent good health to a girl whose legitimacy was openly disputed. Queen Isabella had been instrumental in exposing the infidelity of her sisters-in-law, Margaret (wife of Louis the Stubborn) and Blanche (wife of their younger brother, Charles). She gave each an embroidered coin purse of unmistakable design; when the Aunay brothers, the suspected lovers of the royal sisters-in-law, were later seen publicly flaunting the purses, their adultery was exposed. The Tour de Nesle affair ended with the execution of the Aunays and a cloud hanging over the legitimacy of Joan, Margaret's only surviving child by Louis, born just two years before the scandal broke.

King Edward III's counsellors never accepted the validity of the Salic law. The fact that women had inheritance rights was key to the dynastic policies of every ruling family. Heiresses were necessary for the system to function: they were courted, their husbands able to add their wives' lands to theirs. Women were key players – if not usually personally powerful ones – in medieval politics. Canon law required a dispensation for a marriage between remote cousins; if the betrothed had great-great-great-great-great-grandparents in common, the church had to approve the match. Which meant that the pope had to approve most dynastic marriages. He was not a neutral observer; he could and did block or promote the marital ambitions of kings, dukes, and counts.

The descendants of Hugh Capet were as unusual as they were fortunate; the Capetian kings produced an unbroken line of male heirs for twelve generations, with fathers living long enough for their sons to take over without the need for regencies (with a single exception: Blanche of Castile acted as regent for her twelve-year-old son, Louis IX). The run of good fortune ran out with Louis IX's grandson, Philip IV. Although three of Philip's sons survived to adulthood, none produced a male heir who lived longer than one week. When Philip IV's youngest son, Charles IV, died in 1328, his Valois cousin, Philip VI, had the strongest claim under Salic law to succeed him.

At the accession council, Edward III's representative disputed the validity of Salic law, but Philip of Valois was everyone else's choice. Edward waited until Philip tried to deprive him of Gascony, his French province, before reasserting his claim and quartering the three lions of England with the three lilies of France on his coat of arms. He attracted support from others with a quarrel with the French throne (mostly in Flanders), but the peers of France never wavered in their preference for Philip VI; they did not want a foreign king.

The English were organised and focused enough to challenge France repeatedly. Edward III recruited a volunteer army at a time when most princes relied on mercenaries. His sons were more interested in victory than chivalry. On three occasions English armies, specifically their longbow archers, inflicted comprehensive defeats on the French and rocked the French state to its foundations. Despite spectacular victories, the English never stood a chance in the long run: too small, too alien, and too intermittent in their fighting. And the pope at Avignon remained the puppet of the French king. Edward planned a brilliant marriage for his fourth son, Edmund of Langley: Margaret of Mâle was heir to the county of Flanders; if Flanders had fallen under English control, the tide of the war might have been diverted. But Pope Innocent VI withheld the necessary dispensation. Instead, a French pope favoured the cause of Philip of Burgundy, favourite son of John II of France.

Throughout the war, English tactics were designed to discomfort rather than displace the Valois. Their main military operation was the *chevauchée*, a brutal long-distance raid, mounted with no intention of holding territory, designed rather to terrify the locals and deprive the king of France of revenue. Successes were generally smaller than was celebrated at the time. King John II was the biggest ransom prize of the age of chivalry, taken prisoner at the Battle of Poitiers, but the treaties he negotiated in captivity in London were not endorsed by those who had to implement their provisions in France. Eventually, the hostage died in Savoy Palace with the desired ransom largely unpaid. Throughout history, victors have found it difficult to resist the temptation to exploit their (usually temporary) dominance. Even though they may be able to extract crushing concessions from the frazzled negotiators of the defeated, these rarely survive long in practice.

King Henry V got closest among English pretenders to securing the prize of the French throne; in 1420, the Treaty of Troyes named him as heir to the feckless Charles VI of France, but he predeceased his French rival by two months. His infant son was proclaimed king of France in Paris but never crowned in Reims. Joan of Arc embraced the cause of the son Charles VI had disinherited when recognising Henry V as his heir; she called him 'Dauphin' until his coronation as Charles VII in Reims in 1429.

Hostilities flared occasionally for another generation. The Battle of Castillon on 17 July 1453 is less well known in the UK than Crecy, Poitiers, or Agincourt but proved more decisive historically. The English took more than 100 years to surrender the last of their French territories, losing Calais only in 1558, but France remained Britain's European bogeyman until Germany united towards the end of the nineteenth century. The British invaded occasionally (usually at the invitation of some French faction) but never again held French territory for long (occupying Corsica only briefly in the 1790s). The rivalry was conducted principally in the two countries' colonies.

King Henry VIII was one of the most consequential English monarchs yet is these days best remembered for the consequences of marriage to him for his six wives. He broke with Rome in a peculiarly English way, resisting the Lutheran, Calvinist, and Zwinglian forms of protest. He dissolved the monasteries. He raised commoners with the humblest origins to the highest offices in government: Thomas Wolsey ended as a cardinal but started life as the son of an Ipswich butcher; Thomas Cromwell ended as an earl but started as the son of a Putney brewer. Henry increased the distance between monarch and subjects (being the first to be addressed as 'Majesty') and increased the power of the executive. Debating the practicalities of 'taking back control' after the UK's exit from the EU, Parliament in the 2020s spends much time disputing the government's preference for 'Henry VIII clauses' in legislation, clauses that enable ministers to amend or repeal provisions in an Act of Parliament using secondary legislation, which is subject to less parliamentary scrutiny than most parliamentarians would like.

Henry VIII was the last English king to aspire to the imperial throne. After the death of Maximilian I, Holy Roman Emperor, on 12 January 1519, three candidates presented themselves in Frankfurt the following June: Charles, archduke of Austria and king of Spain; Francis I, king of France; and Henry. Charles prevailed with stronger ties of blood (being grandson of the late emperor) and territory (boasting more land within the Holy Roman Empire's borders than either of his rivals; Henry had none), and much deeper pockets for the bribing of the seven electors. After Frederick III of Saxony publicly declared for Charles, the other six prince-electors fell quickly into line and Charles was elected unanimously on 28 June.

The election was the last time the imperial succession was seriously contested until the death of Charles VI in 1740. But contemporaries had no reason to suspect that would be the case. Henry believed that having a male heir would bolster his claim next time the imperial throne fell vacant. The English throne had already been occupied by a woman, but women were specifically excluded from the imperial succession (in 1745, after the brief reign of Charles VII, electors chose Francis I, the husband of Maria Theresa, who was the elder surviving child of Charles VI and ruled over most imperial territory).

By the end of the 1530s, Henry VIII was father to two girls and one sickly infant boy. After one dynastic marriage and two love matches with English women, he was persuaded to seek a second dynastic marriage. Cromwell's choice was Anne, sister of the duke of Cleves. He recognised that England faced new dangers. While Henry's relations with Charles V and Francis I had see-sawed over time, England had always benefited from the fact that the Empire and France were traditional enemies of each other. But in the late 1530s this was no longer reliably the case.

Cromwell advocated an alliance with the Schmalkaldic League of German Protestant principalities in order to deter invasion. Henry accepted the strategic case that the connections of a new wife might deter his enemies from launching an attack but wanted to be sure that the German princess selected by his chief adviser would make a pleasing wife. He wanted a pretty bride. He despatched Hans Holbein to the Rhineland. Holbein's portrait of Anne is astonishing: beautiful and profound – and yet the viewer cannot be sure that the subject is either beautiful or profound; she looks enigmatic and worth getting to know better. Anne and Henry married on 6 January 1540. But dynastic considerations could not override the groom's personal distaste for his bride; they divorced on 12 July, just over six months later, making this his shortest marriage. Henry did not complain about the work of his court painter (blaming instead the written descriptions of his ambassadors): the portrait was truthful; its shortcomings lay in the imagination of the viewer rather than the artist.

Henry was already forty-eight years old at the time of his marriage to Anne, in a time when anyone over the age of forty-five was considered old. He was obese and suffered an ulcerated leg; only his status made him an appealing consort. After a marriage to the teenage Katherine Howard which lasted barely twice as long as his marriage to Anne, he settled for companionship with Catherine Parr at the end of his life.

His teenage son, Edward, and middle-aged daughter, Mary, followed him as monarchs in quick succession. No one was particularly surprised when Mary's marriage to Philip II of Spain, her first cousin and eleven years her junior, failed to produce an heir. Under Catholic Mary, the Protestant cause bided its time; although Mary acquired the sobriquet 'Bloody', her slaughter of Protestants was not nearly comprehensive enough to dislodge the new national church, which became entrenched under her half-sister, Elizabeth I.

Queen Elizabeth I gripped the national imagination as much as her father, exciting as much admiration overseas as adulation at home. Pope Sixtus V opined:

BRITISH HISTORY THAT MATTERS   35

She certainly is a great queen, and were she only a Catholic she would be our dearly beloved. Just look how well she governs; she is only a woman, only mistress of half an island, and yet she makes herself feared by Spain, by France, by the Empire, by all.

His admiration reached fever pitch in the wake of the defeat of the Armada, when he remarked, aged sixty-eight: 'What a valiant woman – she braves the two greatest kings by land and sea. A pity we cannot marry, she and I, for our children would have ruled the world.'

The queen herself and Robert Cecil, her chief adviser, managed the succession of the childless monarch. Her nearest heir was the Protestant son of Mary, Queen of Scots, the Catholic rival she had executed in 1587; that did not prevent the king of Scotland from becoming king of England. Under James VI and I, half an island became a personal union of the whole British Isles.

James commissioned the best translation into English of the Bible, survived the attempt on the lives of parliamentarians at the State Opening in 1605 (which has necessitated a Beefeaters' inspection of Parliament's cellars for gunpowder kegs before every subsequent State Opening), and witnessed the establishment of the first permanent European settlements in North America (at Jamestown, Virginia). He also fathered Charles I, the country's most energetic and least effective proponent of the doctrine of the divine right of kings.

An equilibrium between monarch and legislature took some generations to achieve. Necessary for the Restoration after a short-lived republic was the monarch's recognition of his dependence on Parliament – for money and, ultimately, legitimacy. But the king still sat atop the system; his personal choices still resonated. In 1661, Lord Clarendon negotiated

Charles II's marriage contract with Catherine of Braganza. His sense of geography was imperfect. When he accepted the offer of Bombay, he believed he was acquiring a safe harbour in the South Atlantic; instead he got the best harbour in the subcontinent and cemented Britain's presence in India.

Catherine's inability to produce a child meant that Charles, having converted to Catholicism on his deathbed, was succeeded by his younger brother. King James II's vicious incompetence, including conversion to Rome while in vigorous good health when his personal choices had wider consequences, spurred Parliament into action. The end of the seventeenth and beginning of the eighteenth centuries saw the rolling invention of a British constitutional monarchy.

In 1688, Parliament dictated terms to William of Orange (fortuitously married to James II's elder and still-Protestant daughter). William and Mary died childless and were succeeded by Mary's sister, Anne. In 1701, Parliament chose Anne's heir. (Although the queen had been pregnant seventeen times, only three babies survived more than one day; the longest-lived was the Duke of Gloucester, who died aged eleven in 1700.) Electress Sophia of Hanover was favoured over seventy Catholics with a stronger claim in blood. Because Sophia predeceased Anne (by less than three months), her son was summoned to London as George I in August 1714. Ill winds prevented quick passage from The Hague, so he did not land in his new capital until 18 September.

The new monarch's precarious position was underlined by the rioting in more than twenty towns which accompanied his coronation in Westminster Abbey on 20 October 1714. Despite thirteen years' preparation time, his English was poor. The position of the king's chief minister rapidly increased in power in relation to the monarch. The enhanced status achieved during Robert Walpole's time was recognised by a new title;

the start of Walpole's tenure as prime minister is traditionally dated 3 April 1721, when he succeeded Lord Sunderland as first lord of the Treasury (a title prime ministers still hold).

Still the longest-serving prime minister, Walpole established the essentials of the job (even though the title was not acknowledged in a royal warrant until 1905). Other chief ministers had been the monarch's chief policy adviser, but Walpole was the first to get the Crown to hire and fire other ministers at his overt direction. He involved himself in the major decisions of other ministers without their effectively being able to object. He also accepted 10 Downing Street as an official residence (rather than a personal gift) from George II. Apart from the flagrant corruption to benefit himself and his allies, the job was identifiably the same as it is today by the time he left office in 1742.

Two of Walpole's eighteenth-century successors make most lists of the most effective prime ministers: the Pitts, father and son. After the Acts of Union between England and Scotland in 1707, they helped accelerate the process of Great Britain becoming a coherent nation – one that was Protestant, commercial, innovative in agriculture and industry, anti-French, bellicose, naval, expansionist overseas, and determined to prevent the dominance of the European mainland by any one continental power. (Away from politics, social reform started slowly in the eighteenth century; Jeremy Bentham coined the dictum 'everybody to count for one, nobody for more than one', which inspired John Stuart Mill and the utilitarians in the next century. Under the influence of his wife, Harriet Taylor, Mill wrote *The Subjection of Women* (1869), making the case for equality between men and women.)

The Seven Years' War marked a turning point for Britain on the international stage. It was the first truly global war and ended with major territorial exchanges everywhere except

Europe, home to the major belligerents. Britain's overseas pos-
sessions expanded massively: the French were effectively cleared
out of Canada (after the Battle of the Plains of Abraham) and
India (after their Mughal allies ceded Bengal to Britain).

Pitt the Younger had even more trouble with the French than
his father, but his ultimate triumph (though he failed to live
to see it) was even more complete. The Congress of Vienna
was the UK's greatest diplomatic success: magnanimity to
the defeated French ushered in a century of peace (more or
less) in Europe. Apart from in Crimea, the UK fought its wars
further afield, against adversaries whose ultimate defeat was
hardwired before hostilities started: the yawning gulf in technology proved impossible for weaker opponents to bridge. One
striking exception was the mountainous terrain beyond the
North-West Frontier Province in central Asia, the gap between
the maximum extent of the Russian and British Indian empires.
Neither side being able to subdue Afghanistan's stubbornly
independent inhabitants, they accepted it as a buffer state.

At the end of the eighteenth century, whatever his merits
as monarch, George III was an indifferent parent. He fathered
nine sons and six daughters. The daughters were kept close to
home. Three rebelled and married in middle age, in the teeth of
parental opposition; only one had a child (a stillborn daughter).
George's sons ran wild, most siring large numbers of children
by their mistresses but refusing to marry in accordance with
the king's wishes and the law; none of their offspring was in
the line of succession. The sole exception was Charlotte, only
daughter of George III's eldest son, conceived during the few
weeks her parents deigned to live together. Charlotte's parents
were estranged by the time of her birth, but at least her father
had supplied a legitimate heir.

The royal family went into a tailspin in 1817 when Charlotte died in childbirth. Under paternal pressure, three of

George III's sons quickly contracted legal marriages with German princesses. The wedding stakes produced seven children in the late 1810s and early 1820s. By the time William IV became king in 1830, aged sixty-four and with no surviving legitimate children, it was clear that Victoria, only child of his younger brother Edward, would not be supplanted as heir.

Constitutional monarchy took another stride forward under long-lived Victoria. Her husband, Albert, invented the job of private secretary to the monarch. Through her nine pregnancies, he assumed greater power as her principal adviser. She never recovered from his death, aged forty-two, when their youngest child was just four years old. During Victoria's forty-year widowhood, her court failed to keep pace with the UK's expanding empire and prosperity. She lived relatively modestly in the houses Albert had built, principally Balmoral Castle on Speyside and Osborne House on the Isle of Wight.

Under Victoria, British explorers reached all unknown parts of the globe with the exception of the poles. They were the first Europeans to uncover the sources of the rivers Nile (John Hanning Speke) and Congo (David Livingstone). After the loss of the first British Empire when thirteen North American colonies broke away in the 1770s, the Victorians assembled a second, massively bigger empire with India at its heart. In common with imperialists through the ages, they co-opted local leaders and groups to consolidate their control: Sikhs in India and Hausa in Nigeria, for example, were raised above other groups and recruited into local armies and police forces.

In common with most empires, the British Empire had slavery as part of its business model. In compiling their historical narrative, Britons find it easier to remember the roles of William Wilberforce and other abolitionists in ending the transatlantic slave trade in 1807 than the centuries when slavery was an accepted fact and fundamental to economic growth.

They also forget the resistance, including within the Church of England, to the anti-slavery campaign, and the fact that, after abolition, the only people compensated were those who had claimed people as property.

Not only did Victorians expand the areas under British administration, whose markets were then dominated by British goods, but they proselytised the Anglican faith. Missionaries energetically and unapologetically urged the replacement of local religions and traditions; in their view, the Church of England and Victorian morals were self-evidently better. Colonised peoples generally adopted the new codes with alacrity; earlier tolerance and plurality were replaced by a narrower, more inflexible British way of seeing the world, which has persisted even when the UK has moved on. African provinces in the Anglican Communion, for example, have a more intolerant attitude to homosexuality than their ancestors practised before British missionaries arrived.

Queen Victoria's son Edward VII, taking his cue from a constitutional historian (Walter Bagehot) and a flamboyant courtier (Reginald Esher), reinvented the monarchy for the imperial age. His coronation in 1902 set the template followed ever since (much of the sumptuous needlework produced then by the Royal School of Needlework is still in use). The pageantry of the State Opening of Parliament was laid down during Edward's reign. The consort's throne was created as an exact replica of the original sovereign's throne, but one inch shorter (between State Openings, it is entrusted to the safekeeping of Lord Cholmondeley, who serves as lord great chamberlain in alternate reigns). Esher supervised the layout of The Mall and the building of Admiralty Arch; the architect Aston Webb completed the remodelling of the east facade of Buckingham Palace in 1913, putting into place the final piece of the architecture of ceremonial London.

All the loos and washbasins in my primary and grammar schools were stamped in sloping blue letters 'Armitage Shanks'. But before Armitage Shanks, there was Shanks of Greenock. In the early twentieth century, Shanks's ubiquity reached further than municipal contracts in the North of England. In 1967, Ronald Hyam of Magdalene College, Cambridge used the company to illustrate the informal power of the British Empire to students in the Mill Lane lecture theatre. Among his audience was Peter Hennessy, who later quoted Hyam's opening verbatim:

> It is very difficult for people of your age to appreciate the British Empire at its zenith. There is no shortage of clichés – quarter of the earth's surface on which the sun never set – but they are as banal as they are misleading because they only give you a sense of the territorial expression of British power. A better test is this. If you were a chap almost anywhere in the world around 1904 and you went for a pee, you would point your cock at a piece of porcelain on which was written 'Shanks of Greenock' ... Not for nothing was Greenock called 'the arsehole of the British Empire'.[8]

On the eve of the First World War, the UK hit its peak but already felt keenly the challengers snapping at its heels. Across the Atlantic, the US had organised itself 'from sea to shining sea'; New Mexico and Arizona were admitted to the Union as its forty-seventh and forty-eighth members, respectively, in 1912. The US economy was growing more rapidly than that of the UK. On the continent, imperial Germany was also enjoying rapid economic expansion. Kaiser Wilhelm II was obsessed by the Royal Navy. The British became fixated on German motives and capabilities. At the pinnacle of its power, the UK was more aware of the growing strength of its rivals than its own weaknesses as a power on the turn. But, despite the nervousness of successive first lords of the Admiralty, the fact is that, until the outbreak of the First World War, the Royal Navy achieved its ambition to be as large as the next two largest navies combined, with HMS *Dreadnought* (launched in 1906) setting the standard for battleships to which other navies aspired but failed to match.

The UK is capable of making strategic choices only when it is not aware of making the choice. As a power whose pre-eminence was ending, the UK could have thrown support to either of the rivals in the tussle to displace it, giving that power a decisive edge. In the second decade of the twentieth century, the UK favoured the US over Germany. The continental neighbour was too close to be acceptable as a replacement hegemon. Graham Allison postulated, following Thucydides, that war was difficult to avoid when an emerging power threatened the pre-eminence of an established one. The UK walked into the mother and father of Thucydides Traps. The way the UK played its hand during the twentieth century's Thirty Years' War (in two instalments) ensured that the US rather than Germany would be the ultimate beneficiary of British decline.

The Second World War is the period in British history about which Britons feel proudest, the easiest war in history to justify, the only war whose rationale I understood as a ten-year-old. It was a war that had to be won if the values the UK embraced and embodied were to survive, and in which the UK played a pivotal role in the defeat of the only adversary in modern history universally branded evil. Yet misremembering what had just happened was essential to the UK's high view of its performance. In 1945, the UK was completely exhausted. To defeat the Nazis, the UK acquiesced in, even facilitated, the triumph of Soviet Communism in half of Europe. Containing, confronting, and eventually defeating the Soviet Union was a longer game than destroying Nazi Germany; the UK's role in the longer war was more marginal. From the moment the Allies convened at Potsdam, ten weeks after VE Day, it was clear that the US would be the decisive power in taking on Stalin and his successors in Moscow.

The Second World War was a victory from which the UK could not recover; the price of coaxing the US to join us – indispensable to victory – was the liquidation of the British Empire and the acceptance of American leadership in every field where previously the UK had led. The Second World War was at one and the same time the apotheosis of British leadership and effectiveness and the abrupt end of the UK's long run as top nation.

3

Losing an Empire

Patriotism is a problem for anyone examining the UK's changed standing in the world. It seems a vociferous love of country is required before a commentator is qualified to comment on a country's foreign policy, and the love must be unconditional. To note a decline is to invite accusations of 'declinism', of believing that the UK is defined by irreversible decline. When I was PUS at the FCO, I occasionally featured in a newspaper story. In June 2018, when taking part in a debate at the Institute for Government, I observed that the UK was a medium-sized power: 'One fact that will not change is that we are a medium-sized country and most of what we want to do on the international stage we can only achieve with partners.'

In the audience, Bob Seely MP objected: 'I just get wound up when I hear this medium-sized power stuff.' I explained that I was not saying that the UK was small; indeed, the UK was still among the biggest six powers by any measure apart from population. But the fact was that the world's two largest powers – the US and China – were so far ahead of the field that even the third-placed power could only honestly be cate-gorised as medium-sized. The next day the *Daily Express* took issue with my analysis under the headline 'Don't BELITTLE Britain! Tory MP LAYS INTO top mandarin over comments on post-Brexit future'.

One reason the UK's changed status is difficult to process

is that, even at its peak, the UK was nitpicking and penny-pinching. Individuals had swagger but government did not (indeed, the government objected to the swagger of individuals who were government employees). The UK did not generally behave as if it were the world's number-one power. Even ambassadors in the capitals of countries the government was trying to impress had trouble persuading London to see the importance of a dignified residence to their conduct of business.

Enterprising ambassadors took matters into their own hands. In 1814, the duke of Wellington, newly named as ambassador at Paris after Napoleon's exile to Elba, bought the Hôtel de Charost from Napoleon's sister, Pauline Borghese. She wanted one million francs; he beat her down to 861,500 including contents (equivalent then to £46,500). Borghese used the money to help finance her brother's return to power the following year. The duke had to persuade the Treasury to pay her in instalments. When Kemal Atatürk moved the Turkish capital to Ankara, the diplomat Hughe Knatchbull-Hugessen promptly bought the best house in the city and then spent years cajoling the Ministry of Works into reimbursing him.

As consul-general, Evelyn Baring effectively ruled Egypt for twenty-four years at the turn of the twentieth century. In common with many newly arrived excellencies, he complained about his accommodation. Head office was not immediately responsive. Three years into his posting, he returned to the charge:

> The house which I at present occupy is in no way adapted for an Agency [embassy]. The reception rooms are far too small for the number of people whom I am obliged to entertain. As regards sleeping apartments there is only just enough room for my family which only consists of my wife, two children and a governess. If I have to receive any visitors

as was the case when the Viceroy returned from India I am
obliged to go to the trouble and expense of sending my children to an hotel.

London did not come up with a definitive, satisfactory reply
for another six years. By the time building on a new embassy
began in 1892, Baring had coaxed Whitehall into purchasing
a bigger plot in the best part of the city, sandwiched between
two riverfront palaces. Highfalutin neighbours expected the
interloper to match their standards. They demanded extensive
snagging. Water seepage meant the basement floor had to be
raised above the Nile flood level. Providing a reliable source
of constant electric power that did not regularly plunge the
neighbourhood into darkness required the installation of a
steam-driven generator, which proved expensive to maintain.

Early in its history, the imposing new addition to the Nile
riverbank acquired the nickname Bayt Al Lurd (the lord's
house); Baring had been made earl of Cromer in 1901, six years
before he left Cairo. Four other lords subsequently lived there:
Kitchener, Allenby, Lloyd, and Killearn. In 1942, Lord Killearn
left the house accompanied by a military cortège which proceeded to surround Abdeen Palace, where he presented King
Farouk with a choice: appoint a pro-British cabinet or abdi-
cate. The young monarch complied and kept his throne for an
additional decade.

The UK's standing in Egypt fell with Farouk. In October
1954, Ralph Stevenson (Killearn's successor-but-one) awoke
one morning to discover that his embassy compound had lost
its bomb shelter, its swimming pool, its Nile-side dock, and
5,000 square metres of manicured lawn. In their place, Gamal
Abdel Nasser's government had begun construction of a corniche. Contrary to diplomatic legend, the Egyptians paid for
the land they took, transferring to Her Majesty's Treasury the

sum of 300,000 Egyptian pounds, approximately sixty Egyptian pounds per square metre for land originally purchased by the British at three Egyptian pounds per square metre.

The corniche was barely two years old when Britain and France, allied with Israel, occupied the Suez Canal area in October 1956. Of all the steps downwards, the Suez Crisis was the most difficult to present in any other way and therefore the most humiliating. Prime Minister Anthony Eden launched an adventure with Prime Minister Guy Mollet without taking either his cabinet or the UK's main ally fully into his confidence. US opposition led swiftly to the withdrawal of British and French forces and Eden's resignation; Mollet's followed six months later. Almost fifty years on, the former Israeli prime minister Shimon Peres told me that for Israel the operation was a strategic success: Israel's Arab neighbours left it alone for the next decade. Nasser severed diplomatic relations and for three years the Union Jack stopped fluttering above Bayt Al Lurd. By the time it was rehoisted, the house was just another poorly maintained historic pile; guests went there to meet trade delegations rather than decide the fate of nations.

For some people, even noting the UK's changed position in the world amounts to defeatism. But facts cannot safely be denied. In 1902 the final event of Edward VII's coronation was a review of the fleet at Spithead. Using only ships deployed in home waters, the Royal Navy mustered twenty battleships, twenty-four cruisers, and forty-seven destroyers. In 1953, also at Spithead, Elizabeth II reviewed over 200 ships (most smaller than their Edwardian predecessors), moored over 22 km, and over 300 aircraft from the Fleet Air Arm flew in formation over the newly crowned queen. In 2023, the coronation of Charles III was not marked by a review of the fleet: not enough ships could be spared from active operations.

British sensitivity to the idea of reduced standing did not

begin with Bob Seely or MPs in the European Research Group. Perhaps the most famous assessment was Dean Acheson's throwaway remark at the end of a speech at West Point about the future of NATO in 1962: 'Great Britain has lost an empire and has not yet found a role.' The historian Emily Lowrance-Floyd explored the impact of Acheson's comment (the quotations from newspapers and politicians in the next six paragraphs were cited in her doctoral thesis). Her analysis of why a retired US secretary of state said what he said, and how different parts of the UK establishment responded, is eerily familiar. It could apply to any number of transatlantic spats over the last sixty years: an oversensitive reaction to a factual-but-crass American statement of the obvious.

Even though Colonial Office forecasts in the 1950s had envisaged independence for African colonies many decades hence, the end of British rule in Africa was suddenly and irrevocably imminent by the end of 1962. Acheson's comment was a statement of disagreeable reality. Because the change in the UK's role was externally imposed rather than internally planned, its reality was energetically disputed. Prime Minister Harold Macmillan's answer – to apply for EEC membership, so the UK could make its way in the world as part of the main European club of nations – generated fierce domestic opposition.

Most people hate criticism from their friends; when that criticism is public and unintended, it wounds even more deeply. The pithy observations of Acheson, retired but renowned, commanded greater attention than he expected. In a letter to Arthur M. Schlesinger Jr, he expressed sarcastic surprise at the severity of the British reaction: 'I wonder who the unsung reportorial genius was who read through the whole speech and found that paragraph to cable to London.'[9]

In his diary, Macmillan lamented the widespread upset as 'not a good sign, for we ought to be strong enough to laugh off this kind of thing'.[10] Nevertheless, he publicly chided Acheson for denigrating 'the resolution and will of Britain and the British people. [The same mistake was] made by quite a lot of people in the course of the last 400 years, including Philip of Spain, Louis XIV, Napoleon, the Kaiser and Hitler'.[11] He went on to say that Acheson seemed 'wholly to misunderstand the role of the Commonwealth in world affairs' and to argue that the doctrine of interdependence among nations was not exclusive to Europe but applied to all nations, including the US.

Critics claimed Acheson belittled not only the world role of the British Commonwealth but also the 'special relationship' between Britain and the US. Lord Hailsham, leader of the House of Lords, speaking at a lunch in Glasgow, said he was tired of friends 'who have got so used to our friendship that they cease to care about our feelings'.[12]

The Kennedy administration found itself engaged in damage limitation, denying that Acheson's views reflected its own. Dean Rusk, secretary of state, reassured a press conference a few days later that America viewed Britain as 'one of the great Powers in the Atlantic Community' and that the strength of the 400-year-old special relationship was as potent as ever.

The *Daily Express* led the attack from the right (some things don't change), and the *New Statesman* objected loudly from the left. Simultaneously, a counter-reaction agreed with Acheson. *The Spectator* stated that Acheson's 'plain truth ... hardly justifies the reactions it excited in the United Kingdom'.[13] And *The Economist* criticised anti-American commentators by arguing that Acheson's points 'were plainly true ... The ability frankly to own up to what is clearly the case would be the ideal gift for Britain this Christmas'.[14]

Nearly thirty years later, sipping whisky with George Busby in Königswinter in 1989, I wondered whether the UK needed a foreign policy at all: our approach to most foreign policy issues had been fixed a generation earlier, and our approach to anything new was dictated by the US. Half a dozen years after that, working in the embassy in Washington, I answered my question: yes, the UK needed a foreign policy, because when new problems appeared the US did not immediately know how to react; there was a moment when partners could influence them. The Americans listened to the countries that were most useful to them – those with insight and the resources and willingness to help. In diplomacy, influence on the powerful can be almost as useful as power.

In the 1990s, the UK continued to fret that the special relationship might no longer be special. My first ambassador in Washington, Robin Renwick, forbad British diplomats from using the phrase but added, 'I don't mind if an American uses it.'[15] More recently, the diplomat Robert Cooper has observed that every country has a special relationship with the US because the US is their single most important partner. Throughout history, the foreign policy of most countries has been dominated by their neighbourhood and by relations with the hegemon, which for most countries has been the US for the last century; latterly, relations with the ex-colonial power have hovered in the foreground for ex-colonies and in the background for the ex-colonial power.

Fifteen years after I posed my callow question in Königswinter, the director-general of the Israeli Foreign Ministry made a similar observation. Yoav Biran summoned ambassadors from EU member states to Jerusalem. I cannot remember what the EU had done to upset Israel that month, but Biran was scathing about European posturing. In his peroration, he remarked that only two and a half EU member states had a foreign policy at all. I remember the German and Italian ambassadors looking furtively at each other, trying to work out which of them represented the half.

Now, more than fifteen years after that, I think two other questions need answers first: (a) how many countries need a foreign policy in the twenty-first century? And (b) how many countries have a foreign policy worth the name? My answers are: (a) not many, and (b) even fewer. In Europe, most EU member states could step back and entrust their foreign policy formation and implementation wholly to the European External Action Service (EEAS) without suffering a diminution in their foreign-policy clout. Since Catherine Ashton was chosen as first high representative of the EU in 2009, the EEAS has shown ever greater willingness to step up. It is the only international organisation that insists its representatives are treated in the same way as ambassadors from sovereign countries, presenting credentials to heads of state.

No matter that global power is concentrated in a few capitals, all capitals want to grace the international stage – even if, in reality, they are mere spear-carriers while the leading players strut their stuff. No matter how little a Luxembourg foreign minister has to do or how small a difference they can make, the grand duchy always has an energetic foreign minister. Jean Asselborn has held the job since 2004. Apart from one caretaker, Luxembourg had just four foreign ministers in the thirty-eight years I worked for HM Diplomatic Service. Smaller countries seem to specialise in keeping their foreign ministers in place for longer; the experience and extensive personal networks of their top diplomats make bigger countries pay more attention to their concerns.

Often benefiting from more stable government at home, small states also enjoy the advantages of long tenure of their envoys to key international organisations. At the United Nations (UN) in New York, Christian Wenaweser has represented Liechtenstein since 2002; over twenty years he has become one of the best-known and most effective operators in Turtle Bay, a master of procedure, exercising influence far greater than is suggested by the size of the state he represents. Even if objectively their foreign policy needs are meagre, Luxembourg and Liechtenstein are effectively represented on the international stage.

Superficially, international organisations disguise the realities of differential power. The two main founding principles of the UN denied (or corrected) the main principles on which European order had rested since the Congress of Vienna in 1814–15: the UN subscribes to the idea of sovereign equality of states no matter their size, and to respecting member states' right to organise their internal affairs as their governments wish. At Vienna, participants had no trouble in dividing countries into great and small powers; over the nineteenth century the second category was itself divided between medium-sized and small powers. Great powers were defined by success in war, specifically war in Europe (skirmishes further afield did not count). Great Britain, Russia, Austria-Hungary, Prussia, and France were the original great powers. After unification in the 1860s, Italy claimed the status (not always persuasively).

Medium-sized powers had armies capable of mounting a credible defence, if not a plausible attack. Small powers had only token defence forces, such as smaller German duchies and grand duchies, many of which had been absorbed by Prussia before unification in 1871. At congresses and conferences, medium-sized and small powers were treated differently; they were excluded from key meetings and explicitly needed the help of the great powers to defend their interests. The division persisted at the Paris Peace Conference in 1919–20. The last acknowledgement of powers treated as greater than others was the establishment of five permanent members of the UN Security Council in 1945. Just as the statesmen Lord Castlereagh and Klemens von Metternich had recognised (defeated) France as a great power in 1815, so American and British negotiators insisted that (once again defeated) France be included in the exclusive club. The material expression of Soviet resistance was the fact that, within Germany, French zones were carved out of what had been assigned to the US and UK rather than being an equal quarter-share of the whole.

The pretence of equality has complicated the functioning of the international system. Smaller states overestimate their influence on proceedings; just because larger states are obliged to give them equal time does not mean they pay close attention to how smaller states use their time at the podium. And smaller states cannot staff all the meetings to which they have access. So they accept briefings from non-governmental organisations (NGOs); some smaller states are captured by lobby groups. The relationship is generally symbiotic rather than parasitic: the small state benefits from the greater research capacity and presentational savvy of the NGO, which makes their case with greater fluency and impact than they could achieve unaided. Although making their client's overall case, the NGO is able to feed its detailed ideas into the negotiation.

As well as misleading smaller states into thinking they carry greater clout than they actually do, the international architecture flatters the pretensions of the founding fathers, particularly the previously powerful. At the UN in New York, the five permanent members of the Security Council (the P5) rule the roost. Early on, the drafters made accommodations that helped the durability of the structures they were designing. They included the Republic of China and France in the P5, despite the weakness in 1945 of both.

In the next quarter century they made two essential adjustments. First, they expanded the elected element of the Security Council to give better geographical representation as colonies became independent countries. And second, as part of the long, slow process of recognising the reality of the Chinese Communist Party's victory over the Kuomintang, Beijing replaced Taipei as a P5 member in 1971. The switch was made before Beijing's massive economic expansion. International policymakers are more comfortable anticipating the requirements of incipient change than being forced to recognise the consequences later.

A third vital adjustment came much later, in 1991, when the Soviet Union imploded. With minimal debate, the UK's permanent representative engineered the substitution of Russia for the Soviet Union; the membership quickly acquiesced in the idea that Russia inherited all the Soviet Union's international status. The manoeuvre was so deft and swift that no one disputed Russia's right to be treated as the successor state. It might also help the UK in the longer term: if Scotland were to become independent or Ireland to unite, then London could cite a precedent when arguing that the residual UK should enjoy the same status it held pre-fragmentation.

Nearly eighty years after the UN General Assembly first gathered in the Methodist Central Hall in Westminster, three of the original P5 are objectively hanging on by their fingertips. If the UN Charter were negotiated afresh, the UK, France, and Russia would not persuade the rest of the membership of their continued eligibility for permanent membership of the Security Council.

But the winners of the Second World War wrote the rule book to suit themselves. In the face of Muscovite hostility, which faded to grudging quiescence after extracting concessions, the Soviet Union accepted that France should be a permanent member of the Security Council; France's (restored) overseas empire was half the size of the UK's but bigger than anyone else's, home to 10 per cent of the world's population. France was grateful to be included, but the Soviet Union (and US) would not have joined unless the Charter allowed them to protect their interests as they saw them.

High-minded resistance to the power of the most powerful scuppered the League of Nations before Eric Drummond moved into the Palais Wilson in Geneva as its first secretary-general in November 1920: the US Senate didn't like the fledgling organisation's egalitarian governance, so senators would not ratify the founding treaty.

By contrast, at the UN, nothing that has the force of international law can happen if one of the P5 opposes it. With the single exception of authorisation for humanitarian action in Libya in 2011, the Security Council has been deadlocked and sterile since Russia's invasion of Georgia in 2008. Russia single-mindedly protects its interests at the UN, no matter the obloquy that attracts. So what if 141 countries condemned them in the General Assembly? Resolutions there are advisory; no country is obliged to do anything, even when a draft is passed by an overwhelming majority. By ignoring international condemnation, Russia makes itself look tough and the UN look weak.

Similarly, all the P5 vigilantly guard their interests when anyone mentions Charter reform. Formally, at least, all five can block any proposed change. Which is why reform of the Security Council focuses on adding permanent members rather than subtracting or replacing them. At least six countries openly aspire to join the Security Council permanently; the four whose candidacy attracts most apparent support are India, Japan, Germany, and Brazil (a group known as the G4). The UK (and others) also embrace some form of permanent representation for Africa, 'along lines that African countries themselves agree'. A larger group than the G4 aspires to permanent Security Council membership but is coy about publicly voicing those ambitions; they want other countries to recognise their manifest qualifications.

The UK plays honest broker, working with both aspirant permanent members and the so-called Coffee Club of countries who oppose G4 ambitions, which generally cut across their own. Generally, when legitimacy is declining or disputed, the UK implicitly relies on the legitimacy of competence (consider the House of Lords). The justification may be lost in the mists of time and no longer strong, but British performance – constructive, imaginative, consensus-building, and effective – means those who might object do not.

The Security Council needs more radical overhaul than ditching a couple of founding permanent members or a second enlargement. It needs to acknowledge wider changes on the international scene. In 1945, the UN plugged the gap at the global level that the League of Nations failed to fill. There were no permanent regional organisations to speak of and only fifty-one member states. Now regional organisations energetically and increasingly assertively represent the interests of their members, and 193 countries are member states. A membership of fifteen is already testing the bounds of efficient working at the Security Council. For more countries and organisations to have a more regular voice in its working, it might in future also have a new category of semi-permanent membership.

I propose that France, Russia, and the UK stop being permanent members. Instead, the EU (via the EEAS) would become a permanent member; Russia and the UK would be alternate members, each serving two years on, two years off. The same arrangement might apply to India and Japan. One of the two seats now earmarked for Africa might rotate between Egypt, Nigeria, and South Africa. And one of the two seats reserved for Latin America might rotate between Argentina, Brazil, and Mexico. Each of these African and Latin American countries would be Security Council members in two out of every six years. Security Council membership would hold steady at fifteen; eight seats (a majority) would still be elected, the whole membership choosing among smaller member states, one Latin American/Caribbean, one Middle Eastern, two African, two Asian, and two European and Other (the Western Europe and Others Group and Eastern European Group would merge).

I realise I am presenting something for everyone to hate (Europe as a whole, not merely the UK, would lose out), but I am trying to achieve three objectives: to reflect power in the mid-twenty-first rather than mid-twentieth century; to maintain a size compatible with efficient work; and to give more regular and certain membership to larger non-European states.

Adapting to straitened circumstances is among the toughest tasks for anyone or any country. In international relations, declining powers still have power, sometimes enough power to lull them into thinking they do not need to address their changing status. For twenty years after the end of the Second World War, the UK's international ambition continued undiminished; in policy terms, reverses such as the Suez Crisis in 1956 were treated as temporary. Successive Labour and Conservative governments tried to maintain all commitments they inherited on the world stage while simultaneously cutting the defence budget. By the mid-1960s, overstretch could no longer be disguised. Denis Healey, who took over the new Ministry of Defence six months after it was set up in 1964, was the first unblinkingly to confront the new reality. His defence review in 1966 remains the most honest, thorough, and consequential in the MoD's history.

A low-profile ministerial statement on 26 July 2023 dramatised the outcome of that long, slow change. On behalf of His Majesty's Government, Andrew Mitchell, minister for Africa, reacted to a coup in Niger. He made three points:

The UK is closely monitoring events taking place in Niger's capital.

The UK condemns in the strongest possible terms any attempt to undermine stability and democracy in Niger.

The UK joins the African Union and Economic Community of West African States [ECOWAS] in their calls to end the unacceptable events seen today, and to ensure the full and swift restoration of Niger's democratically elected institutions.[16]

The habit of telling other people what to do dies hard. I can imagine the collective shrug of the shoulders in Niamey: why would Abdourahmane Tchiani, who named himself as head of a transitional government on 28 July, pay attention to Mitchell? The UK will not intervene militarily. The Nigerien need not fear British sanctions (Niger is the UK's 197th largest trading partner) nor the loss of British aid (there is none). The only reason coup leaders might take account of British views is because of the UK's partnerships – its role in the P5 and its links to ECOWAS leaders, to the US, France, and the EU. Acting alone, the UK is essentially powerless in other people's affairs these days.

Losing an empire requires a massive and evidently disagreeable psychological adjustment, but only by accepting the new reality can a country develop an effective new role.

4

Not Finding a Role

Through the last year of the Second World War, Alec Cadogan (PUS at the Foreign Office) and Gladwyn Jebb (Cadogan's private secretary, who became the UN's first secretary-general) laboured on designing a new world order. Washington was the focus of their attention. British reliance on America to win the war was plain to see, but the UK wanted a decisive part in operating the post-war world. Britain was aware it was a supplicant, but it was a confident supplicant.

In many ways, the British Empire between the world wars was at its peak. After the American War of Independence, no part of the empire had broken away. India tried in 1857 but failed. One consequence of the failed rebellion was the end of the peculiar rule of the East India Company, replaced by formal rule from Whitehall. Queen Victoria was declared empress of India, and her viceroy held sway in Calcutta. In 1867, Canada became the first dominion, a status also granted to Australia, New Zealand, Newfoundland, and South Africa in the first decade of the twentieth century; the status satisfied the short-term sovereignty needs of the oldest colonies that were most thickly populated by Britons. British-controlled territory was augmented by the treaties after the First World War. New additions were called 'mandates' rather than 'colonies', because their temporary control by the UK had been mandated by the international community as a whole through the League of Nations. The UK's explicit task was to prepare these territories for independence; meanwhile, British officials were clearly in charge.

British overseas services were larger than ever before. Individual officials juggled multiple tasks and were thinly stretched, but the power they exercised over the people in their districts was undeniable. A cadre of district commissioners, trained in the newer public schools (notably Haileybury) and Oxford and Cambridge fanned out across Africa and Asia providing basic administration and justice, and authorising public infrastructure projects.

My grandfather admired these men as selfless public servants. Because of their work, he ranked the British Empire as the best European empire. The Netherlands was second, France third, Portugal and Italy poor from what he saw, Germany irrelevant because it was no longer a colonial power by the time he was sailing to Africa, and Belgium dead last. He judged colonial empires by the durability of the institutions they established, the quality of the physical infrastructure they left behind, and the level of local admiration for the metropolitan country. He did not pretend to be objective, but one merchant seaman's opinion made a great impression on me.

Despite his contempt for imperialism, George Orwell wrote sympathetically about the young men who served as district commissioners. By their own lights, they were doing admirable things. Their lives were hard from their point of view. But the rewards made it worthwhile. They judged their own lives exclusively from their point of view, and were assessed by contemporaries the same way. More recently, commentators have taken others' perspectives into account. People like Nobel laureate Abdulrazak Gurnah and journalist Sathnam Sanghera have begun to redress the balance, asking why their ancestors were denied the opportunities they now have.

Of all the changes in human affairs since humans began recording their history, the greatest is ordinary people all over the world having greater power over their own lives. The change was a long time coming. In *Leviathan*, Thomas Hobbes distilled the life of almost every person who had lived up to the middle of the seventeenth century into five adjectives: 'solitary, poor, nasty, brutish, and short'. The truth of that assessment changed slowly over the next three hundred years. The change does not apply everywhere, nor does 'greater control' mean 'complete control'. Afghan and Kurdish refugees biding their time in camps near Calais, hoping to cross to England, clearly have limited control over their own lives, but at least they were able to leave Afghanistan and Iraq; they have more options than their ancestors. People know more, about both their immediate surroundings and personal circumstances, and what is happening and what is possible further afield. They cooperate more. They are able to make time for what they care about rather than being forced, every day, to focus on food and their most basic needs.

The knowledge that the status quo was not immutable, that power did not inevitably have to be wielded by outsiders, fuelled decolonisation. Local leaders were supported in their demands for freedom by outsiders, including from the colonial power but particularly from the US. President Woodrow Wilson launched his Fourteen Points in the last year of the First World War. Self-determination was their common thread. The US had its own colonies and inconsistencies, but the promotion of self-determination has been the lodestar of American foreign policy since Wilson.

One explanation for the UK finding it difficult to accustom itself to its reduced status is the strange pacing of its decline. It set in so long ago, overlapping with the final phases of territorial expansion, and developed so slowly that Britons were not

forced to acknowledge what was happening. Winston Churchill stoutly opposed independence for India until it happened;
Enoch Powell aspired to be viceroy even after Clement Attlee's
government had announced the timetable for the transfer of
power. But Indian independence in 1947 was a watershed.
Because Britons, by and large, chose not to acknowledge that
fact, it is not surprising that the school curriculum, along
with the imagination of leading politicians, failed to keep
up with the suddenly accelerated pace of change, leaving
Britons like my grandfather fiercely proud of but largely ignorant about their imperial past, and disconcerted and largely
uncomprehending about their decolonising present.

The elite, particularly the most thoughtful politicians and
civil servants, knew better what was happening and contemplated new strategies to replace empire in the 1960s. Like *The
Economist*, they recognised the truth in Acheson's jibe. Shorn
of empire, and aware of the UK's inability to stand alone,
Macmillan commissioned a study of the UK's options in the
early 1960s. He did not believe that a closer relationship with
the dominions would fill the gap and he did not care for more
explicit subservience to the US. He persuaded the cabinet to
choose Europe.

The EEC rejected his government's application for membership in 1963 and Harold Wilson's renewed application in 1967.
In retirement in 1969, with a general election in the offing,
Macmillan visited Corpus Christi College, Cambridge, where
he was hosted by the former permanent secretary to the Treasury Frank Lee, then master of the college. Over dinner, guests
discussed at length the desirability of a new Conservative
government applying for a third time. Frank Lee's son-in-law,
Richard Wilson (later cabinet secretary), was the youngest
person present.

Fifty years later, Wilson told me that the gathering agreed

that Edward Heath should apply a third time for EEC membership, if the Conservatives won the election. But they were uncertain about the UK's prospects. Lee thought the biggest risk was the French maintaining their veto, despite the glimmer of hope offered by the recent arrival of Georges Pompidou to replace Charles de Gaulle. Macmillan, on the other hand, felt the biggest problem lay closer to home: the Conservative Party membership in the country would never forgive the leadership for preferring membership of someone else's club to making our own way. The UK had won the Second World War; victors were not supplicants.

For forty-seven years after finally joining the EEC in January 1973, Europe was the single biggest component in the UK's overseas policy. In intelligence policy and cooperation, the US always loomed largest; in defence policy and cooperation, it was NATO, with the US the biggest single ally; but in economics and trade, it was increasingly the EEC/EU, with only Turkey, Norway, and Australia interrupting the EU-dominated run of the UK's twenty next-most-important defence partners.

After leaving the EU, the UK discovered that different areas of overseas policy have different weight in determining the UK's prospects and status: economics and trade are most important. And British diplomats had recognised at least as early as the 1980s that London's standing in Washington was largely a function of how decisive UK influence was over its European neighbours (Antony Acland repeatedly made the point when he was British ambassador in Washington). Even in intelligence, foreign, and defence policy, our absence from the EU affects our standing with our main ally. Senior American officials are urged by British counterparts to assert the contrary, but the pattern of contact and business has shifted since Brexit. Diplomats and politicians in larger EU member states would be privately unhappy if their opposite numbers in Washington answered Henry Kissinger's question, 'Who do I call if I want to call Europe?' with 'Brussels', but only Brits hope the answer is 'London'.

Decline was punctuated with moments of brilliance and times when the UK successfully persuaded more powerful countries to do what it wanted. London played a full part in designing the post-Second World War order. Just before Cadogan and Jebb attended the meetings at Dumbarton Oaks in 1944, which resulted in the agreement of the UN Charter in San Francisco in 1945, John Maynard Keynes dazzled transatlantic colleagues during negotiations to agree the rules of the post-war economic system. Keynes's hatred of Washington's summer climate was so acute and his reputation there so high, that the Americans chose instead a venue in New Hampshire outside Bretton Woods. Negotiators established the International Bank for Reconstruction and Development (later part of the World Bank Group) and the International Monetary Fund.

The Falklands War was a moment of brilliance from which the UK managed to draw the wrong conclusions. Every military memoir acknowledges that it was a close-run thing. The UK was at the extreme edge of its capabilities. The Argentinians fought bravely; the Battle of Mount Tumbledown teetered on a knife edge. When I toured the battlefield nearly four decades later, my guide paid tribute not only to the organisation and doggedness but also to the reputation of the Gurkhas in particular: ordinary Argentinian soldiers were terrified of them. The war in a soldier's head is at least as important as their equipment to the outcome of the fight.

Although British success in the Falklands required substantial American help, it was essentially a British deployment. No deployment at scale has been exclusively or predominantly British since then. Deployments to Timor-Leste in 1999 and Sierra Leone in 2000 were smaller and shorter in duration.

Also in 1999, the UK led a NATO deployment to Kosovo. On all other occasions, UK deployments have been part of wider international action led by the US. Even when the UK seemed to be leading (with France, in Libya in 2011), the US was doing substantially more while not wanting publicly to take the credit (in the initial attack on Benghazi, the US fired 108 cruise missiles to the UK's three).

Sometimes it feels as if the UK is taking inspiration from Stacey King, a journeyman basketball player, who played for the Chicago Bulls at the start of his professional career. His debut season coincided with the prime of Michael Jordan. On 28 March 1990, Jordan scored sixty-nine points against the Cleveland Cavaliers, his best-ever performance. Late in the game, King came on to court and scored one point through a free throw in overtime. Afterwards he told reporters, 'I'll always remember this as the night that Michael Jordan and I combined to score seventy points.'

No one doubts the excellence of the UK's armed forces; the best are as good as the best anywhere in the world. But these days they lack strength in depth. They are trading on their old reputation. As the Prussian general Carl von Clausewitz pointed out, this is legitimate and important: there is no downside to persuading an adversary that it is in their interest to yield without fighting. But deterrence is effective only if you are willing and able to fight if necessary – and not only to fight but to suffer losses in the fighting. Since the Second World War, Western countries have become increasingly reluctant to contemplate, still less sustain, casualties. During the Falklands War, Margaret Thatcher was told by Clive Whitmore, her principal private secretary, that she would struggle to maintain popular support if losses crept into four figures. By the end of the war, total British losses were 255 military deaths.

The causes for which the British public are willing to suffer

British casualties are fewer than in the 1940s or even the 1980s. Fighting in Afghanistan always had more support than fighting in Iraq, despite the fact that casualties in Afghanistan (457 British military deaths) were higher than in Iraq (179), due to its objective. The conflict in Afghanistan was easier to justify: the Taliban government gave shelter to Osama bin Laden while he planned the 9/11 attacks and then refused to hand him over; in Iraq, the British public was not convinced that George W. Bush and Tony Blair had exhausted all the alternatives to conflict before launching the invasion in March 2003 and was hopping mad when coalition forces failed subsequently to find viable weapons of mass destruction.

The UK's armed forces could not now fulfil the expectations politicians and parts of the public still have of them, apart from training allies and partners, deploying peacekeepers as part of UN operations, and (crucially) defending the UK itself.

With Brexit completed and a general election in the offing, the UK would do best to confront its changed status on the international stage. The reckoning has been so long delayed that political parties may see no penalty in a further postponement. Partial reckonings in the past – such as the withdrawal from East of Suez, which Denis Healey initiated in 1968 – may lull manifesto writers into thinking there is no urgency. But such reviews often felt more radical at the time than they look in retrospect. Partial reassessments disguise rather than solve the problem. An inadequate response may mollify us, but it does not impress other countries, who are not obliged to share our self-delusion. It's time for change.

5

Still Not Finding a Role

History matters most, but geography matters almost as much. History has bequeathed the UK a series of responsibilities that geography makes increasingly difficult for the UK to discharge. For example, on 3 July 1767, a teenage midshipman aboard HMS *Swallow*, sailing the South Pacific, spotted a volcanic island. Captain Philip Carteret later described the island as 'small, high [and] uninhabited, not above four or five miles round ... scarce better than a large rock in the Ocean'[17] and named it Pitcairn's Island after Robert Pitcairn, the eagle-eyed fifteen-year-old. Because the ship's equipment did not include the recently invented marine chronometer, Carteret miscalculated the island's longitude by 3°, placing it 338 km to the west of its actual location and misleading James Cook, who failed to find it in 1773 during his second voyage across the Pacific. Nine mutineers from HMS *Bounty* (with eighteen Tahitians, including eleven women) had greater luck in 1790. Carteret's description of high volcanic cliffs which prevented voyagers from landing appealed to the fugitives, who deliberately beached their ship; the wreck is still visible beneath the waters of Bounty Bay.

The UK formally incorporated Pitcairn and nearby islands into the empire in 1838; at the same time, women on the island became the first in the British Empire to acquire voting rights. In a small, remote, hardscrabble community, everyone had to be engaged if anyone was to survive. The island's population never exceeded 233 (in the 1930s); these days it hovers around fifty, relying for economic survival on the occasional visits of cruise ships, whose passengers are partial to their honey, lobster, and wooden models.

Pitcairn's status as a British Overseas Territory in the twenty-first century is anomalous. Its future is unresolved. Four models are regularly debated and rejected. Independence is not viable for an island with a population in double figures, without a permanent water supply or an airport, thousands of miles from the next population centre. Administrative transfer to New Zealand, where its governor lives (doubling as the UK's high commissioner), has a logic and neatness resisted by the locals. They are equally unenthusiastic about their physical transfer elsewhere; their community is now over 200 years old; the commonest family name is 'Christian', denoting descendants of Fletcher Christian, the leader of the mutiny on the *Bounty*. Attracting new settlers is also controversial. While isolation appeals to many people in theory, in practice it rarely works out (although the island's mayor, for the first time, is someone who arrived on Pitcairn as an adult). Meanwhile, the island suffers many of the problems common to remote, unobserved communities; in the 2000s, the investigation of sexual abuse of minors ended with the imprisonment of half a dozen leading islanders.

However, the islands have become more important geopolitically. No country wants to establish a base there or to exploit local (and plentiful, but difficult to extract) raw materials. Rather the islands command a vast tract of relatively unspoilt ocean. Around them, the British have declared a marine protected area larger than the US. Remoteness and a new status in international law have not protected the area from pollution, however. Henderson Island, the largest in the Pitcairn group, is uninhabited, but its beaches are clogged with plastic waste. The South Pacific Gyre is an ocean current that collects waste from across the southern hemisphere before depositing it on the island. Research published in 2017 suggested that Henderson suffered 'the highest density of plastic rubbish anywhere in the world'[18], with an estimated 37.7 million items weighing nearly 18 tonnes. A (curtailed) operation in 2019 cleared some 6 million tonnes from the eastern beach. Covid-19 put paid to a second expedition.

The fact that the UK and Pitcairn are near antipodes – diametrically opposed on the globe – complicates administration from London. The governor generally visits just once a year; no governor has managed more than four visits in his or her tenure. The resident administrator stays for two years at most and sometimes for only a few months (for example, seven served between February 2022 and February 2023). The only time in my tenure in the FCO when Pitcairn featured in ministerial in-trays was during the child abuse scandal. In common with all other Overseas Territories (OTs), it is a relic of history where geography suggests the UK should have a more distant future relationship. It's time for a grown-up conversation between London and Wellington, with the full participation of islanders. But, again in common with other OTs, islanders need to understand that their views are not pre-eminent: choices that have expensive consequences for others give the others a greater say.

Without its empire, the UK needs to look at the globe again. The UK has carried out periodic and partial reviews of its overseas policy for many decades, but the first formal National Security Strategy (NSS) was published only in 2008. At the time, I was Prime Minister Gordon Brown's foreign policy adviser and discussed my boss' intentions with Condoleezza Rice, then US secretary of state, during a visit to Washington.

She roared laughing. Her crisp advice was, 'Don't bother.' As national security adviser, she had supervised the US's first NSS in 2002 and found it a dispiriting process. She feared that the UK attempt would suffer the same shortcomings, the review becoming a focal point for vested interests hotly to defend the status quo, determined above all else to prevent their field from being deprioritised. The American powers that be had achieved their purpose, ensuring her report was devoid of useful recommendations. She predicted a similar fate for the UK's NSS. She was right.

Since then, British NSSs have been longer and more persuasive on analysis than policy prescription. Hard choices have essentially been avoided. Palmerston would have recognised the breadth of ambition, seeking decisive impact everywhere on all major issues. The UK remains transfixed by the idea of British leadership in every sphere we care about. But a cooler analysis reveals that, at any point in the last fifty years, the UK's major interests and markets have been close to home. Any robust foreign policy for the rest of the twenty-first century should begin with our neighbourhood in Europe and the North Atlantic.

Every British government for the last fifty years has found it difficult to accept that constraint. Post-Brexit, the constraint is even more difficult to acknowledge: having chosen voluntarily to leave our main regional club, the UK looks further afield for its organising principles. Immediately after the 2016 referendum, Boris Johnson talked of 'Global Britain'[19]. In our first conversation after his appointment as foreign secretary, he coined the phrase for the first time in my hearing.

Although the idea excited his supporters, it landed poorly with most audiences. I detected two basic problems. First, the emphasis on 'global' made the UK sound as if it were turning its back on its own continent. Having sloughed the shackles to the organisation that dominates our neighbourhood and demanded too much of British attention, the UK was apparently happy to focus on opportunities further afield for new or reinvigorated traditional markets and for partnerships in everything from tech to development assistance.

Second, the idea of 'taking back control' caused critics to fear that Global Britain was a blueprint for Empire 2.0. The UK, liberated from Europe, would be free to rediscover an abandoned imperial mission. For two years, in every meeting with one particular minister, they would claim that everywhere they went in the world their interlocutors were glad 'to have us back'. An ability to filter diplomatic pleasantries is not a requirement for ministerial appointment.

On 23 October 2022, interviewed in *Le Journal du Dimanche*, Nicolas Sarkozy said: 'Brexit is a major historical aberration. The United Kingdom had won the battle of languages, the battle of finance, the battle of symbols. It is in the process of losing everything with its exit from Europe.'[20] The bleak analysis was widely shared overseas, and by remainers in the UK, to the sneering irritation of leaver leaders. But Brexit is a problem. A few years after leaving the EU, the UK is not better off by any quantifiable measure. Sovereignty may be better than vassalage in theory, but sovereignty is not what it used to be, and the tangible benefits of greater sovereignty are hard to come by.

Brexiteers were right about some things. They were right that the EU is an imperfect project, whose leaders are not open and honest about their ultimate ambitions. They were right that the EU paid less attention to UK concerns than German or French concerns and that that problem had been exacerbated by the launch of the euro without sterling. They were right that the EU's legitimacy is fragile: the European Parliament (EP, the only body elected by EU citizens), although it was made increasingly powerful by treaty changes in the 1990s and 2000s, is still the least powerful of the central organs of the EU, lagging behind the European Commission (which retains the right to initiate legislation) and the European Council (which still controls the purse strings). They were right that, probably as a consequence, the EP fails to command the interest and respect of most EU citizens; turnout for EP elections is habitually low, much lower than for national elections, and between elections few newspapers and fewer television stations report proceedings in any detail. They were right that many council meetings are talking shops whose statements have little impact on the problems they are trying to address.

But they were wrong more than they were right. They underestimated the clout of the EU on the world stage. When the EU is united, its policy choices demand the attention of the US, China, and others. And the UK was often the swing voter when building an EU position. When the UK agreed with either Germany or France, that view prevailed; the trouble was that it was equally true that when Germany and France agreed with each other but not the UK, that view generally carried the day.

Brexiteers underestimated the EU's penetration into the UK's economic life. In 2016, the EU absorbed about 43 per cent of British exports; the trade agreements negotiated by the Commission accounted for an extra 11 per cent of British trade. The best the UK could aspire to in leaving was replicating those arrangements. Nowhere has it improved them. As the EU's first post-Brexit representative in London often said, the EU–UK Trade and Cooperation Agreement was the first trade deal in history whose aim was the reduction in trade between signatories. Liz Truss built a leadership campaign on the scores of bilateral trade treaties the Department for International Trade negotiated with countries further afield, but in not one single case were a new treaty's provisions better from the UK's point of view than the multilateral agreement being replaced. In retirement, some of her cabinet colleagues at the time are voicing their assessment that the (usually smaller) countries on the other side of the table got the better of the negotiation: the UK was so keen to sign that it made key concessions to, for example, Australian and New Zealand agriculture.

Brexiteers spoke passionately about the problems and limitations of UK membership of the EU that they knew about. But none of them saw the whole picture; none saw the balancing advantages in other areas, or was prepared to acknowledge publicly UK successes over the decades, particularly in designing and launching the single market. When it came to negotiating the UK's exit, David Davis, Dominic Raab, Michael Gove, and Co discovered that disentangling the UK went much further than their bugbears. In the end, Brexiteers believed in impossible things, almost as if *Alice in Wonderland* were their inspiration. In *Through the Looking-Glass*, the White Queen invites Alice to believe that she is one hundred and one years, five months, and one day old. Try as she might, Alice cannot believe it:

> 'Can't you?' the Queen said in a pitying tone. 'Try again: draw a long breath, and shut your eyes.'
>
> Alice laughed. 'There's no use trying,' she said: 'one can't believe impossible things.'
>
> 'I daresay you haven't had much practice,' said the Queen. 'When I was your age, I always did it for half-an-hour a day. Why, sometimes I've believed as many as six impossible things before breakfast.'[21]

Displaying more restraint than the White Queen, Brexiteers believed four impossible things: (a) that Brexit would take place in a benign environment, (b) that the rest of the world would give the UK a better deal than it had given the UK as a member of a much larger trading bloc, (c) that the UK could exercise sovereignty again in the way it had done when ruling one-quarter of the Earth's landmass, and (d) that globalisation and the reality of greater interdependence between countries was optional and reversible. They learned the impossibility of their beliefs the hard way, by trying and failing to negotiate them into existence. Sadly for the UK, Brexiteers were articulate, passionate, and persuasive in their belief of impossible things.

Although the reputation of experts has taken a knock in recent years, British voters have tended to respect expert views, especially when experts agree. I remember in the 1975 EEC referendum that nearly every talking head – from Catherine Cookson to Margaret Thatcher – campaigned for continued membership. From Cookson's homespun wisdom ('Whatever you do in life, whether you sink or swim, it's better to do it in company'[22]) to Thatcher's detailed economic prognosis, the overwhelming weight of the argument was pro-Europe, and the result was 2:1 in favour of staying.

By 2016, experts were split. Michael Gove pooh-poohed the importance of their contribution ('I think the people of this country have had enough of experts'[23]), but the key for voters was that the talking heads they trusted were divided; people they would expect to know more than they did were arguing confidently for exit. Politicians who turned out not to know as much as they thought made it easier for voters to take a step into the unknown.

When these politicians triumphed, they looked dazed. At their first post-result rally, Boris Johnson, Michael Gove, and Gisela Stuart looked like naughty schoolchildren outside the headmaster's study, who could not quite believe that they had pulled off the jolly jape they had planned with maximum devastation. Ever since then, a slice of British opinion has claimed that foreigners are 'laughing at us'. But, at least initially, the overseas reaction was different; many observers gave the UK the benefit of the doubt. As a leading foreign businessman said to one of my old bosses: 'We're talking here about the United Kingdom. The United Kingdom always has a plan, even when it's not immediately clear to outsiders.'[24]

But once in office, the naughty-schoolboy politicians discovered two crucial truths about negotiating: in most negotiations, the bigger party generally gets the best of the deal; and in any negotiation, the guys on the other side of the table have a say, and they will defend their interests as doughtily as the home team. In the Brexit negotiation, the EU held all the picture cards. The UK held two decent cards, but for political and, separately, honourable reasons we played them early and cheaply.

At every opportunity after the referendum, EU leaders and negotiators loudly asserted that no part of the negotiation could begin until after the Article 50 trigger had been pulled. Well, they would say that, wouldn't they? They knew that, as soon as the time-limited negotiation started, they held the whip hand. They knew that any sober analysis of UK interests would quickly lead the government to conclude that a no-deal Brexit hurt the UK more than the EU. Of course, that did not prevent some ministers from enthusiastically advocating the no-deal option in the endgame. But the 'reverse Brer Rabbit' strategy only works if you can persuade your adversary that the outcome you most fear is the one you most want. In 2019, Michel Barnier and Co knew that that was nonsense. As soon as the negotiation became time-limited, the UK had more to fear from a disorderly end to that negotiation.

The UK could have delayed pulling the trigger much longer. More than anything else, the EU finds an obstreperous member state its most difficult challenge. For the last several years, its biggest internal (and unresolved) problems have been governments with authoritarian tendencies in Hungary and Poland. The UK could have joined the awkward squad, snarling up business until the key principles and maybe even conclusions of the forthcoming exit negotiation had been agreed. It would have been ugly and disagreeable, it might not have succeeded, but it could not have been less successful than the playing-by-their-book approach actually adopted.

The UK's second trump card was foreign, defence, and security policies. The EU wanted the UK to be involved in the first and needed the UK to be involved in the second and third. Her Majesty's Government decided, honourably, that security and defence issues were simply too important to become bargaining chips. As a result, Prime Minister May took off the table the set of issues where the EU most feared the consequences of the UK's departure. Honourable behaviour about something they cared about did not reap any benefits elsewhere in the negotiation.

The EU referendum involved only UK voters, but it did not affect only the UK. The twenty-seven other member states followed the campaign closely and were deeply affected by the result. By and large, their leaders hated it. As a consequence, they felt no inclination to be helpful during the exit negotiation. Shortly after Theresa May formed her government on 13 July 2016, a senior EU figure visited London to meet the new foreign secretary. With Boris Johnson walking slightly ahead of us, I accompanied him up the Grand Staircase in the FCO. Although Johnson did not speak his visitor's language, he might have detected the hostile tone as he fumed:

> This man has despoiled the political project I most care about, a project I have worked all my life to promote, and now you launch him at us as your foreign minister. I can barely bring myself to talk to him. I don't know how it is going to be possible to do business.

Subsequent events showed that the sentiment was widely shared. The EU was never going to be helpful in the negotiation. Why on earth would it be, when we were casting doubt upon and damaging its great project? As it turned out, the EU was pretty hostile. There was no need for the EU (in my view) to make the integrity of the single market absolute, but it did, with consequences in Northern Ireland for all to see. But, in the end, it had to demonstrate beyond argument that being a member of the EU was better than not being a member, and that leaving was a mistake. It was an existential issue for the EU. Although that was never an explicit part of the referendum campaign in the UK (I never heard the argument 'where the UK leads, others will follow'), EU leaders are gratified by the fact that no other member state has been tempted to follow, and regularly cite opinion polls in the remaining twenty-seven showing that support for EU membership is at historic highs.

Brexit is the central new fact as the UK contemplates its future options on the international stage. The EU will continue to think we made a mistake. Most Brexiteers continue to think we made the right choice. Whether or not Nicolas Sarkozy is right to say the UK is losing everything is beside the point: many of our partners think that way. The UK has to face up to that thinking as it makes its case for a different international role.

Throughout my time in the FCO, inertia was the most powerful force at work in policy formulation and execution. The default settings favoured the status quo and the US; the most accurate guide to any budget in any given year was what the same budget had been the previous year. Policy was confident and unimaginative. Now, in new circumstances whose newness no one can dispute, at the very least the UK has the opportunity to consider new options. And we should at least look at those options before reverting, like Linus van Pelt to his comfort blanket, to the old, familiar, and reliable. We may decide in the end that it is not time for change, but at least that should be a decision after a debate.

PART II

External Challenges

6

Russia/Ukraine

The world faces three long-term mega-challenges and one immediate challenge which demands overwhelming attention and resources in the short term.

Ukraine is the second biggest country in Europe after Russia. For most of its recent history, it has been part of the Russian/Soviet empire. Key events in Russia's founding myth took place in Ukraine, in particular the baptism of Vladimir the Great in 988. Scholars dispute Vladimir's motivation: Russian accounts stress the prince's weighing of the relative merits of different faiths for his people, rejecting Islam ('Drinking is the joy of all Rus') and Judaism (the loss of the Jewish temple in Jerusalem supposedly indicating God's displeasure) and western Christianity (he found no beauty in German churches) before settling on eastern Christianity (describing divine liturgy in Hagia Sophia, his envoys 'no longer knew whether [they] were in heaven or on earth'[25]). Arab sources ascribe more political motives: Vladimir answered Emperor Basil II's appeal for help against growing rebellion in exchange for the emperor's sister's hand in marriage, which required his conversion to Christianity. The victorious alliance subsequently proved hugely useful to the newly converted prince.

Ukraine had been independent from Russia for enough of its history that it could become a founding member of the UN, with its own vote in the General Assembly (admittedly, this was a ruse to boost the Soviet Union's voting heft rather than an acknowledgement of Ukraine's separateness). For decades, the seat at the UN was largely inactive; a Ukrainian foreign minister would occasionally address the General Assembly to make a point, and the delegation automatically followed the Soviet Union whenever it voted. But the fact that it existed made all the difference in 1991 when the Soviet Union collapsed. Ukraine (and Belarus) were able to activate an existing membership and become independent UN members; other constituent republics had to wait for resolutions in the Security Council and General Assembly. The referendum in Ukraine on 1 December confirming Ukrainian secession signalled the complete collapse of the Soviet Union.

For more than a decade, Russia accepted the dissolution of the Soviet empire. George Robertson recalls that, in his nine meetings with Putin when he was secretary-general of NATO, the Russian president signed accords guaranteeing nations, and Ukraine specifically, 'the inherent right to choose the means to ensure their own security, [and] the inviolability of their borders'[26]. But, during his second term, Putin changed his tune. In private and then in public, he called the collapse of the Soviet Union 'the greatest geopolitical tragedy of the twentieth century'[27]. By 2007, in particular in his speech to the Munich Security Conference, he was making the case that the new order was not permanent and could be reversed. Russia had had enough of being pushed around. Things would be different in future.

The world did not have to wait long for evidence of a new Russian approach. In the summer of 2008, Russia invaded Georgia. For years, Russia had stoked up Russian-speaking separatists in the Georgian territories of Abkhazia and South Ossetia. As the August holiday began, the Russian army sent troops through the Roki Tunnel; they had been on

Georgian territory for up to a week before Georgia responded on 7 August. Fighting was intense and not entirely dictated by Russia before President Sarkozy negotiated a ceasefire five days later. By October, Russia had withdrawn from territory that it acknowledged was Georgian but had recognised the independence of Abkhazia and South Ossetia and allowed the ethnic cleansing of Georgians from its two new satellite states.

Putin learned two main things from the brief Russo–Georgian War: first, Russia suffered almost no international penalty (condemnation was routine and toothless; diplomatic life moved on swiftly), and second, Russian soldiers and weapons were less efficient than he had expected. The first conclusion meant he could plan further territorial expansion; the second meant he had to improve Russia's forces before implementing those plans.

In 2012, the interim government in Kyrgyzstan requested Russian help in their second city of Osh after armed clashes between Kyrgyz and Uzbeks had left dozens dead and hundreds injured. Russian peacekeepers restored calm, and remained.

In 2014, Putin set his sights on Crimea after popular protests in February dislodged his ally, Viktor Yanukovych, from the presidential palace in Kyiv. Within a week, Russian forces had captured strategic sites across Crimea. A puppet government was installed on 27 February. A referendum on 16 March asked whether voters wanted to rejoin Russia or reassert the 1992 constitution under which Crimea was a self-governing republic within Ukraine. To no one's surprise, the official result reported 97 per cent of voters, on an 89 per cent turnout, preferring incorporation into the Russian Federation. The state council immediately declared Crimea's independence from Ukraine, simultaneously requesting to join Russia. Russia annexed the peninsula two days later, on 18 March 2014.

The international response was not notably stronger than in

2008. Part of the reason was the history and status of Crimea. Ukraine's principal administrative division is into twenty-seven regions: twenty-four oblasts (provinces), two cities with special status (Kyiv and Sevastopol), and one autonomous republic (Crimea). Crimea's difference had always been acknowledged by a special status. More Russian speakers than Ukrainian speakers lived there. For 200 years, the Russian Empire tried to wrest control of Crimea from the Ottoman Empire before Catherine the Great's fleet destroyed the Ottoman fleet in 1774. Nine years later, Catherine formally incorporated Crimea into the Russian Empire. The territory remained administratively part of Russia until 1954, when the Presidium of the Supreme Soviet transferred Crimea from the Russian Soviet Federative Socialist Republic to the Ukrainian Soviet Socialist Republic in commemoration of the tricentennial of Ukraine's union with Russia. At the time, Nikita Khrushchev, born just 11 km from the Russo–Ukrainian border, was in his first year as first secretary of the Communist Party and the most powerful man in the Soviet Union.

Western countries lamented the implausible speed and prejudice in the organisation of the status referendum, but in effect conceded that Putin had a point: Crimea had been part of Russia for much longer than it had been part of Ukraine, and its transfer had been a ceremonial act within the borders of what was then a united sovereign country. The annexation was reasserting the historical order. There were strong statements and some sanctions, but again Putin would have observed that the international community was compliant in the face of his determined will.

The annexation sparked a war in the Donbas. Already it was clear that Putin's ambition in Ukraine was not limited to Crimea. Policymakers in the West speculated that Russia might be able to provoke rebellion in half the country, everywhere east of Kyiv, where in many areas Russian speakers were more numerous than Ukrainian speakers. That did not happen. Ukrainian resistance was already surprisingly (to Moscow) dogged. Russian forces failed to secure even the two most easterly and most Russia-dominated provinces of Luhansk and Donetsk. A grinding war of attrition set in, complete with trenches reminiscent of the Western Front in the First World War. When I visited Kyiv in 2019, I saw the monument on Independence Square to honour the memory of over 4,000 Ukrainian soldiers killed in the Donbas since 2014.

As attrition turned to stalemate, Putin looked for a way to break through. The enforced isolation of the Covid-19 pandemic gave him time to think, combing through old maps and old books in the Kremlin, which reinforced his view of Russia's mission in the world and increased his determination to reclaim Ukraine as the cradle of Russian civilisation. In 2021, as the pandemic released its grip, Putin upped the tempo of his planning.

The seeds of the special operation in February 2022 were sown in 2014. The annexation of Crimea was an announcement of wider intent. Putin regarded the 'hoodlums' who displaced Yanukovych as enemies: Petro Poroshenko, an oligarch, was bad enough as Yanukovych's immediate successor, but Volodymyr Zelenskyy, a former comedian who denied Poroshenko a second term, was much worse. Many of Putin's criticisms (despite their 'mote and beam' quality) had substance. Ukraine was undoubtedly a corrupt and poorly run country. Government ministers and senior administrators were undoubtedly lining their pockets. Indeed, Putin's lieutenants had some success in buying up and buying off key players.

Even as war still rages, it is clear that Putin miscalculated all-important factors. Although in early 2022 he had reason to think that all factors were where he needed them to be, he was wrong about (a) his external partners, (b) his external adversaries, (c) his military's capabilities, and (d) his Ukrainian target. Over the following twelve months, all four revealed themselves to be fundamentally different from his apparently reasonable expectation.

First, before launching the invasion, he took care to secure the tacit support of his main partner, China. On 4 February 2022, he flew to Beijing for the opening ceremony of the Winter Olympics. At a carefully prepared meeting, he and President Xi Jinping signed a 'no limits' partnership; in sixty-four paragraphs, the two leaders agreed about every important international issue, and showed complete respect for each other's key international interests. Putin recognised that Taiwan remained an inalienable part of China and opposed any form of independence for Taiwan.

Given the fact that more than 100,000 Russian troops were already massing on the Russo–Ukrainian border, it seems implausible that Ukraine was not discussed, even though it did not make its way into the communiqué. I suspect but cannot prove that Putin outlined his plans for later that month. Ukraine would have been classified as a 'renegade province' (à la Taiwan) rather than a sovereign state (à la repeated international agreements signed by Russia). The adversary would have been portrayed as weak, compromised, and ready to accept the Russian embrace at the first invitation. Putin would have predicted a swift victory and sought Chinese support for his explanation for the need to act (to snuff out a Nazi regime and reunite the greater Russian people) against the double standards which the West might indulge.

But China is a bigger international player than Russia these days. The joint statement was long on words but short on concrete commitments. Chinese understanding remained private and conditional on success. In the first year after the invasion, China ensured that Russia was not entirely isolated on the international stage. Because of Russia's veto, there was never any question of action at the UN Security Council. But Western allies moved diplomatic action smartly to the General Assembly, where Russia could not block discussion or exercise a veto. In three high-profile votes, Ukraine secured the support of over 140 UN member states. Only a handful of countries supported Russia: Belarus, Eritrea, Mali, Nicaragua, North Korea, and Syria. But a bloc of thirty-odd countries, led by China, abstained. In the febrile world of the UN Assembly Hall, where piling up opposition to Russia was the name of the game, the abstentions gave more comfort to Moscow than to Kyiv.

China also benefited economically from Russia's plight. With sanctions biting, Russia found it increasingly difficult to sell its raw materials internationally. China, and other abstainers, picked up oil and gas on the cheap at a time when most of the world was paying record prices. Russia became China's cheap petrol station, selling oil at up to a 50 per cent discount, saving China over $3 billion in the middle two quarters of 2022; Russia thus fulfilled John McCain's jibe in 2014 that it was 'a gas station masquerading as a country'.[28]

When Xi visited Moscow in March 2023, Putin rolled out the most scarlet red carpet. The words spoken were as honeyed as in the joint statement, and the pictures depicted harmony. But Xi gave Putin nothing of what he really wanted. Arms would continue to be supplied, but in neither the quantities nor categories Putin most wanted. Putin could direct all Russia's economic assets to the war effort, but what Russia generated would not be substantially supplemented by Beijing.

Second, Putin underestimated the West. After feckless reactions in 2008 and 2014, Putin thought he had Western governments where he wanted them: blustering on the sidelines. Outraged diplomatic statements were not worth the paper they were no longer printed on. He did not even need to shrug his shoulders in response. And since 2014, he had reason to think that the West was even less likely to mount a muscular opposition.

The Americans had retreated, hurt, inside Fortress America. The final withdrawal from Afghanistan in the summer of 2021 had been a humiliation. The Washington-backed local government had not even managed a brief interlude in charge without training wheels. As soon as Uncle Sam left, they collapsed. On his final day in office, President Ashraf Ghani told his staff at the presidential palace in Kabul that he was going to take a short nap, before slipping out the back door and into exile. In the US, former presidents and potential presidential candidates were competing to rule out most stringently the idea of further overseas troop deployments. Newer deployments in the twenty-first century had been wound up and older deployments from the twentieth century were in question, likely to be reduced if not ended. Putin calculated that his main adversary had no stomach effectively to object, and that he would benefit from an unarguable demonstration that Russia was advancing at the same time as the US was retreating.

After the withdrawal from Kabul, NATO looked like a busted flush. Its most significant out-of-area operation had ended in failure. Americans, especially Donald Trump, were increasingly vocal in their unhappiness at the burden the US continued to shoulder within NATO. In the 2010s, the US continued to supply 40 per cent of the alliance's military capability within Europe. Trump's threats to walk away had encouraged European allies to re-examine their defence budgets, but Putin was entitled to note that the recommitment to the defence spending target of 2 per cent of GDP was made with varying degrees of enthusiasm and credibility.

At the same time, allies in the EU were talking of 'strategic autonomy'. Aware that the US would not hang around Europe forever, President Emmanuel Macron was urging EU partners to focus their defence efforts on the EU rather than NATO. He imagined a day when the US would not automatically come to Europe's defence; the EU had to anticipate that day by becoming more capable in advance of an American withdrawal. The theoretical need was clear, but a timetable to replace America's contribution was conspicuously lacking. To Putin, it might have appeared Europe was debating rather than acting on its defence interests.

But NATO's reaction to Putin's invasion was instantaneous. Existing training and equipping programmes were ramped up. And NATO looked to its own defence. High-profile assurances were given to the Baltic States and Poland, and NATO reached out to Russia's neighbours who were not NATO members. In Finland and Sweden, the debate about NATO membership had been simmering inconclusively for years. The Finnish and Swedish governments had consistently concluded that membership would serve no vital interest: all it would do was annoy Russia at a time when Russia posed no direct threat. Suddenly that changed. NATO's popularity rapidly increased.

In October 2021, the advisory board for defence information in Finland had reported that 24 per cent of Finns wanted Finland to join NATO; by October 2022, that figure had risen to 85 per cent. By the end of 2022, all allies apart from Hungary and Turkey had ratified enlargement to include the two Nordic countries. Finland secured Hungarian and Turkish support in March 2023 and joined the following month, but Sweden had to wait until after the Turkish general election in May; at NATO's Vilnius summit in July 2023, President Recep Tayyip Erdogan finally signalled his willingness to admit Sweden, clearing the way for the alliance to grow to thirty-two members.

Bilaterally in Europe, Putin had long focused on Germany. He had met Gerhard Schroeder during his first term as president. And Schroeder became chairman of Gazprom's North European Gas Pipeline company in 2005, shortly after stepping down as chancellor. After the successful commissioning of Nord Stream 1 in November 2011, Schroeder became an enthusiastic advocate for Nord Stream 2. In the teeth of opposition from allies, Germany ploughed ahead with the second, even larger pipeline to bring Russian gas to western Europe. By the end of 2021, work was largely completed at a total cost of almost €11 billion and, at the start of 2022, the pipeline was ready to be commissioned. Putin complacently calculated that a country that had taken flak for more than a decade for its economic ties with Russia, a country that was addicted to cheap Russian energy, whose gas was more than 60 per cent Russian in the winter of 2021–22, would suck up one more disagreeable political embarrassment. He was wrong.

Third, Putin overestimated his own military. The reforms after the uninspiring performance in Georgia in 2008 were meant to forge the best army in the world. But it turned out that merely increasing budgets and ramping up expectations did not address the fundamental problems of the Russian military. Like the society it fought for, it was corrupt. Equipment (like tyres) that needed to be regularly renewed to maintain reliability was customarily not renewed. Instead, old kit was recertified as new and the money for its replacement pocketed by commanders. As a fighting force, the Russian army looked better on paper than in the field.

In the face of an opposition suffering poor morale and poor equipment, the Russian army could still acquit itself adequately. In Kyrgyzstan and Kazakhstan, it helped pro-Russian forces maintain control. But facing an army supported to the hilt by its people, fighting for a cause its soldiers believed was worth dying for, the Russian army quickly fell short. One week after the invasion of Ukraine, it was already clear that the operation was not going according to plan. One early piece of evidence was the unusually high number of senior military deaths. Generals rarely appear in the thick of the action, but when multiple armed columns became bogged down, some went to the front to investigate. Unhappy commanders, gesticulating wildly in the open, provided clear targets for Ukrainian snipers. A dozen one-, two-, and three-star officers were killed in the first six months of the campaign.

Russian losses mounted quickly. Elite forces were deployed early and were shredded. Casualty figures produced by the two sides are wildly implausible, each claiming fantastical losses suffered by the other side. Every day the *Kyiv Independent* newspaper tweets daily and cumulative death tolls. By 1 April, its estimate of Russian deaths stood at 173,990, including an unverified 630 Russian deaths in the previous twenty-four hours. Moscow is mostly mute about Russian losses.

Because each side has an interest in minimising its own losses and inflating its enemy's, most external sources shy away from offering estimates. But some facts still emerge through the fog of war. The sinking of the *Moskva*, the flagship of Russia's Black Sea fleet, on 14 April 2022 is a verified fact. The number of casualties among its 500-strong crew remains disputed, Russia admitting to one, *Naval News* estimating about 240, and *The Insider* giving a range starting at 400. Russia also organised an ad hoc round of conscription. Before it was suspended three months later, however, as many young Russian men had left the country as had joined the army. In 1995, Russia and Mongolia had signed a bilateral investment agreement in which both sides agreed to visa-free travel for their citizens; the agreement came into force in 2006. Sixteen years later, the border was clogged with cars carrying young Russians to Ulaanbaatar.

From the start, a substantial part of the Russian effort was subcontracted to the Wagner Group, a private military company of mercenaries led by Yevgeny Prigozhin, who supplemented his forces by touring Russian prisons and offering the inmates the chance of freedom – if they fought in Ukraine.

While sustaining significant casualties, Wagner forces played an increasingly prominent role in the Russian effort. No dictator relishes military dependence on forces not completely under his control; so, in the spring of 2023, Putin attempted to tighten official control over the Wagner Group. Objecting, Prigozhin mutinied; on 23 June 2023, his forces captured Rostov and threatened Moscow. Next month, Richard Moore, head of the UK's Secret Intelligence Service, publicly analysed Putin's treatment of his adversary that day: 'Prigozhin started off as a traitor at breakfast; he had been pardoned by supper; and a few days later he was invited for tea.'

For a time, Prigozhin went unpunished in a country where the tariff for hoisting a 'no war' placard is seven years in prison. That made the president look weak. But the powerful can avenge their humiliation. On 23 August 2023, the private plane Prigozhin was flying on crashed between Moscow and St Petersburg, killing everyone on board. In tasking his henchmen to rid him of this turbulent mercenary, Putin was exacting his usual punishment for disloyalty, but he forgot that some enemies are as troublesome dead as alive.

Putin has reasserted himself. The control he continues to exercise over the thoughts and actions of the citizens of Russia in 2023 is comparable to the control Big Brother enjoys over the citizens of Oceania in *1984*. But Prigozhin's rebellion has damaged him domestically and internationally. Domestically, Prigozhin let the cat out of the bag: in a series of excoriating videos, he conceded that Ukraine was not run by Nazis and had posed no threat to Russia when the special military operation was launched on 24 February 2022; venting snarling contempt, he accused the minister of defence and chief of the general staff of launching that operation to further their personal ambitions and then running it incompetently.

Internationally, 'strong man' leaders noted that a charter member of their club suddenly looked less qualified for membership. Putin's moment of weakness made him a less appealing partner: at the end of July 2023, the second meeting of the Russia–Africa Summit attracted only seventeen African heads of state and government compared with thirty-eight at the inaugural meeting four years earlier.

Fourth, and most importantly, Putin completely underestimated Ukraine. Before setting out the proof, it is important to acknowledge that at the beginning the Ukrainians wobbled. For weeks and months, they watched the Russians make their preparations over the border, and they listened to international commentators opine that, come the day, Russia would not invade. Russia would not invade because Russia had achieved its maximum power and maximum leverage by threatening invasion. The future of Ukraine was on the international agenda in a way comfortable to Russia. Officials were debating how clearly their governments could state their opposition to Ukraine joining NATO without excluding the possibility completely, in some far-off future when Ukrainian membership of NATO would not threaten the interests of its bigger neighbour or the overall peace of Europe. Commentators who contemplated the possibility of war foresaw a swift capitulation followed by a guerrilla campaign, sustained by a population unsympathetic to the ambition of the conqueror to absorb it. Why would Putin embrace such an unattractive future, when the threat was so much more effective from his point of view than the actual use of force?

Ukrainians were shocked when the air-raid sirens sounded in

the middle of the night on 24 February. Going about their ordinary lives in the ordinary way had not really prepared them. Over the next couple of days, the Russians seemed to make quick progress across the flat plain in the east of the country; Kyiv seemed vulnerable to a blitzkrieg attack. Ukraine's external partners seemed united in their gloomy view of the country's short-term prospects. Hundreds of thousands fled the country, mostly heading west. Ukraine wobbled.

Two crucial things happened over the next few days. First, the Ukrainian army held the line. They were able to mount sufficient opposition to force Moscow to re-examine its plans. The training they had received from Britons, Canadians, and others in the years before the invasion paid off. Western partners had not been as generous in supplying the materiel Kyiv wanted in the quantities they needed, but the Ukrainian army had enough to stall the Russian advance. Second, Zelenskyy held firm. Until the outbreak of hostilities, the president had seemed unpromising war-leader material. In advance, no one could be sure that an accidental president would rise to the challenge.

During my visit in 2019, the British ambassador encouraged me to watch *Servant of the People* on Netflix. The first episode of this hit series in Ukraine is prophetic. An everyman figure – a teacher portrayed by Zelenskyy – is recorded by one of his pupils denouncing the corruption of the presidential campaign that is underway as the TV series starts. The video goes viral and the schoolteacher finds himself spearheading a popular movement to cleanse politics. To the astonishment of the manipulators accustomed to running the show (depicted in bespoke suits, smoking cigars), he is elected president.

Zelenskyy enjoyed a similar political trajectory and, like Vasily, his alter ego, made a good and principled head of state. But Putin saw only the raw material, not what office made of that raw material; he viewed with contempt the comedian who won Ukraine's version of *Strictly Come Dancing*, who voiced Paddington in the movie, and who danced shirtless in high heels for one of his comedy videos. Putin and his propagandists wove their view of Zelenskyy as a degenerate into their narrative of Ukraine as a non-state in thrall to gangsters and Nazis. To them, he looked like a contemptible adversary.

The reality has been different. With a background in entertainment, Zelenskyy showed an instinct for effective communication from the first hours of the invasion. Even quotations that might not be wholly accurate have been incorporated into his counter-narrative. For example, at the start, few outsiders were confident in Ukraine's ability to withstand the Russian onslaught. Mounting an insurgency under foreign occupation was the widespread Western expectation. Zelenskyy was seen as a figurehead who would be better deployed outside the country. President Joe Biden offered him passage out of Ukraine with the idea that he might be able to build a government in exile. Zelenskyy's riposte became a slogan to emblazon across t-shirts: 'The fight is here; I need ammunition, not a ride.'

Every day, from day one, he addressed his people – with defiance, with honesty, and with humour. He rallied his government. He spurned the offer of a safe route out for him and his family. He shared the fate of his countrymen, and they were inspired. Of all Putin's miscalculations, the biggest was underestimating Zelenskyy and the Ukrainians he leads.

Over a year later, some unavoidable consequences of Putin's four strategic miscalculations are visible. First, and most important, he cannot achieve his main objective: Ukraine will never be a complaisant component of Russia. The manner of the attack has turned Ukrainians against Russia. The targeting of civilians, the destruction of basic infrastructure, and the casual threat to use nuclear weapons have turned the over-whelming majority of Ukrainians against Russia in a way that makes it impossible to imagine them as docile citizens in a greater Russia. Ukraine's national identity has been forged in this war, in its own eyes and in the eyes of the rest of the world.

Second, although Putin ideally wanted Ukraine to fall into his lap, its citizens glad to be liberated from their 'Nazi' usurpers and content to accept direction from Moscow, old-fashioned conquest was always an option. To decimate the regime clinically, to prove brutally to the population the error of its ways, and to re-educate cynically the next generation was always Option B. But Option B is also a nasty pipe dream. After eighteen months of all-out war, Ukraine has shown that it will not lose. Its people know that unless they fight on, they will suffer the fate of Option B. But, more than that, they have the stomach to keep fighting. What they want from the rest of the world is the means to win.

The appeal is aimed squarely at the West. Even in the first uncertain stages of the war, Zelenskyy paid close attention to relations with the West, particularly the US. Covid-19 had accustomed everyone to remote working and meetings on a screen. Parliament after parliament, starting with the US Con-gress, gave Zelenskyy a remote platform. I was present in the gallery of the House of Commons when he addressed a packed session of MPs and peers, looking down at us from what are now known as 'Zelenskyy screens'. He spoke for less than ten minutes, quoting Shakespeare and Churchill. His audience had been admirers before he spoke, but when he finished we were ardent fans.

At the end of 2022, Zelenskyy began to travel abroad. He started again with the US, and then visited London, Paris, and Brussels in quick succession at the start of 2023. I was in Westminster Hall when he addressed a mass gathering of MPs, peers, and staffers. His appeal for military aid was direct and passionate. He repeatedly paid tribute to the UK, at one point remarking that the UK was fortunate because it had a king who was an air-force pilot. He continued: 'In Ukraine today, every air force pilot is a king – for us, for our families, because they are so few, they are so precious, that we the servants of our kings do everything possible and impossible to make the world provide us with modern planes.'[29] He asked the UK for 'wings for freedom', and his audience lapped it up. By the end of his tour, no category of military help was ruled out. The tanks, fighter planes, high-mobility artillery rocket systems, and multiple-launch rocket systems delivered in 2023 could turn a force that will not lose into one that will win.

On the other hand, the Russians offer dogged determination. They point out that, ultimately, their resources are greater than Ukraine's. In a grinding attritional war, where each side is willing to throw everything it has at the other, the side with the greater resources will win in the end. The Nazis drove the Russians to the brink of defeat in 1941, but four years later the Soviet Union triumphed. Putin can quote the history, but he must hope not to have to test his people.

New players and new factors have always affected the outcomes of armed conflict. The addition of the US in the First and Second World Wars made the decisive difference. In the 2020s, the subtraction of the US might have a similar effect. President Biden's administration has put its money where its mouth is: the US has supplied Ukraine with ten times more military and financial assistance than any other country. The support is confident and increasingly complete. In 2023, Washington still shies away from providing kit with which Ukraine could hit Russia proper from its positions next to Russian lines, but decision-making moves inexorably in Ukraine's favour. American support is essential, and it is demonstrably making a difference, but it is not domestically uncontroversial. Candidates for the Republican Party's nomination for the presidency publicly express their doubts about the administration's policy. They want the US to wind down its support; they advocate negotiation.

Every conflict there ever was ended in a negotiation. But the problem with a premature negotiation is that it starts with the ideas of 'right on both sides' and 'compromise'. Yet Russia has mounted an unprovoked attack, denying recent agreements and rehabilitating a baseless interpretation of history. Russia is wrong. Whatever Russia extracted from negotiations would be undeserved, so dialogue is best begun only when Ukraine has established dominance in the fight and is in a position to limit Russian gains and secure its independent future.

With Donald Trump or any of his Republican rivals in the Oval Office, Putin has reason to hope. The Americans may force the Ukrainians to the negotiating table before they are willing. But I would urge the Kremlin not to hang its hat on such a development for two reasons. First, Donald Trump may be the candidate best disposed to Putin and the one most likely to win the Republican nomination, but he is also the Republican least likely to displace Biden. The midterm elections in 2022 gave a foretaste of how the electorate feels about Trump's possible resurgence. His endorsement carried a slew of attractive-only-to-the-Trump-base candidates to Republican nominations for the positions of senator, governor, and representative. In the general election, with the exception of a House seat in Wyoming, they all lost.

Second, and more important, wars are not always won by the stronger party. As Clausewitz observed, control over territory also involves control over the people who live there. He said that peoples were less and less likely to allow their political destinies to be determined over their heads. The historian Michael Howard elaborated: 'If the people themselves are not prepared if necessary to take part in the defence of their own country, they cannot in the long run be protected; and if they are not prepared to acquiesce in alien conquest, that conquest cannot in the long run be sustained.'[30]

As applied to Ukraine, on the evidence of 2022 and 2023, there are uncomfortable conclusions for Putin: Ukrainians will not accept Russian conquest; at the start, they resisted more effectively than expected; more recently, they have begun to turn the tide. Will Russians allow Putin to persist when they see the war effort failing? Howard's interpretation of Clausewitz's thinking can be adapted and applied to Russia: if the people themselves are not prepared if necessary to take part in the attack of another country, they cannot in the long run be coerced into doing so; and if they are not prepared to make sacrifices to continue the alien conquest, that conquest cannot in the long run be sustained.

Looking further ahead, Putin's main problem is close to home. Every foreign invasion of Russia has shown Russia's infinite capacity to sacrifice in order to defend the motherland, but Putin is engaged in an optional war of aggression. Over time, even Russia's carefully controlled media will not be able to disguise the lack of Ukrainian support for the war. Russia is an unwanted outsider. Young men are being asked to die for a cause that is increasingly difficult to understand (if the Ukrainian government really are all Nazis, why do so few Ukrainians want to get rid of them?); in the end, as casualties mount, it will be impossible to defend.

Meanwhile, much of the international community looks on, somewhat bemused. In the Global South, they wonder why so much attention is devoted to one conflict, when there are many others closer to home. They wonder why they should care. This is Europe's war, or the West's war, the latest instalment in an unloved series stretching back to Afghanistan and Iraq. But, as 2022 wore on, the rest of the world felt the consequences of the absence of Ukraine's crops in international markets. In India, sunflower oil is a staple in every household, usually the cheapest and most widely available cooking oil. When prices began to rise steeply, Indians discovered that Ukraine was the main source of the product.

In his public diplomacy, particularly in sub-Saharan Africa and Asia, Putin makes much of the parallels to Iraq and Afghanistan. He accuses the US and the West of double standards: they went to war to defend their interests despite the misgivings of much of the international community; why shouldn't Russians be allowed to defend their interests? The argument ignores three key facts. First, although the wars in Iraq and Afghanistan were controversial (domestically as well as internationally), President Bush and Prime Minister Blair assiduously built a legal justification. For months, their ambassadors negotiated at the UN and, on 8 November 2002, Security Council Resolution 1441 offered Saddam Hussein and Iraq a 'final chance to comply with its disarmament obligations'. Lawyers still dispute whether the resolution required a further resolution before military force was used, but no commentator disputes the claim that a resolution that clearly required a follow-up resolution would have been much quicker to negotiate. Coalition leaders believed they had a solid legal base when they launched air attacks on 19 March 2003.

On the other hand, apart perhaps from a private conversation with Xi Jinping, Putin made no attempt in advance to make an international case for attacking Ukraine. When the international community was consulted, through resolutions at the General Assembly of the UN, its condemnation of Russia's action was overwhelming. In the Iraq scenario there was a disputed legal basis, but in the Ukraine scenario there was no legal basis at all.

Second, the parallel with Iraq and Afghanistan ignores the unhappy outcome for the outside forces. In the end, the key fact in both Iraq and Afghanistan was that the local population did not want the permanent presence of outside forces; some might have welcomed their help in ridding them of an oppressive government but, in both countries, once that task was accomplished, the majority objected to foreigners trying to dictate their future.

Third, Russia is not confronting the US or NATO in Ukraine. Despite its imaginative claims, it is confronting Ukrainians. No NATO troops are deployed in Ukraine. Ukraine is not a member of NATO. The US and all European countries are helping Ukraine because Ukraine has a right under the UN Charter to defend itself, and other UN member states have the right to supply arms to a fellow member state defending itself.

This is Ukraine's fight, but the consequences of what happens there will be felt far beyond Ukraine. If Putin succeeds, his ambition will not be satisfied for long. Fourteen republics broke away in 1991; he will have reabsorbed one and will have another (Belarus) under his thumb. He will have acquired a border with Moldova, which already has a pro-Russian breakaway government in Transnistria. Moldova will likely be next on his wish list. And, at the least, Russian pressure and informal control will increase in the Transcaucasus and Central Asia.

If Putin fails, the consequences will be equally important. How Russia fails is relevant. Russian humiliation will not help global security and stability: the Russian bear at bay will look for opportunities to lash out. The image of Russia's president in the dock at the International Criminal Court in The Hague is beguiling for Russia's opponents, but unhelpful. Its realistic prospect will be an incentive for Putin to continue fighting when otherwise he might consider a negotiated settlement.

Russia's 'failure' must be framed entirely in terms of Ukraine.

Russia must be thrown out of all territory occupied since 24 February 2022. It would be desirable for Russia to be forced from all territory occupied since February 2014. A complete Ukrainian victory would restore Ukraine's internationally recognised borders from before the annexation of Crimea.

Neither Ukraine nor the wider international community need demand more. Russian territory is not threatened. Russia's government is not threatened. Russia will continue to choose its leader without interference from the international community. Russia's standing in the international community will not change formally; until the UN Security Council is comprehensively reformed, it will remain a permanent member.

It is vital that Russia understands the limits of the war aims of Ukraine and its partners. Mission creep undermines the coherence and legitimacy of any military operation. And mission creep that included the invasion of Russia and overthrow of Putin would be the only possible theoretical justification for Russian use of nuclear weapons.

Since President Harry S. Truman authorised Enola Gay and Bockscar to drop atom bombs on Hiroshima and Nagasaki on 6 and 9 August 1945, no other nuclear bomb has been used in a conflict. President Kennedy and Secretary Khrushchev got closest in the Cuban Missile Crisis in 1962 but stepped back from the brink. The number of nuclear powers has grown to nine: the US, Russia, China, France, the UK, India, Pakistan, Israel, and North Korea. Nuclear doctrine is national rather than governed by international rules. Only China and India have ever explicitly accepted a 'no first use' policy, reserving their use for a second strike in response to an enemy targeting them or their allies with weapons of mass destruction.

However vague nuclear-weapon states are about the circumstances in which they would use their arsenal, they generally agree that nuclear weapons can be used only in extremis, when the territory and indeed the continued political existence of the nuclear-weapon state is under direct attack. In the years since the Manhattan Project gave the US a nuclear-weapons capability, other states have wanted the capability, principally to give them invulnerability at home; nuclear weapons are the ultimate deterrent to external interference. Israel destroyed Iraq's nascent programme, and the West persuaded Libya to give up theirs; Saddam Hussein and Muammar Gaddafi saw their regimes disintegrate before their own ignominious executions, filmed on mobile phones. The lesson the Kim family drew in Pyongyang was that a viable device was the best protection a regime could buy. The ayatollahs in Tehran (pursuing a policy initiated by the Shah) have evidently drawn the same conclusion.

Putin has publicly mentioned the possibility of deploying nuclear weapons several times since the invasion of Ukraine. Each mention grabs the international community by the throat. Each word is parsed. Every Russia expert is asked to opine. The foreign-affairs specialist Fiona Hill judges that Putin is capable of pressing the button: in his words, 'Why would we want a world without Russia?'[31]

The issue is not the continued existence of Russia but the continuation of Russia's adventure in Ukraine. The international community needs to make it plain that the use of a nuclear weapon to retrieve a desperate position in a war of choice outside Russia's borders is utterly unacceptable. It seems that, in different ways, the US and China have both made that point, Washington saying that any nuclear deployment – no matter how 'small' or 'tactical' – would be met by a massive conventional response. The use of a nuclear weapon beyond Russia's borders would be a declaration of war against the world. Beijing, too, has repeated the very limited circumstances in which the use of a nuclear weapon might be justified, no doubt adding that China, having acquired the capability in 1964, was the first country to embrace 'no first use'.

For practical purposes, the possession of nuclear weapons has not helped Putin in the war against Ukraine. He might make their flesh creep and give nervous Ukrainians another reason to lose a night's sleep, but he has not cowed them into surrender. As Zelenskyy and his war cabinet have war-gamed the possibility, they will have concluded that the use of a nuclear weapon would not materially help Putin's campaign. First, a nuclear explosion would irradiate significant territory of a country Putin claims as his own, a curious way to treat land you purport to care about. Second, the circumstances in which the use of a tactical device would advance the Russian campaign are highly circumscribed. If Ukrainian generals were to concentrate significant forces in one place, a nuclear explosion would destroy them. But Ukrainian forces are dispersed across the thousands of kilometres separating them from Russian troops. Wiping out a few hundred or even a few thousand troops would not make a significant military difference, especially as, third, using a nuclear weapon would end such international support as Putin continues to enjoy and would irradiate farmland that has become Africa's breadbasket.

My FCO career was punctuated by conflicts involving the UK that were controversial at the time, and even more controversial in the rear-view mirror. British deployments in Iraq and Afghanistan failed to achieve the objectives that those deployments were eventually saddled with; more limited objectives, perhaps limited to what was achieved in the first weeks of the deployment, might have helped. But expanding objectives led to failure. Removing enemy regimes that had directly harmed the US, the UK's principal ally, was one thing; trying to dictate to the locals what should replace those regimes was quite another. British experience in Iraq and Afghanistan has dulled the UK public's appetite for foreign deployments at scale for the foreseeable future.

The war Ukrainians are fighting – to defend and reclaim their country – is the best for British interests in my adult lifetime. The fact that we are not direct participants is part of its appeal. It is in the UK's strategic interest to supply Ukraine for as long as Ukrainians are willing to fight. The British role is key but indirect: the training of combatants, the supply of materiel, and the corralling of international opinion. A Russian victory would be disastrous for British and Western as well as Ukrainian interests. A Ukrainian victory would open the possibility of consolidating the post-Cold War order, with all countries accepting their internationally recognised borders. A Ukrainian victory would lead to renewed efforts to solve the 'frozen conflicts' in other former republics of the Soviet Union, particularly in Georgia and Moldova.

For the last twenty years of my career, I said that the West's victory in the Cold War was bigger than we needed it to be. We needed the Soviet Union to release its grip on the eastern half of Europe; we needed Russia, reasserting itself after the collapse of the Communist system, to see that the West was not its implacable foe; and we needed to begin tackling common challenges together. But we did not need Russia to disintegrate to make our victory secure. I remember the glib thought that, with its empire in pieces, Moscow would be fully occupied with rebuilding relations with the successor states and less able to make trouble elsewhere.

But the completeness of Russia's humiliation was always resented in the Kremlin. As soon as Russia picked itself up after the heady but ultimately drunken and misleading Yeltsin interlude, it was able to act on its resentment. However much it concentrated on its near abroad in the former Soviet Union, there was always capacity to make trouble elsewhere. The

West felt that diplomatically, as the Security Council became a decreasingly effective forum for dispute settlement and even management, and as Russia cosied up to the West's adversaries in Syria, Iran, and North Korea.

In 2023, we are where we are. Lamenting too big a victory will not help us. Understanding the effects of that victory on Russia, however, might help us deal with Putin. Russia remains the biggest country in the world, with the largest reserves of most raw materials. Russia keeps its seat at the top table. But thirty years after the dissolution of the Soviet Union, republics that left will not come back. In thirty years, they have consolidated their separate national identities.

After Putin ordered the invasion of Ukraine, someone asked his foreign minister who Putin listened to. Sergey Lavrov replied that Putin had just three advisers: Ivan the Terrible, Peter the Great, and Catherine the Great. Perhaps he is currently incapable of giving up an outdated imperial vision, but a Ukrainian victory would force him to do so. The West would do well to signal that only the vision has ended; Russia within its borders could quickly become a respected partner again. The magnanimity of Vienna in 1815 rather than the malice of Paris in 1919 would be the guide: if Russia accepted Ukraine's permanent independence within the borders of 1991, then Russia could resume its place on the international stage. It would offer a chance to relive the 1990s, but with the West understanding the responsibilities and limitations of victory, even if the victory this time was Ukraine's rather than our own.

7

China

The most striking item in the dining room of the British ambassador's residence in Beijing is a portrait of George Staunton, an Irish baronet, who, as a boy of twelve, accompanied Lord Macartney on his embassy to China. The second most striking artefact in the dining room is Macartney's framed official commission from George III.

George Macartney (1737–1806) was a distinguished colonial administrator, remembered these days for one aphorism and one failed diplomatic mission. After the Treaty of Paris in 1763 formalised British conquests made during the Seven Years' War, he remarked that Britain now controlled a 'vast Empire, on which the sun never sets'.[32] And in 1792 he was appointed first British envoy to the Qianlong Emperor in China.

Since Marco Polo in the thirteenth century became the first European to survive long enough to write about his experiences travelling to China, various European rulers had tried to open a channel of communication and encourage trade. All of them came to nothing. The Chinese were used to treating outsiders as underlings, in business as well as in politics. They were the hegemon in the only part of the globe they knew. For them, foreigners were vassals rather than equals. A foreigner might arrive in a well-equipped ship with intriguing gifts, but every visitor looked puny measured against the Son of Heaven (the sacred title of the Chinese sovereign).

In the seventeenth and eighteenth centuries, Qing emperors opened trading routes slowly. The Canton System channelled trade through a guild of thirteen trading companies, known as the Cohong (Hong in Cantonese), selected by the imperial government. As British prosperity increased, so British taste developed. By the end of the eighteenth century, British appetite for Chinese spices, silk, porcelain, and tea was not satisfied by the quantities Britain was able to import.

In the 1780s, to encourage the opening up of trade and encouraged by the East India Company, Pitt the Younger decided to send an ambassador to Beijing, but his first choice, Charles Cathcart, died on the journey. Macartney suggested an alternative replacement to his friends in the East India Company before agreeing to take on the mission himself, on condition that he be allowed to choose his companions and be raised to the rank of earl in the peerage (he had been made a baron in 1776, shortly after becoming governor-general of the British West Indies).

Macartney chose George Staunton (father of the subject of the portrait) as his deputy, on the understanding that Staunton would replace him as leader should he suffer the same fate as Cathcart. Their one hundred-strong delegation included doctors, scientists, and artists who would record their impressions. Interpretation was a challenge, because the Chinese authorities forbad Chinese people from teaching Chinese to foreigners. Staunton nevertheless managed to recruit four Chinese Catholic priests, whose task was complicated by the fact that they spoke Latin but not English. With these captive tutors, Staunton junior began Chinese lessons on the voyage.

A flotilla of three ships, led by HMS *Lion*, left Portsmouth on 26 September 1792. A storm in the Channel led to the temporary loss of the smallest vessel – the *Jackal*, which later caught up with the flotilla in Batavia (present-day Jakarta)

– and necessitated emergency repairs at Torbay. The full squadron arrived in Macao on 19 June 1793. Before its arrival, representatives had begun negotiating the route of the final leg of the journey with the local governor. Customarily, foreign delegations disembarked at Canton and travelled north overland. But, because of the large and fragile nature of the gifts Macartney was bringing, the emperor exceptionally gave permission for his ships to dock at Tianjin, the closest major port to Beijing. Macartney's oceanographers were able to use the opportunity illicitly to improve their charts of the Yellow Sea.

The delegation arrived in Tianjin on 11 August. They negotiated final arrangements for their reception by the emperor with the local viceroy. He told them that they would be received in a summer palace in Chengde rather than in the capital. They persuaded him to allow some of the more fragile gifts, including a planetarium, to stay in Beijing rather than be transported to Chengde. The viceroy was ordered not to accompany the embassy on its final leg; according to Qianling, 'Treated too favourably, a barbarian becomes arrogant.'[33]

In the days before the meeting with the emperor, the Chinese urged Macartney to kowtow, downplaying the significance of the ritual as 'mere exterior and unmeaning ceremony'.[34] But he objected: he would not do anything before the emperor that he would not do before his own sovereign. He suggested that whatever he did before the emperor, a Chinese official should do before the portrait of George III that had accompanied the embassy, as an acknowledgement of the equal status of the two sovereigns. The Chinese objected: as Son of Heaven, their monarch could have no equal. Eventually, Macartney agreed to genuflect before the emperor, as he would before his own king, but not to kiss his hand as he would the king (no one kissed the emperor's hand); in addition, he would prostrate himself once (as opposed to the usual nine times). British accounts of the subservience Macartney was prepared to show are kinder to his independence of spirit than has been corroborated by later academic research.

The meeting took place at Chengde, beyond the Great Wall of China, on 14 September 1793. Macartney and his retinue left their lodgings at 3 a.m.; the emperor arrived at 7 a.m. Thousands waited outside the yellow yurt where the emperor received his guest and three of his companions – Staunton and his son, and an interpreter. Having knelt before the emperor, Macartney handed over George III's letter; the translators had made the text more acceptable to imperial eyes, ditching references to Christianity and referring to the emperor with the elaborate politeness he expected. The emperor was apparently impressed by young Staunton's proficiency in Mandarin; he gave him a present. At the subsequent banquet, the British delegation was seated (perhaps only briefly) to the emperor's left, in the position of honour (which is why even a brief placement was worth boasting about).

In his written replies to the letter, the Qianlong Emperor disappointed the British; he did not grant their immediate objectives of (a) relaxing constraints on British trade, (b) granting them the use of a 'small, unfortified island' for the exclusive use of British traders, or (c) establishing a permanent embassy in Beijing: 'Our Celestial Empire possesses all things in prolific abundance and lacks no product within its borders. There is therefore no need to import manufactures of outside barbarians in exchange for our own produce.'[35] His final words commanded George III to 'tremblingly obey and show no negligence',[36] using the standard formulation for a Chinese subject.

But the British had got their foot in the Chinese imperial door towards the end of the era when the Chinese could treat the wider world in the same way they treated their neighbourhood.

In the nineteenth century, Britons and other outsiders would become more successfully insistent, and the Chinese would discover an appetite for Western products, including – disastrously for them, and despicably encouraged by the British – Indian-grown opium.

The Chinese narrative is that the nineteenth and twentieth centuries interrupted the natural order in which China was the centre of the world ('the Middle Kingdom'). The recent past has been an aberration; the twenty-first century is witnessing a return to normality. Even though it is true that China was the centre of its world before Europeans were able to dictate terms 200 years ago, China's world was discrete from other civilisations. Only India impinged, and India was separated from China either by the (unscalable) Himalayas or a treacherous journey across two oceans. The size and capabilities of Macartney's ships impressed the Qing Chinese, whose junks were capable only of short journeys that hugged the coastline. In earlier centuries the Chinese may or may not have outstripped Aztec, Inca, Bugandan, European, and other civilisations, but comparison was impossible at the time, because the Americas, Africa, and Europe were completely closed to them.

China roaring back to reclaim its rightful place at the pinnacle of the world is central to China's contemporary view of itself. Its external relationships do not easily accommodate the idea of equality; when China has its way, it dominates any bilateral relationship and any organisation of which it is a member. Other countries find themselves playing the subservient role China assigns them in their relationship because of China's massive economic success since Deng Xiaoping embraced capitalism with Chinese characteristics.

Alongside tentatively expressed but rampantly implemented support for capitalism, Deng also launched a twenty-four-character strategy to guide China as it re-emerged on the world stage: 'Observe calm; secure China's position; handle affairs [with the US] calmly; hide our capacity and bide our time; maintain a low profile; and never claim leadership [on the world stage].'[37]

For Xi Jinping the formulation is too passive, but also too revered to be ditched. He has come up with his own twenty-four-character strategy, a recasting of the original: 'Be calm; keep determined; seek progress and stability; be proactive and go for achievements; unite under the Communist Party; dare to fight.'[38] Domestically, Xi stresses the centrality of the Chinese Community Party (CCP), which Deng had assumed without feeling the need to state. Internationally, he implies that, having bided its time, China is not only ready for a leadership role and able to match the achievements of any other country but prepared to fight to claim its rightful position.

During the Great Chinese Famine of 1959–1961, China's economy shrank (by nearly 30 per cent in 1961). Having recovered in the early 1960s, the economy shrank again in 1966 and 1967 due to the initially devastating effect of the cultural revolution. Growth was erratic until the end of the cultural revolution and Mao Zedong's death in 1976. After Deng put China on a new economic path, growth picked up; after 1978 it dipped below 5 per cent in only two years (1989 and 1990) before the Covid-19-induced slump to 2.24 per cent in 2020.

Chinese economic growth was not only spectacularly high but consistently maintained. In the forty years after Mao's death, China overtook all other economies in nominal GDP apart from the US. By the 2010s, the Chinese economy grew by the equivalent of a medium-sized G20 economy (such as Argentina) each year.

Every country has had to pay attention to the new behemoth in East Asia. For centuries, outsiders acknowledged China's potential. In exile on Saint Helena, Napoleon is alleged to have observed: 'China is a sleeping giant. Let her sleep, for when she wakes, she will shake the world.'[39] The first person to ascribe the full quotation to Napoleon was the screenwriter Bernard Gordon, who put the words into the mouth of David Niven's character in the 1963 movie *55 Days at Peking*. Earlier, the *Time* magazine cover on 1 December 1958 had cited part of the quotation.

But it seems that later generations attributed a foresight to Napoleon that he never fully expressed himself. The closest Napoleon got, according to a contemporary account, was advice to Great Britain recorded by his Irish doctor on Saint Helena; Barry O'Meara recalled the emperor doubting the wisdom of Britain going to war with China:

> It would be the worst thing you have done for a number of years, to go to war with an immense empire like China, and possessing so many resources. You would doubtless, at first, succeed, take what vessels they have, and destroy their trade; but you would teach them their own strength. They would be compelled to adopt measures to defend themselves against you; they would consider, and say, 'we must try to make ourselves equal to this nation. Why should we suffer a people, so far away, to do as they please to us? We must build ships, we must put guns into them, we must render ourselves equal to them.' [They would] get artificers and shipbuilders from France and America, even from London; they would build a fleet, and, in the course of time, defeat you.[40]

Even when his words were long-winded but accurately recorded, rather than pithy and polished by admirers, the ex-emperor was on to something. The stubborn and protracted conservatism of the imperial court followed by revolution, civil war, and Maoism delayed China's emergence on to the world stage but, by the 2000s, Beijing was activating its latent power. The Asian financial crisis, starting in 1997, eventually blighted the whole world. When Gordon Brown visited Beijing in 2008, he paid tribute to the role of his hosts in ensuring the world did not fall into a 1930s-scale slump: China had become every country's key trading partner.

Even though I disagree with the assertion by the Chinese that they are restoring China's natural place at the centre (or top) of the world, that hardly matters; China is exercising a power globally that it once felt was its right to exercise in the part of the globe known to its rulers. The keynote in its external relations is dominance.

First, Beijing wants direct control of all territory that was once part of the Chinese imperium. At the end of the twentieth century, Hong Kong and Macao returned to the fold. Taiwan is the most obvious outstanding example. But all its neighbours feel the keenness of China's interest in border areas. The nine-dash line delineated China's ambitions in the South China Sea, ambitions that in 2016 the Permanent Court of Arbitration deemed to have no basis in law, overlapping as they did the territorial waters of Brunei, Indonesia, Malaysia, the Philippines, and Vietnam. When the arbitration failed to go China's way, it briefed noisily against the objectivity of one of the panel whose wife was Filipina.

India, too, is targeted. As the prime minister's foreign policy adviser, I worked closely with colleagues in the office of Prime Minister Manmohan Singh. On one of my visits to Delhi, my main interlocutor was uncharacteristically relaxed; he explained that recent contacts with Beijing had confounded his natural pessimism; relations had improved and were their best ever. Ten years later, I saw him in retirement. Over lunch, he warned me about China. The rapprochement of 2008 had been the high point. Shortly afterwards, Beijing reactivated its interest in long-standing border disputes. He expanded: 'Simon, they claimed an entire Indian state. Arunachal Pradesh is over 80,000 km² in the eastern foothills of the Himalayas. They reckon they have documentary proof that it was once under Chinese suzerainty and want it back.'

At the end of our lunch, my Indian colleague said that after long reflection he had concluded that China's objective vis-à-vis India was quite simple: 'They want to kill us.' In the long term, India – because of the size of its population – is China's only plausible rival. Strategically, China has an interest in eliminating the threat before India mobilises its immense latent power.

On a subsequent visit to Dhaka, a conversation in the margins of the UK–Bangladesh Strategic Dialogue provided grist to the mill of Indian disquiet. One of my Bangladeshi interlocutors said that he had made a study of the memoirs and journals of British travellers in the subcontinent in the early Victorian era. But the works of one author had always been denied him, because they were still classified as secret nearly 200 years after they were written. He had concluded that the only explanation was that the explorer had described as Chinese various settlements that India now considered inalienably Indian.

China's neighbourhood feels its ambition most keenly. But its preferred way of doing business with countries further afield is similarly high-handed; the basis for diplomatic relations is mutually acknowledged Chinese superiority. The Chinese treat their junior partners with greater respect than in the eighteenth century but still make their view of disparity in status unmistakably plain. When I visited Beijing in 2007 to prepare for the prime minister's visit, I dealt mainly with Dai Bingguo, who was recently appointed state councillor (effectively President Hu Jintao's foreign policy adviser). He was the calm centre surrounded by the frenetic activity of underlings.

Like most good diplomats, he was not only interested in

the formal agenda. In the middle of a seven-course banquet, he began comparing my origins and my age with his; I was a forty-six-year-old northerner. He explained that he, too, was an outsider; his surname was not one of the Hundred Family Surnames (also known as Bai Jia Xing – a list of Chinese surnames compiled nearly one thousand years ago). Outsiders could make their way in the system, but they had to be more accepting of the system than insiders. He was sixty-six; he had the position he had always wanted but no longer the energy to do the things he had wanted twenty years earlier: 'In China, we think forty-six is the best age for a man, old enough to carry authority, vigorous enough to carry out his plans.'

In dealing with the formal agenda, Dai made his points gently but firmly. He commended the work of the Shanghai Cooperation Organisation (SCO). I had never heard of it. For me, it became a charter member of Clubs to Which We Do Not Belong. For all our history, the UK has been used to being in the room – at every congress in the nineteenth century, at every conference and in every club in the first half of the twentieth. But in the second half of the twentieth century, the world began organising itself in new ways.

The first clubs from which we were excluded were regional. The UK held back from joining the regional organisation of its own region in the 1950s. Elsewhere, although the UK had colonies in the regions organising themselves, membership of new organisations was restricted to independent states: the Arab League (1945), the Organisation of American States (1948), the Organisation of African Unity (1963, replaced by the African Union, 2001), the Association of Southeast Asian Nations (1967), and the South Asian Association for Regional Cooperation (1985).

In the late twentieth century, leaders acquired a taste for summit meetings to discuss economic questions. Valéry Giscard d'Estaing convened the first meeting of the 'group of six' (G6) leading industrial economies at the Château de Rambouillet in November 1975. Four European heads of government (Giscard, Helmut Schmidt, Harold Wilson, and Aldo Moro), plus the president of the US and prime minister of Japan, met for three days. For the next meeting in Puerto Rico in 1976, the six invited Pierre Trudeau of Canada (the world's seventh-largest economy). From 1997, the group expanded from G7 to G8 (before reverting to G7 in 2014). Including Russia was the West's strongest signal that relations with the Soviet Union's main successor state were moving on; excluding Russia from 2014 was the strongest political signal of displeasure after the annexation of Crimea.

Regional economic groupings began organising at the end of the twentieth century: the Asia-Pacific Economic Cooperation (APEC, 1989), the Southern Common Market (Mercosur, 1991), and the Southern African Development Community (1992). APEC was the only one to make much of an impression outside its region: with the US, China, and Japan meeting, every country not at the table felt the possibility that decisions directly affecting them were being taken.

I was working for Gordon Brown when Lehman Brothers crashed and the world economy tanked in 2008. Brown quickly concluded that the existing machinery for dealing with the world's economic problems would not suffice: the G8 was too small and, with fifty-four members, the UN Economic and Social Council was too big. The existing group that included most of the key players was, for him, the G20. After the Asian financial crisis in the 1990s, Brown had been instrumental in organising the inaugural G20 meeting of finance ministers and central bank governors in Berlin in December 1999.

As the world grappled with an even bigger economic crisis, the G20 format – which included the G8, China, and India

– was the best available. At a meeting with prime ministers Kevin Rudd (Australia) and José Luis Rodríguez Zapatero (Spain) in the margins of the UN General Assembly in September 2008, Brown proposed revitalising the G20, with heads of government leading national delegations. To acknowledge the upgrade to leader level, he suggested calling it the L20. The idea (if not his relabelling) flourished. After the New York meeting broke up, Brown wondered aloud whether Zapatero, swept up in the general enthusiasm to endorse everything Brown had proposed, realised that Spain was not a G20 member.

The G20 quickly established itself as a fixture among annual summits, with members competing to play host. From the outset, the shortcomings in its membership were acknowledged by hosts including others in their invitation lists. Key international organisations (initially the UN, EU, International Monetary Fund, World Bank, and World Trade Organization) are always present, plus representation from under-represented regions (Africa, South East Asia). Partly because it was there at the creation, Spain has become a permanent participant. At the summit in New Delhi in September 2023, permanent membership was offered to the African Union, which had been a regular participant since the fourth summit in 2010.

Most new groupings that survive achieve significant results in their initial meeting (one reason for their survival) but, over time, become part of the international furniture, prestigious but a bit boring, looking for an agenda and grabbing attention only when their timing coincides with an international crisis on which they can comment or lead. For example, President Biden and President Xi met in the margins of the G20 summit in Bali in November 2022 and agreed to work to deter Russia from using nuclear weapons in Ukraine.

The agendas become routine, but the habit of summitry is essential to the healthy functioning of international politics.

Successful diplomacy is impossible if people do not know each other personally. And summits are the best way for leaders to get to know other leaders. The formal sessions may be formulaic, the summit statements may strive unsuccessfully to be fresh and worth reading, but the meetings in the margins, breakfasts, 'pull asides', quick coffees, and cheeky beers are invaluable and irreplaceable.

Most countries do not have the luxury of choosing the clubs to which they belong: size, geography, and history decide. The UK remains a member of some of the most effective international clubs – the P5, the G7, and the G20 – but it has excluded itself from its regional club. David Cameron may have found European Council meetings irredeemably dull, but they meant he was able to get to know regional leaders well. It is easier to pick up the phone and have a quick (or difficult) conversation if you already know the person you are calling. Cameron's successors are penalised by the lack of regular contact with the chancellor of Germany, president of France, and prime ministers of the rest of the EU.

In the twenty-first century, China has been most active in creating new international groupings. The Beijing invitation is generally irresistible, and the Beijing ambition is generally to promote groupings in which it is the pre-eminent participant. In 2001, the economist Jim O'Neill coined the term 'BRICs' for the emerging economies of Brazil, Russia, India, and China. In 2009, the four met at summit level in Yekaterinburg. One year later, they invited South Africa to join (the hanging 's' at the end of the acronym had long been presumed to denote South Africa), and the five have met annually at the head-of-government level ever since.

At their summit meeting in August 2023, the BRICS invited Argentina, Egypt, Ethiopia, Iran, Saudi Arabia, and the United Arab Emirates to join their club. In selecting among nineteen aspirant countries, leaders appeared to apply one key criterion: that new members possess the ability to annoy the US sufficiently for the US to pay attention. The BRICS exist to prove that the American way is not the only way.

The SCO belongs to this flurry of Chinese diplomacy. The grouping began in 1996 as the Shanghai Five with a treaty on deepening military trust in border regions, signed in Shanghai by China, Russia, Kazakhstan, Kyrgyzstan, and Tajikistan. In 2001 the Shanghai Five became six with the admission of Uzbekistan, and the six became the SCO with headquarters in Beijing. From 2005 other nations have attended the SCO's annual summits as observers, and in 2015 two of those initial observers – India and Pakistan – became full members. Chinese and Russian remain the organisation's official languages.

Dai Bingguo commended the SCO as a useful new piece of the international architecture in which two big members could defuse potential problems and their smaller neighbours could be included in their deliberations and thinking. Sixteen years later, the UK feels no penalty at failing to develop any kind of relationship with this Beijing-focused and -controlled grouping, but more informal groupings are appearing in which British interests are more directly engaged, and initiators do not always think of London when putting together their proposals.

The example that felt most significant at inception was the initial meeting in February 2014 of what became the Minsk Group. Germany's foreign minister, Frank-Walter Steinmeier, suggested to Catherine Ashton, EU high representative, that she endorse a trilateral German-French-Polish initiative to help defuse tensions between Ukraine and Russia. Steinmeier conducted talks alongside his French and Polish counterparts, Laurent Fabius and Radosław Sikorski, which culminated in the signing in Kyiv on 21 February of an agreement to end the crisis in Ukraine. Within days, it became apparent that it had not done so. Ashton was not the only significant European player missing from the signing ceremony at the presidential palace; William Hague, then the UK's foreign secretary, preferred to maintain a planned visit to Brazil rather than join his colleagues. It is true that Steinmeier was not clamouring for him to join, but at that early stage he would not have been able to resist Hague's muscling in.

Having been absent at the start, the UK did not take part in the subsequent 'Normandy process' – a series of meetings with the Russian and Ukrainian leaders through which the Minsk signatories hoped to broker peace. A feeling that Steinmeier's initiative was doomed (proved quickly enough when Russia annexed Crimea within one month) lulled London into complacency. No matter how rose-tinted the spectacles of the observer, everything that succeeded the 21 February document was a failure. But sometimes in diplomacy being there is the point, a proof of relevance no matter the outcome, and for years the UK was not in the room when others were discussing Ukraine's future.

The UK was, however, always a member of any group dealing with the Balkans. Even after the Brexit vote, London continued to host key meetings. One of the signals that Boris Johnson was teetering on the brink of resigning as foreign secretary on 9 July 2018 was his failure to turn up on the first day of the Western Balkans Summit, which he was supposed to be chairing. Five years later, the UK holds on implausibly as a participant in the Berlin Process, whose main purpose is to prevent Balkans participants from losing heart as their prospects for joining the EU disappear into the remote future.

More and more diplomatic work is done by subsets of the international community, quads and quints which generally include the US and EU. The P5 of the UN Security Council is the longest standing. In the last decade, the P5+1 (Germany being the addition) has been one of the most consequential, the focus of international efforts to deny Iran a nuclear device while permitting Iran a civil nuclear programme. Unacknowledged in the name but crucial to the working of the P5+1 (or E3+3; take your pick of titles) was the EU, whose high representative chaired the grouping and gavelled the Joint Comprehensive Plan of Action to conclusion on 14 July 2015.

After Barack Obama was elected as US president, he asked the former secretary of state Madeleine Albright to lead outreach to international partners during the presidential transition. I was with Gordon Brown when he met her in the margins of the Washington G20 summit on 14 November 2008. She spoke about international groupings, wryly observing that every foreign government representative she met commended working through such groupings, and urged the new administration to pay particular attention to the smallest grouping of which both the US and their government were members. In 2008, the former secretary of state and serving British prime minister could share a chuckle at other countries' expense: invariable members of exclusive clubs could be complacent. But in the 2020s, the UK's access is no longer automatic. The UK must now make a persuasive case.

As London surveys the international landscape, the group to which it does not belong and to which it would most like access is probably the Quadrilateral Security Dialogue, initiated in 2007 and known as the Quad, comprising the US, India, Australia, and Japan. The challenges posed by China prompted the Japanese prime minister, Shinzo Abe, to seek this group of partners. Aware of that motivation, Beijing has never much cared for the Quad, which is one reason other countries might hesitate before publicly lobbying to join. But, if the tilt to the Indo-Pacific trumpeted in the UK's 2021 Integrated Review and its 2023 refresh – two texts setting out the government's vision for the UK's current and future role in the world – is to mean anything, then some sort of association with the Quad looks necessary for the UK.

Alongside Quad members, the UK, too, is grappling with what the rise of China means for it. Anticipating China's rise, London sought a more equal relationship with Beijing from the 1980s. The FCO recommended, and Thatcher accepted, that once the New Territories were returned to Chinese sovereignty in 1997 at the end of their ninety-nine-year lease, Hong Kong Island should also revert to China. The lease on the territories had been secured in the first place because of the vulnerability of the island, with an inadequate water supply and outside communications controlled entirely by the mainland. The prize of getting something back that was not due automatically to revert encouraged the Chinese to negotiate how Hong Kong would be governed after the handover.

But, even in the 1980s, Beijing was a slippery and assertive negotiating partner. The meaning of the somewhat ambiguously worded Sino-British Joint Declaration has been disputed since it was signed in December 1984. The British are clear that the declaration allowed it a continuing political-oversight role after the handover in 1997; the Chinese are equally clear that it did not. The truth is that the dispute shows the limits of the usefulness of ambiguity in diplomacy: both sides can argue to their own satisfaction that their interpretation is correct, leaving third parties to scratch their head.

In the first decade of the twenty-first century, the FCO judged that China's economy would develop in ways that would play to the UK's strengths. In the first heady decades of industrial development, China needed to import machine tools and heavy equipment, products that Germany had generally made better than the UK for at least a century. British car manufacturers might have done well in the Chinese market, but their sales always lagged behind German competitors. However, economic historians recalled that the UK had fuelled Germany's industrial expansion in the second half of the nineteenth century, before this main export market turned into Britain's main competitor in other markets. The reasoning went that a similar fate would now befall Germany in China. At some point, earlier than Germany realised, its main export market for industrial goods would become sated with German products, which it would copy, improve, and make more cheaply. At that point, German exports would peak and decline, and the UK would come into its own, with China's more mature market craving the business services at which the UK excelled.

The projection was persuasive – but life did not turn out that way. Chinese planners had also read economic history; they planned their growth along different lines. Instead of importing business services (insurance, accountancy, lawyers, consultancy), they would generate this business themselves. No matter how attractive the UK made its offer, China saw greater advantage in developing these sectors domestically.

The Chinese ambassador to Germany, Wu Hongbo, explained the plan to me over lunch in Berlin in 2011: where the Chinese identified a growing Chinese need, they were better these days at satisfying it themselves. He used the wine industry as an illustration. The Chinese had been drinking wine since the Han dynasty over 2,000 years ago, but their partiality for wine had developed with their economy over the last thirty years. Because their landscape was so varied, they had been able to plant vineyards in areas with similar soil and climate to France and Italy. China now accounted for almost half the world's grape production and had the third-largest vineyard area worldwide. He did not talk in terms of 'bottles produced' but 'tonnes produced': 13.2 million in 2011. China was drinking its own wine.

A decade later, things have not panned out quite as Wu predicted. In 2021, China's wine market was the second largest after the US. But Chinese tastes have become more sophisticated; despite the size and potential of their domestic industry, consumers are drinking better-quality vintages, especially from France, Australia, and Italy. Foreign producers can prosper if their product is good and well marketed. The City of London still has reason to hope.

Politically, British Sinologists also saw the prospect of Chinese development in a way that would make China an easier political partner. Economic liberalism under Deng and his successors had not been accompanied by any political relaxation; the CCP retained a monopoly on political power. But British experts saw hope in China's rapid urbanisation: every other country whose farmers had migrated from countryside to towns had witnessed political change; urbanisation of 50 per cent was almost an automatic trigger. With the majority of its population living in towns and cities, the Chinese government would face irresistible calls for political change.

But, again, the CCP had read the textbooks and prepared its defences. The penetration of the CCP into every nook and cranny of life meant it could keep control over political debate. British political parties had been niche rather than ubiquitous at the time of the UK's urbanisation in the nineteenth century; the Whigs and Tories had never thought about the demands of an expanding electorate before they were forced to address those demands. In China, peasants had always been the part of Chinese society most impervious to Beijing's diktat (the one-child policy, for example); town dwellers had always been more malleable and easily controlled. And, as prosperity and cities ballooned, town dwellers continued to accept the party line.

Internationally, British Sinologists speculated that China might buck the predicted trend in another way. Throughout history, increased economic power has been accompanied by increased political ambition. In the 2010s, an FCO director-general responsible for China policy briefed a meeting of senior British ambassadors; in their presentation, they wondered whether China might not already be providing evidence of a different choice, happy to amass material prosperity, benefiting from and seeing no advantage in challenging the Pax Americana: 'We might be witnessing one of those rare moments in history when economic and political power are wielded separately.' Simon Fraser, my predecessor as permanent secretary, challenged the thesis.

Ten years later, he has been proved right. As Deng had advised, China hid its potential and its intent while it accumulated power; Xi is happy to wield that power openly. Just as every country in the twentieth century had a special relationship with the US because the US was every country's most important relationship, every country in the twenty-first century must have a bespoke relationship with China. China is the steeply rising power; if it has not already displaced the US in foreign-policy planning (as it has for most countries in Asia and the Pacific), it is either on course to shunt aside the US (for most countries in Africa and Latin America) or poised uncomfortably to complicate the relationship with the US (for most countries in Europe).

During the 2010s, the UK performed a volte-face towards China. Prime Minister Cameron and Chancellor Osborne bet big on Beijing. The UK had clearly failed to profit as handsomely as Germany (or France or Italy) from the first three decades of China's economic expansion. But China was now looking for political as well as economic relationships. The UK would reap the advantage of 'first mover', embracing Beijing while others hesitated. The UK would not exclude sensitive technologies from bilateral cooperation; the UK would be happy for China to build and own its nuclear power stations, and build and own its communications networks. The new

Sinophilia would be cemented with an incoming state visit; President Xi would get the full House of Windsor treatment.

Chinese protocol lived down to its reputation for making unreasonable demands. As usual, the guest himself proved more amenable to doing things in the traditional Windsor way. That did not prevent a scuffle on Horse Guards Parade when Chinese security officers tried to clamber aboard a horse-drawn carriage to which they had not been assigned; the Metropolitan Police held firm. That evening, at the state banquet in Buckingham Palace, harmony had been restored. To the prime minister's and chancellor's evident delight, Xi spoke of a 'golden era' in Sino-British relations.

That was the pinnacle. Sitting in foreign policy discussions as home secretary, Theresa May had been consistently unhappy with her colleagues' rampant Sinophilia; she argued that possible economic benefits had been prioritised over actual security concerns. When May became prime minister, the change in tone was immediate; the change in substance took longer – and was muddied by Boris Johnson's ambivalence towards China – but in the 2020s the UK is consistently taking a hard line.

The reassessment has been general across the Western world, led by President Trump. However controversial the forty-fifth president's other foreign policy choices, his harder line towards Beijing has been welcomed across the US political spectrum, and by most of the US's Western allies. Countries are now less bothered about spending time in the Beijing doghouse. In the 2010s, European countries appeared to take turns in attracting Chinese opprobrium, often associated with too warm a welcome for the Dalai Lama.

Inherently problematic relationships always acquire a touchstone issue by which opponents of too cosy a relationship judge official behaviour. Authoritarian regimes (those without free elections, freedom of speech, equality before the law) always have question marks over their respect for human rights. But campaigners find it difficult to galvanise public opinion in support of groups (such as, for example, the Uyghurs), which tend to be faceless and difficult to relate to. Individuals – especially individuals who photograph memorably, speak enigmatically, and win Nobel Prizes – generate more copy.

In his flowing saffron robes, the Peace Prize laureate and twinkly eyed fourteenth Dalai Lama fits the bill. Not everyone is impressed: a long-serving European foreign minister once asked me whether the charlatan was worth the fuss. But for years human-rights defenders were in no doubt that he represented Tibet, a country under the suzerainty of China (but controlling its domestic policies) from 1720 until 1951, when Red Army troops marched into Lhasa.

In the early 2010s, European countries were prepared to learn their lesson, do their porridge, and forego future official contact with the Dalai Lama, but, as the decade wore on, governments became less supine in other policy areas. By 2020, it had become fashionable to defy Beijing, usually in a way that would grab a headline without making a difference on the ground. Or at sea. When the UK sent its new aircraft carrier through the South China Sea in July 2021, the Chinese were vociferously displeased. After three days, HMS *Queen Elizabeth* steamed on towards Korea. A point – but no difference – had been made.

The 2010s were the decade when parts of the international community began to have second thoughts about the benignity of China's rise. In some places the One Belt One Road initiative – China's policy of investment in international infrastructure to facilitate trade routes – was greeted with open arms. But it quickly became apparent that strings were attached. In Sri Lanka, China invested $1.3 billion in Hambantota Port, the first part of which opened in 2010. From the start, the new port struggled to make a profit, and the Sri Lankans found it impossible to service their debt. In 2016, their government tried to strike a deal selling 80 per cent of the port to China Merchants Port Holdings Company, but withdrew in the face of mass popular protests. One year later, in 2017, defying the protesters because of its financial desperation, the government recast the deal, this time handing over a 70 per cent stake in a joint venture with its state-run Sri Lanka Ports Authority. At the time, Constantino Xavier, a fellow at the think tank Carnegie, told the *Financial Times*:

> This is part of a larger modus operandi by China in the region. Beijing typically finds a local partner, makes that local partner accept investment plans that are detrimental to their country in the long term, and then uses the debts to either acquire the project altogether or to acquire political leverage in that country.[41]

Also in 2017, Myanmar, Nepal, and Pakistan cancelled or stalled hydroelectricity projects worth $20 billion in total. The region was reassessing, but not before its government elites had mortgaged its future to Beijing. The network of ports across the Indian Ocean included Gwadar in Pakistan, the centrepiece of the $55 billion China–Pakistan Economic Corridor; the redevelopment of Gwadar proceeded.

Every capital I visited as PUS in sub-Saharan Africa seemed to have a foreign ministry built by China. More security-conscious countries would hesitate to ask foreign contractors to provide them with a building where they might want to hold conversations that would not be heard in other capitals. New Chinese investment has outstripped American investment in Africa since 2013. And China accounted for 22 per cent of Africa's trade in 2022. China is now the largest foreign investor in Africa. The most memorable contribution to the FCO's Senior Leadership

Forum in 2018 was from an ambassador posted to Latin America, who told colleagues that China was buying up the continent, with a particular emphasis on energy and media sectors. As in Africa, China has hoovered up business in Latin America while no one outside the continent was paying attention.

The touchstone issue for relations with China now is Taiwan. President Xi has reaffirmed Beijing's long-standing ambition to see the reincorporation of the island into the People's Republic of China by 2049, the hundredth anniversary of the triumph of the CCP. Any country that wants a relationship with Beijing routinely subscribes to the One China policy, ruling out full independence for Taipei. After the revolution, both Beijing and Taipei claimed to represent the whole of China. Until 1970, most of the world agreed with Taipei, which occupied China's (permanent) seat at the UN Security Council.

After Richard Nixon went to China, most of the world rapidly reassessed, recognising the Communist rather than the Kuomintang government. In the 1970s, Beijing was not strong enough to object effectively to those countries maintaining a trade office in Taipei; they contented themselves with the major prize. For a time, some parts of the world – the Middle East (Islamic governments hesitated to confer legitimacy on a militantly atheist partner) and the Pacific (where Taipei worked energetically to maintain its primacy among the island states) – continued to prefer Taiwan.

Despite Nixon's conversion, the US never gave up entirely on its erstwhile ally. Taipei's democratic credentials ensured continuing congressional support. As relations with Beijing soured, individual senators and representatives made their way to Taipei to reaffirm old ties, and occasionally to collect a Taiwanese decoration. The uptick in American interest coincided with an increasingly bellicose approach from Beijing. Xi began to sound impatient with the centenary as a deadline.

No doubt Taiwan featured prominently in Putin's talks with Xi in the margins of the opening ceremony of the Beijing Winter Olympics. No doubt Putin drew a parallel between Ukraine and Taiwan as inalienable parts of the motherland, ripped away in war, ruled by fascists, and able to maintain their separate status only because of Western interference. No doubt Putin offered his special operation as a blueprint for later Chinese action: offensive forces, better-drilled, better-equipped, and better-motivated than their adversaries would quickly overthrow the local government; international opponents would wring their hands as they had done in 2008 (Georgia) and 2014 (Crimea) but quickly accept the new status quo; life would go on.

Putin would probably have given little space in his presentation to the views of the local citizenry. In the end, they would do as they were told – happy to be a part of a stronger country, indifferent to who collected their taxes, or sullen but respectful in their dislike of the new arrangement – because the manner of conquest would remind them that the bigger state knew how to deal with troublesome internal opponents. Putin's pitch would have been designed to appeal to his eastern neighbour: confident, logical, and undemanding. He would not have asked for direct support in the way of armaments; he did not think he needed it. Rather he would have asked Xi to protect his back diplomatically.

To cement their understanding, the two leaders signed the 'no limits' partnership, in which the two professed complete respect for each other's vital interests. The agreement also boldly presented China and Russia as champions of democracy, defined as governments that respond to the vital needs of their people (with no mention of elections).

If things had turned out as Putin predicted, the Ukrainian special operation might have been a useful precedent for Xi: a renegade province swiftly reincorporated with minimum negative international consequences. But Putin was wrong. The two men take trouble to ensure that no one learns what they say to each other, but it is easy to imagine Xi withholding praise for the conduct of the war. He does not want his neighbour to lose humiliatingly (which would be a victory for his international opponents), but equally he sees no advantage in being identified with Putin's fight.

As Xi and his advisers analyse why Putin's predictions were wrong, the factor that should give them greatest pause is the role of the locals. It turns out that millions of people have a say in how they are governed. If they do not want new rulers, they can fight, and outsiders can help with the full justification of the UN Charter. Ukrainians have proven that national identity does not have to be old to be precious; it does not have to be wholly distinct to be worth fighting for. Russians and Ukrainians share much history; their languages are as closely related as many of their families – but enough is different for them to want to remain separate. Russia's conduct of the war, targeting civilians, killing over 8,000 in the first year after the invasion, has driven all Ukrainians further from Russia, including those Russian speakers who might theoretically have been predisposed to a takeover by Moscow.

Whatever Putin said to Xi, there are clear parallels between Ukraine and Taiwan. The local population has the key say in whether its more powerful neighbour can absorb it. A key condition for Western countries accepting the One China policy was that reincorporation could only take place if it were the manifest wish of a majority of Taiwanese people. Perhaps Beijing has paid too little attention to that condition of late.

Even more alarming from Beijing's point of view than a lack of international acquiescence will be determined and effective local opposition. Since 2016, the Taiwanese president has been a member of the Democratic Progressive Party, which increasingly advocates a separate Taiwanese identity. What if this were a canary in the coal mine of China's plans, early warning that the Taiwanese would not accept a political fix made over their heads or a blitzkrieg invasion?

Every country has to decide what it would do if Beijing made a move against Taipei. Most would shrug and do nothing, recognising (a) their greater dependence on Beijing than Taipei and (b) their inability to affect the outcome, no matter their private preference. Most of Asia, Africa, and Latin America would fall into this category.

The US would be most bellicose. Some there might be tempted to treat a move against their old ally as the moment for a showdown. Even if the administration did not treat it as a casus belli, it would react strongly. An American-led sanctions regime could cut China out of the Western economic system and lead to the rewiring of world trade; it would cost Western economic growth dearly, but sometimes the right thing to do comes at great personal cost. As usual, the most effective action would probably precede any decisive Chinese move. There is always warning time, even if it's shorter than policy planners would like. Washington would make crystal clear in advance the consequences of a Chinese move. One danger is that such preliminary threats might box Washington in later; it may find itself obliged to turn blood-curdling threats into action.

Europe would be caught in the middle. No matter the ultimate decision in Washington, no European country would fight. In advance, all European countries could make that plain to Washington. The Ukraine precedent is helpful: reverses in Iraq and Afghanistan made it clear that the deployment of Western troops did not help the side favoured by the US and its allies to win. But Ukraine shows that when Western troops remain far from the battlefield, the side favoured by the West can still prevail. The US would supply the Taiwanese with materiel if they were willing to fight. Individual European nations would face tricky decisions about how much help to offer should China invade.

Until then, all governments can repeat ad nauseam the basis of their One China policies: only peaceful unification, in a choice exercised exclusively by the Taiwanese through a plebiscite adhering to the highest standards of democratic elections, would convince these governments to accept Taiwan's new status.

I suspect that Putin's lack of success has put a major spoke into Xi's plans. Military exercises continue, the formal policy remains unchanged, but there is less urgency about an accelerated timetable. Xi wants to see the return of Taiwan on his watch (now formally extended to be his lifetime). But he does not want a bloody, expensive, protracted mess; he does not want to endure what Putin now endures. And he knows that a lot can happen in twenty-five years. He can afford to wait.

Meanwhile, other countries need to recalibrate their relationships with Beijing. Having previously tried to be China's best friend in the West, the UK has now flirted with public hostility towards it. The hostility was mostly expressed in words (critics might even say 'rhetoric') rather than actions. But the UK has decided to exclude Chinese technology from UK comms infrastructure, to the consternation of external experts familiar with the actual capabilities of the kit being excluded.

Looking ahead, I advocate wary engagement: respectful, transparent, knowledgeable, and limited by national security considerations, but also enthusiastic. As Napoleon may or may not have foreseen, China is of a size and dynamism that, once roused, cannot be ignored. The UK can benefit from a close relationship with Beijing, but London must not concede the whip hand. In sectors where Beijing is dominant, the UK makes itself vulnerable (some universities, for example, are over-reliant on Chinese students to fill their courses and balance their books).

China is not an enemy of the UK; it must never become an enemy. It should be unnecessary to type that, but recent statements by retired British politicians suggest otherwise. At key moments, the UK has been a friend of China: in January 1950, London was the first capital to recognise the new Communist government in Beijing (and break diplomatic ties to Taipei). China has never been an enemy, even when the British treated the Chinese with mercantilist contempt, as necessary customers for Indian opium if British traders were to slake the British thirst for Chinese tea. The Chinese remember the Opium Wars more clearly than the British, but even the bitterest and most justified quarrel loses potency over centuries if new reasons for sustaining the quarrel are lacking; these days the Opium Wars do not determine China's view of the UK.

In the 2020s, China can be a partner. The UK can no longer aspire to an equal partnership – China is far too big, well resourced, and resistant to that idea – but we can have a partnership over which we have sufficient control. As long as we can say 'no' when we need to, we can work together to mutual advantage.

8

Planet

All my life, the health of the planet has been on the international agenda; for most of my career, it has been an item discussed when there is time, when everything else has already been discussed: important, but not most important. As an agenda item it was associated with youth, liberal politics, the West – basically with people whose life ran on rails, with no conflict, no struggle to survive. People with time on their hands to preach.

The world has come relatively late to thinking about the Earth itself. My German teacher taught me that the German for environment (*Umwelt*) was a twentieth-century invention (from 1909); English lexicographers coined the equivalent word about a century earlier. When I was a child, nascent green parties fretted about acid rain; the Black Forest was dying. Fifty years later, the Black Forest seems historically healthy, and 'acid rain' is better remembered as Diana, Princess of Wales's nickname for her stepmother, Raine Spencer. I remember 'planting a tree in '73', 'planting some more in '74', and 'keeping them alive in '75'. I returned to peer through the fence of my childhood garden in Eccles thirty years later and spotted a rather spindly rowan, hanging on.

The first efforts of environmentalists failed to persuade the general population and enraged the developing world. It was unacceptable for countries that had done all the polluting they wanted in order to make their people prosperous to turn around and tell other countries that new rules applied, that no one was permitted to pollute any more. The industrialised world admitted that transitional periods and rules were necessary, and accepted that it had to help pay for the developing world's transition.

The Earth Summit in Rio in 1992 was a watershed moment, the key opening reference point for international debate. Rio launched the Conference of the Parties (of those who signed the protocol), or COP, which has taken place almost every year since. The summitry has been marked by swelling attendances and increasingly frustrated ambition for scientists and organisers. Targets have always been set for the remote future, binding but designed so that the unpleasant practical effects will be suffered by the decision-makers' successors.

In 2005, while working for Gordon Brown at the Treasury, the economist Nick Stern began gathering evidence, comparing the problem with the response, and assessing whether the response was having the necessary impact. The Economics of Climate Change: The Stern Review (2006) remains a seminal document: dense, long, coherent, and persuasive. The next year, the foreign secretary's climate adviser asked to brief me before I took over as Brown's foreign policy adviser. He knew I would have heard of the report but presumed (correctly) that I would not have read it. 'Don't bother,' he advised. 'All you need to know is that it proves two things. First, man-made climate change is real and getting worse. And second, it will be more expensive to tackle later than now.'

In three years working for the prime minister, climate change as a policy issue barely impinged on my life. It was a big deal elsewhere in Number 10 – a group of impassioned and knowledgeable special advisers and officials worked tirelessly; the Copenhagen COP was a major moment in Brown's premiership – but essentially it remained compartmentalised with a negligible read-across to the main foreign policy or international economic issues of the day.

And so we went on. As ambassador in Germany and as PUS, I followed the climate issue; I was (I felt) plausible when lobbying or negotiating a detail. But as an agenda item it always played second fiddle. I noted that even those politicians (such as Angela Merkel) who were best informed generally allowed other considerations to trump climate concerns: cheap and reliable energy to fuel industry was a more pressing concern (the exception for her was ordering Germany's exit from civil nuclear power in the wake of the Fukushima nuclear disaster).

As I flew around the globe (feeling guilty only in retrospect for my expanding carbon footprint), I was disturbed by some sights. As a child, I pored over atlases and wondered how much of the Earth's surface had never been touched by humans. The pages devoted to Siberia and Antarctica seemed most promising. Flying to Japan forty years later, I gazed at thousands of square kilometres of polluted Siberian forest, interrupted by industrial complexes careless of their impact on their surroundings. Zimbabwe looked scarred and scorched from above, difficult to imagine as Africa's breadbasket. And most frustrating was the Falkland Islands, because the damage was most easily rectified, it was just not rectified. Flying low on a short hop to Bleaker Island, I was struck by the countless figures of eight obvious in the scrub. The pilot explained that life was boring for teenagers in Stanley, so at the weekend they would borrow their parents' SUVs and spin doughnuts in the lichen. The problem was that lichen took decades to grow in the hostile climate close to the Antarctic Circle; the damage inflicted during one mindless weekend could take years to repair.

I looked, I sighed, I did nothing. I played the part of the

devout parish priest in the old joke, who took to the roof as the rain flooded the ground floor of his presbytery. First, his curate offered to take him to dry land in his little boat. 'No!' said the priest. 'The Lord will rescue me.' Next, as the rain fell steadily and the floodwater rose past the first floor, the village police officer rowed by and offered a lift. 'That's very kind, but I am waiting for my Lord.' Finally, with rain still falling in stair rods and water lapping at the priest's feet, the local firefighter reached him, suggesting he was his final hope. 'No, you are wrong, for I know that the Lord will provide.' The firefighter sighed and rowed away. Shortly afterwards the priest drowned. Arriving somewhat crestfallen at the pearly gates, he met God. Being also somewhat indignant, he asked the Lord why he had not come to his rescue. 'Well,' replied God, 'I sent your curate, the village police officer, and a firefighter for the sole purpose of saving you, but you chose to ignore me.'

I had seen firsthand evidence that should have made me act, but I chose to ignore it. I was luckier than the pig-headed priest; I saw the light before the waters closed over my head. My personal epiphany happened in South Africa. Edward Roman, consul general in Cape Town, recommended I see a long-resident Brit at the end of my official programme. We met Lewis Pugh at his home near the beach.

Only a few people can meet Pugh and feel in person the persuasive power of this particular force of nature, but those who do become proselytisers of his message. Over the remnants of a cake strewn across a table on his veranda, he explained the climate crisis more compellingly than anyone I had met before. With the aid of a map of the Arctic, a dinner plate, a side plate, and a saucer, he demonstrated the retreating summer Arctic sea ice: the dinner plate covered much of the map and represented the extent of summer ice in the year Pugh was born; the side plate covered 50 per cent less and represented the extent of summer ice at the turn of the millennium; the saucer represented ice coverage in 2018 when we met. Removing the saucer, Pugh said that the Intergovernmental Panel on Climate Change predicted that before 2050 the Arctic Ocean would become almost ice-free in September. Pugh recounted his own Damascene conversion, a swim across the North Pole on 15 July 2007; at the end of the expedition, his skipper told him he had emerged from the water a different person. He had just done something that would have been impossible even ten years earlier. The experience distressed and shocked Pugh even more than it excited him. Since then, he had been making the case for putting climate at the top of the international agenda.

After retiring from the Royal Navy, Pugh's father relocated his young family to South Africa, where Pugh began swimming long distances in cold water as a teenager. His first endurance swim started close to home and finished on Robben Island. He had been surrounded by African penguins for all twelve kilometres. He began connecting swimming with environmental campaigning; popular intrigue at the idea of prolonged spells in freezing water generated publicity. When he first swam in the Arctic off the north coast of Svalbard in 2005, the water temperature was 3 °C. He repeated the same swim twelve years later, horrified to discover that the sea temperature had risen by 7 °C. The Arctic was warming faster than any other place on the planet, up to four times as fast in parts of Greenland.

In 2021, I accompanied Pugh on his last long cold-water swim, across the mouth of the Ilulissat Icefjord in western Greenland. He phoned just a week before he was due to leave for his final training camp in Iceland. Less than one year after leaving the FCO, I found I had nothing in my diary that could not be postponed.

The group accompanying Pugh was small: a doctor, a skipper for the boat, a stills photographer, a drone pilot for moving pictures, and a film director. The team leader, managing the logistics, stayed in South Africa. Everyone had a clear role apart from me. I was given tasks that felt made up but, before I left the expedition halfway through (though flexible, my diary wasn't completely clear), I worked out that I was there to keep conversation going and to keep Pugh motivated. His core team was terrific and reliable – and a bit too familiar.

For the first few days in Greenland, Pugh acclimatised himself. He was not daunted when water-temperature measurements fluctuated between 2 °C and 0 °C. The salt in seawater lowers its freezing point to -1.3 °C. Pugh swam for the photos (spectacular) and explored the neighbourhood. I accompanied him on a helicopter flight to the ice sheet. Everywhere was glistening, because everywhere was melting. At one landing spot, the pilot put down next to a mighty waterfall, one that had not existed in his childhood, when everything we could now see up to the glacier a kilometre away had been under frozen water. The most devastating consequences of climate change occur out of sight, where they are easily ignored.

After I left, Pugh swam 7.8 km over two weeks, in ten-minute bursts, twice a day. Guinness World Records was satisfied that he was the first person to swim across the mouth of the fjord. In advance of COP26 at Glasgow later in the year, he drew attention to the plight of the oceans, with microplastics now detected everywhere at every depth, with rising temperatures killing coral, and with factory ships targeting the tracts of sea they have not already denuded of fish.

Over the last dozen years, countries have begun to see the importance of marine protected areas (MPAs), pristine seas that need to remain pristine for the health of the planet. Any country is free to declare an MPA in its territorial waters. In 2023, the UK declared three (admittedly small) highly protected marine areas in UK waters (North East of Farnes Deep,

Allonby Bay, and Dolphin Head). Around its OTs, the UK has been bolder, designating marine reserves of 834,000 km² around the Pitcairn Islands, 640,000 km² around the British Indian Ocean Territory, and 445,000 km² around Saint Helena.

Protecting the open sea requires international agreement. In 2015, Pugh swam in the Ross Sea in Antarctica to publicise the case for an MPA there. A photo showing him purple with cold, having swum through an ice tunnel, was picked up in Russia. He was later lionised in Moscow, hanging out with Slava Fetisov (think 'Muhammad Ali meets David Beckham' for local impact) and appearing on Zvezda (the Ministry of Defence's private television station); the following year, Russia became the last member of the Commission for the Conservation of Antarctic Marine Living Resources to agree an MPA for the Ross Sea, which immediately came into being.

Many books have been written and television programmes made to draw attention to the climate crisis. The assessment of the scientific community is so consensual that inevitably the contrary minority view attracts favourable attention from people (often on the political right) who distrust consensus. The task of keeping the international community focused on the topic and active in looking for solutions is hard. The dissenting voices of relatively few are enough to distract attention and delay action, especially when those who make the most money from inaction are politically well connected.

Work to persuade everyone, at every level, to act is the second mega-task for diplomacy. The problem is huge and many-faceted, two features which tend to deter progress. In 2022, the world's population surpassed eight billion. It had taken less than eleven years for the world's population to grow to that size from seven billion. Nine billion will be reached almost as quickly. Queen Elizabeth II was born the year before the world's population hit two billion; during her life, she witnessed a four-fold increase in a number which already in 1926 was the highest in history.

Some experts invite us to take comfort from their projection that the world's population will stabilise at around eleven billion before the end of this century. It is difficult enough for the planet to cope with ever more people, but all of those people are more prosperous and consume more resources than their predecessors in the quite recent past. The economist Thomas Robert Malthus and the makers of the game and television series *The Last of Us* suggest that nature will find a way drastically to reduce numbers. The global experience of Covid-19 suggests that humans could defeat disease or starvation. But human ingenuity to avoid unexpected catastrophe, to get us out of a pickle we've made for ourselves, is not enough. At some point, larger numbers will mean that life on Earth is worse for most people and for most of the creatures that share the planet with us. We need a policy response now.

I am sixty-two years old. In my lifetime, humans have destroyed 69 per cent of the biodiversity abundance of the planet. No one knows for sure how many species have been lost, some before they were known to science. But we know that 832,000 km² of the Amazon (over 20 per cent of the total) have been cleared since 1970, that the rainforests of South East Asia have all but disappeared, and that the main thing protecting the rainforest of Central Africa is lawlessness; outsiders do not invest when local leaders appear to prefer killing each other to turning a profit.

The Caspian tiger and Tasmanian tiger (no relation) have disappeared. The rhinoceros is critically endangered. At the start of the twentieth century, an estimated one million black rhinoceroses from four different subspecies roamed the savannah of Africa. By 2001 that number had dropped to 2,300 and the West African black rhinoceros had disappeared. Smaller flora and fauna have also gone. In the UK, every policy tussle between farming interests and environmental interests in my lifetime has eventually been resolved in favour of the farmers. Every farmer I know would object to that characterisation, but how else can they explain the fact that in two generations the British countryside has lost 50 per cent of its biodiversity?

The scientists have had help lately from the popularisers of science. After decades of David Attenborough television programmes that simply marvelled at the natural world, everything he has narrated recently has patiently explained what is at stake. In 2018, Attenborough gave a talk to British ambassadors gathered in London for the Senior Leadership Conference. Their excellencies were more excited by his address than anything else that week; they began tweeting their enthusiastic appreciation before he appeared on stage. Twitter noted the spike in tweets about David Attenborough and the rumour quickly spread that he had died; the BBC felt obliged to issue a statement confirming Attenborough was in robust good health.

His address was unscripted and profoundly affecting. He was optimistic about the future: new policies had fixed the hole in the ozone layer and saved the whale; the sense of wonder of seven-year-olds would save the planet. The next generation was curious about everything and did not recognise the concept of an insoluble problem. The next generation would fix the harm done since the Industrial Revolution. But he was regretful, even wistful, that no one would be able to experience what he had experienced; too much had changed irretrievably.

He told the story of his first encounter with an indri, the largest lemur, found only in Madagascar. After days of patient tracking in the early 1960s, he had been rewarded with a glimpse – a rare sight, he had been assured. These days anyone who can scrape together the airfare to Antananarivo can go to

Madagascar's eastern rainforest; a guide would be happy to take you to the indri's habitat. These days the indri responds to the guide's whistle, having grown used to human presence and fond of the food the guide gives it. In a way, the indri is a good conservation story, but at the same time it is depressing, proof that nature survives by adapting to the needs of humans, not by remaining as wild as it used to be. Nature will be curated; the wilderness will be a giant safari park.

In the UK more people are interested in the planet than when I was a child, but few vote with that interest uppermost in mind. The green parties in different parts of the UK seem otherworldly; Conservative and Labour politicians routinely attack them for appearing to oppose any sort of economic growth. Their impatience means that at some point in any policy debate the greens will do something that lets older parties off the hook; green politicians think voters must bear consequences they don't like, and they don't hide the thought. Politicians from parties that win elections are more used to compromise and to phasing necessary decisions that the electorate dislikes.

However, the greens are essential in calling out shortcomings and hypocrisy in government policy. On the green agenda, nationally and internationally, the British government talks the talk better than it walks the walk. The government fought to host COP26, and Alok Sharma and his team worked tirelessly to reach agreement, achieving significant progress in agreeing near-term targets (a 30 per cent reduction in carbon by 2030), but every participant knew the UK's lamentable environmental record. British water companies dumped raw sewage into rivers more than 375,000 times in the year the UK hosted the COP.

At the despatch box or in a TV studio, the government spokesperson invariably means well and usually has something plausible to say: offering the prospect of effective action in the near future or indicating a plan in gestation. But the spokesperson is blind to weaknesses and inconsistencies in the government's case. A new mine can be approved in Cumbria even as Glasgow prepares to welcome thousands of delegates to COP26. And it can be defended on green grounds: better to have an uber-efficient modern mine close to the manufacturers who will use the coal dug there than to import from Poland. The idea that a beautiful landscape should be protected rather than disrupted with the promise of restoration later is dismissed; the case for moving away from making anything that requires coal is not acknowledged. But the importance of the planetary agenda demands that we do better, nationally and internationally.

9

Technology

The possibilities of new technology have increased exponentially in my lifetime. At the same time, long-established technologies which in my childhood looked permanent have disappeared. Even more bewilderingly, some of the new technologies of my early adulthood have also disappeared or are disappearing. Three quick examples follow.

The post has been a feature of life for the prosperous in Europe since at least the Middle Ages: the princes of Thurn und Taxis made their money by supplying postal services throughout the Holy Roman Empire. The Royal Mail was established in 1516. Rowland Hill invented the adhesive postage stamp in 1840; the Penny Black gave every Brit the possibility of sending letters. By the 1960s, 98 per cent of British households lived within half a mile of one of about 155,500 pillar boxes, with the majority erected in the reign of Elizabeth II; cast iron, cherry red, they looked as if they would last forever. But by 2016 the only company which cast pillar boxes for the Royal Mail was making just one new box annually; it closed that year.

Unless the Post Office wants to honour Charles III for sentimental reasons, he will never see a pillar box with his cypher: there is no need. Post in the twenty-first century has changed fundamentally; whereas twenty years ago I received all bills, letters, and invitations by post, now I receive only cards – and birthday cards are dwindling because few people rub in the passage of time for a sixty-odd-year-old.

In 1984, I bought a CD player. Proud of the single most expensive purchase I had ever made, I was relieved to find three CDs I wanted to buy: Vivaldi, Eurythmics, and Tears for Fears were just about the only artists I wanted to listen to among the meagre initial offering. Forty years later, you cannot give CDs away, and auctioneers refuse to take them; (nearly) everyone streams their music (except the few who have gone back to vinyl).

The YouTube video that made me laugh loudest in 2022 featured a teenager who had been asked to phone a number and given a rotary phone to make the call.

Technologies have been superseded before, but never so quickly, and hardly ever leaving existing technologies completely redundant. Since the invention of the printing press in the fifteenth century, new technology has generally been on the side of the ordinary person, taking over menial tasks or bringing new experiences within the reach of ever more people. Anything that proved itself quickly became cheaper and more accessible, especially in the twentieth century. Technology was a force for democracy. Now, for the first time in 500 years, new technology is swinging the power pendulum back towards the state from the citizen.

Alan Turing is widely credited with inventing the first working computer at Bletchley Park in the Second World War (although Ada Lovelace worked out some of the underlying mathematics more than a century earlier). Computers quickly combined with older ideas about robots, which for the first half of my life straddled the real world and the world of science fiction. In the 1980s, computers were enormous and slow. I remember an episode of *The Burke Special* in which James Burke startled a member of the audience, who let out a gasp;

Burke said it would require a computer the size of the studio to produce a similar reaction to his simple question. When I was an undergraduate, computer scientists used punch cards and knitting needles; philosophers rather than mathematicians and physicists were discussing what might happen when computers became autonomous, operated by what they began to call artificial intelligence (AI); they were intrigued by AI's ethics.

Though initially cumbersome or otherworldly, computers and AI clearly had potential. Science-fiction writers, whose books fuelled the imaginations of real-world scientists, saw the need for rules and warned what might go wrong if machines were able to control themselves. Isaac Asimov and Arthur C. Clarke still hover in the background of debate. In the eighty years since he promulgated them, Asimov's Three Laws of Robotics remain fundamental to aspirations about what robots and computers should be allowed to do. First Law: a robot may not injure a human being, or through inaction allow a human being to come to harm. Second Law: a robot must obey the orders given it by human beings except where such orders conflict with the First Law. Third Law: a robot must protect its own existence as long as such protection does not conflict with the First or Second Law. Later, Asimov added the Zeroth Law: a robot may not injure humanity or, by inaction, allow humanity to come to harm. Clarke toyed with the laws in his Space Odyssey series, and Stanley Kubrick fixed in the mind of everyone who saw his film adaptation of *2001: A Space Odyssey* the problem with over-mighty computers. HAL (Heuristically Programmed Algorithmic Computer) kills one crewman by locking him out of the spaceship because the mission 'is too important for me to allow you to jeopardise it'.[42] A second crewman, having failed to save his companion out in space, demands that HAL allow him back on board and gets the reply, 'I'm sorry, Dave. I'm afraid I can't do that.'[43]

Our fundamental fears found expression early on in the development of AI and computers; now computer capability has increased to the point where it comes close to matching our fears. In 1965, *Electronics* magazine asked the engineer Gordon Moore to contribute a prediction to its thirty-fifth-anniversary edition about the prospects for the semiconductor-components industry over the next ten years. Looking backwards at the rate of growth since 1955, Moore made what he later called a 'wild extrapolation', saying that the number of transistors on a microchip would 'continue to double every year for the next ten years'.[44] In 1975, looking forward ten years again, he revised his prediction to a doubling every two years. Up to 2022, the prediction made in 1975 held true. In 1975, there were about 5,000 transistors on a microchip; by 2022, there were 100,000,000,000. Microchips with more components can power computers that can do more tasks more quickly.

Computer scientists have written programmes to make the most of more capable computers. The most advanced of these programmes are labelled AI. The debate about how capable and how potentially worrying AI programmes might be has spread from computer scientists to government policymakers. I identify two opposed camps.

In the blue corner is a group – those at once most excited and most fearful – arguing that AI will profoundly shape the future of humanity; change, they say, will be fundamental and inevitable. Intelligent systems already perform tasks we once thought only humans could do, such as comprehending languages, making multifaceted decisions, and generating elaborate images from simple inputs. In science, AI applications are able to see patterns and structures that humans do not see. Eric Schmidt (former chief executive officer of Google, whose work infuses this chapter) claims that these innovations will change industries, from healthcare and finance to education and entertainment, increasing the ability of humans to execute complicated tasks with greater speed and efficiency.[45]

In the red corner are those who judge that the power of thought and creativity is beyond even the most sophisticated computer programmes. In the end, AI is statistical sampling; it can draw on a dizzyingly wide array of sources, but it cannot create anything. Or rather it cannot create anything worthwhile: Emily M. Bender, professor of linguistics at the University of Washington, calls large language models (LLMs) 'stochastic parrots'.[46] And evidence is gathering that when ChatGPT-4 is uncertain and not able to parrot from its sources, it makes up its answer, introducing so-called hallucinations to the system.

In the chapel next to the Master's Lodge where I live, a violinist practises Bach partitas late every evening. He makes an achingly beautiful but imperfect sound. We both know two things: that his interpretation will change with time, and that he will never perform as well as Nathan Milstein. But that does not matter. To hear a live performance of a beloved work of art is one of the things that makes life worth living. AI can sample and stitch, but knowing a performer is not in complete control will always be part of the thrill of listening. Professor Richard Mortier at Cambridge University introduced me to the red corner.

Unlike politicians these days, the two groups work from the same set of facts. They acknowledge that people are adopting new technology faster than ever before, with LLMs currently leading the way. It took two months for ChatGPT to reach 100 million users. Gmail took five years to reach the same number. Students are beguiled by the possibilities of ChatGPT-4 and Bard; the dons who mark their papers are uneasily aware of their potentially transformative nature.

In early 2023 at Christ's College, Cambridge, the Economics director of studies set ChatGPT-4, in its first month, a standard first-year economics essay to write. The resulting piece of work (produced rather more rapidly than would be achieved by a first-year economics undergraduate) was, she reckoned, worth a 2:2. The director of studies conceded that lazy students might be tempted to subcontract work that secured such a mark, but added that they would get their comeuppance: the programme was guilty of a couple of howling errors, which anybody who had actually attended the relevant lecture course would not have committed. The marker would have known that the writer had not been anywhere near her lecture theatre and grade accordingly.

AI is an imitator, a paster-together of other people's ideas, which will never amount to 'intelligence'. So far, so Mortier. But slapdash early products should offer no comfort. The speed of adoption and the pace of improvements (because the programme can 'learn' and spruce up what it does) mean that AI will soon be integrated into every business and every industry. It is not intelligent yet, but one day it might be.

The group in the blue corner predicts a future that looks different even from expectations just ten years ago. Schmidt foresees the following developments:

- A small number of 'intelligent' LLM systems will emerge that are so powerful that policymakers across the world will agree they should be carefully managed and regulated.
- Simultaneously, a much larger number of more specialised LLM systems will appear in every digital device we own, from fruit juicer to 4×4 SUV; their embedded chips will be multilingual, able to understand all the most common languages on the planet.
- LLMs now under development will soon have rapid training abilities as well as memory. Right now, they can

generate an answer which they promptly forget. Schmidt states, 'Once true memory is invented, the system should be able to choose alternative futures for itself by imagining a different future from the past. At that point, these systems will begin to approximate artificial general intelligence.'[47]

The argument over the possible direction of AI and LLMs is overlain by an argument over the future direction of computer hardware. Everyone agrees that, at the same time that computer software is changing, computer scientists are making progress towards quantum computing. Standard computers operate on a binary system; everything is either 1 or 0. The computer may be able to handle billions of pieces of data, but every datum is either 1 or 0. In a quantum computer, each piece of data can be simultaneously 1 and 0. The quantum computer provides the answer to Erwin Schrödinger, troubled by the fate of his cat: it is proof that something can simultaneously be in two different states.

A quantum computer will be vastly more capable than any computer now being used, which is why every nation (and tech company) able to afford the necessary research budget (a minimum of hundreds of millions of dollars per year) is making that investment.

Having agreed the possibility of quantum computing, experts are divided about how it might develop. Shortly after he became the British government's chief scientific adviser (and shortly before he became a television celebrity, dispensing the most compelling advice during the coronavirus pandemic), Patrick Vallance invited permanent secretaries to the Francis Crick Institute for a briefing about quantum computers. Having made the case for their transformative effect, Vallance told us that the first act of the world's first quantum computer would be to turn off all the other nascent quantum computers: the victor would be able to claim a complete victory. Others are not so sure, arguing that achieving quantum computing will not be a single event but slower and more incremental; different groups in different places will be able to achieve usable advances before the first all-singing, all-dancing quantum computer makes an appearance, and will be able to keep those advances even after that appearance.

The British government has a good record in attracting scientists of Vallance's calibre. But not all members of the Royal Society are willing governmental collaborators. The computer scientist Roger Needham (after whom Microsoft Research named its building in Cambridge) advised his doctoral students not to work for the government, or at least never to accept research work that required signing the Official Secrets Act. He told his students that government work meant three things in short order: (a) loss of control over their research, because (b) government always in the end returned to its obsessive interest in defence and security, and so (c) demanded secrecy.

Governments want to lead and control and behave increasingly as if in quantum computing 'the winner takes all'. Governments have stopped cooperating on the development of quantum computing, which is driving a wedge between governments and scientists. Ideas are no longer exchanged, and certain crucial components can no longer be exported to rivals. Because the stakes are so high in a 'winner takes all' world, the first reaction of policymakers in Whitehall and its equivalents around the world is to slow down the competition. But policymakers are not in control, so the race to develop quantum computing and AI gathers pace. All competitors know the importance of winning, even as they feel it is becoming harder to win.

This future brings serious concerns. Even people immersed

in the field are bewildered by the rapid spread of this new
technology, finding it hard to keep up with changes. Several
risks are emerging. Human beings are subject to significant
biases; these new systems reflect the (curated) data they are
trained with. The work is demanding, which winnows down
the number able to compete, so power and influence might be
concentrated in the hands of a few AI developers and corporations. On the other hand, as open-source variations of these
LLMs proliferate, rogue actors might use them to generate
persuasive disinformation at machine speed and scale, or to
create a new deadly virus. LLMs could be used to enhance
cyber threats and exploit human vulnerabilities to steal data
and identities.

Looming over these developments are worries about how the
nation that invests the most in researching and developing this
technology will behave: what would China do if its computer
scientists won the race? China's use of new computer technology to date is not encouraging. Beijing operates a system of
'social credits' with its citizens. The principle is simple: if you
behave, you are rewarded; if you misbehave, you are punished.
Existing facial-recognition technology on public transport
systems means that local authorities can deny transport to
residents who owe money to the local authority. China has
AI programs similar to those already developed and released
in the US. They do not release them the way ChatGPT was
released, because China does not allow its population to have
unfettered access to information. But the West must consider
the national security implications and surveillance issues that
arise from China's development of powerful LLMs.

I am writing in 2023, aware of the possibility that these
technologies will move faster and have a bigger impact than
political, regulatory, and ethical systems can sufficiently understand and effectively manage. Some speculate that the fear of

missing out will produce a 'race to the bottom' in which the competition for new features will cause safety mechanisms to be given too low a priority. LLMs already attract close scrutiny; as governments imagine the impact of more sophisticated future iterations, they will move to regulate them. Italy has already banned ChatGPT for violating General Data Protection Regulation (GDPR) rules.

With the launch of ChatGPT-4 on 14 March 2023, the world woke up to the potential of AI. People had grown used to the idea of technology progressing incrementally. Suddenly, for $20 per month, users could experience the rapid, radical advance in AI capabilities. Among others, Hollywood actors and writers quickly focused on the threat rather than the possibility: in July 2023, they started their first joint strike since 1960, fearing that studios might use AI to replace them in future productions.

Like the nuclear age, the age of AI combines limitless promise with a lurking existential threat. Science, medicine, and energy will be transformed. But not all change is guaranteed to be positive. AI is not aligned with human values, and developers do not agree which human values should guide AI development. The questions posed and hesitations suffered by Asimov and Clarke are still to be addressed.

Faced with something so far-reaching in its consequences, the UK must do two things: first, the government must invest heavily; only by investing can the UK claim a leadership role. Early moves by His Majesty's Government have been baby steps: $1 billion worth of funding compared with a Chinese investment in excess of (so far) $15 billion.

The UK will not lead by going it alone. In the spring of 2023, in an attempt to distinguish the UK from the more prescriptive EU approach, British ministers came up with five light-touch principles to inform responsible development of AI. Yet one thing is already clear: in the world of AI and quantum computing, most players need partners. The only exceptions are the two biggest national players, the US and China. Both are likely to exercise their option to act alone. But the UK would harm its interests by diverging from the set of countries (its neighbourhood) most likely to be its partners.

Second, the UK must press for global agreements on the safe and responsible development of AI. Governments collectively can and must assert their right to regulate. When it becomes impossible to distinguish real and fake images, regulators need to step in to require the labelling or erasing of the fake. In the same month that ChatGPT-4 appeared, an image of the pope sporting a white Balenciaga puffer coat briefly fooled the world; other fakes will be even more convincing and might be considerably less benign. Governments also need to set out where AI may never be used; every country should be able to agree never to allow AI to control nuclear weapons or create lethal pathogens.

With accelerating climate change, the rise of AI is likely to be one of the two main challenges of the twenty-first century. British ministers repeatedly assert that there is nothing to fear from AI. In reality, people know they have reason to fear. From the first disciples of Jesus Christ, through their descendants approaching the year 1000, to sceptical readers of *Protect and Survive*, the timorous have feared impending doom. So far, existential fear has always proved unfounded. Government action can help people to deal with the fear-inducing aspects of AI, and to incorporate AI into a better future.

PART III

Response

10

Capabilities: What's Special About the UK

People who love the UK acknowledge its failings; it is one way that they prove their love for the country. Only a country that is truly special would incorporate its failings into its legend about itself. But we prefer to dwell on the good stuff.

I start with five stories about the UK. No doubt their spirit might be claimed by other countries, but I think they are quintessentially British. They are often retold and yet still, quite reliably, bring a tear to my eye (apart from the one that always makes me smile). The first is the only one that involves a person I have met.

I

Nicholas Winton was a London stockbroker in the 1930s. His family (although he didn't know it) was originally Jewish. His father arrived as an immigrant from Germany in the 1900s, when he changed the family name from Wertheim to something more plausibly English. Doing well in business, Winton senior sent his son to a minor public school, from which he found a job in the City of London. As a young professional in the late 1930s, Winton regularly travelled to Czechoslovakia. He saw at firsthand what the Nazis were doing; he saw the immediate and dramatic difference the German takeover of Czechoslovakia made for ordinary Czechs. He resolved to do something about it. In the first eight months of 1939, with a friend in the same stockbroking company, he arranged for 669 young Jewish Czechs to leave home and find sanctuary in the UK. Only the declaration of war on 3 September curtailed his activities. Forced to stop, he put all the paperwork associated with the evacuation in a cardboard box.

After the war, the cardboard box accompanied him from house to house. It was one of the unexplained objects he brought to his marriage in 1948. For nearly forty years, his wife neither asked about the box nor peeked inside. Then one day in 1988, she took a look. She was astonished by the contents, which she decided she must share. Her chosen vehicle was *That's Life!*, one of the most watched television programmes of the day. In February 1988, Esther Rantzen, the show's lead presenter, told nine million people the story of what Nicholas Winton had done in 1939. Without anybody asking him and without seeking payment or recognition, he had saved the lives of hundreds of Jewish children, children whose families had perished in the war that followed.

Rantzen informed a survivor, Vera Gissing, that the man sitting next to her was the man who had rescued her. They hardly knew how to react: a hug, a tear, a wish that no one else was looking. The story sparked a more overt reaction among the audience at home. Information about the children flooded into the studio from all over the country. The following Sunday, Rantzen presented a follow-up piece. Winton was again sitting uncomfortably in the audience. At the climax, Rantzen asked if anyone in the studio audience owed their life to Nicholas Winton. The camera pulled back so that viewers at home could see about a hundred people in that part of the studio. Applause broke out as the majority stood up. They stood stock still. Winton looked around; suddenly he couldn't see much because he was surrounded by standing people; he stood up himself and wiped his eyes as he resumed his seat, speechless. And the show went on.

Winton's story reverberated for years. In the last quarter of his life he was acknowledged as a hero. Because he was part Jewish, the rules of Yad Vashem meant that he could not be recognised as Righteous Among the Nations for saving Jewish lives (only non-Jews are eligible for the title), but the State of Israel and the Czech Republic honoured him. I met him in Israel when he visited in 2006. He was a spry widower in his nineties. His daughter accompanied him, called him 'Nicky' throughout, and was clearly able to keep his feet on the ground as he listened to strangers sing his praises.

I asked him why he had kept quiet about what he had done for so long. He reminded me that it hadn't been his choice to go public, even forty years later. And then he said that, through all those years, all he could think of when he remembered those days in 1939 were the children he had failed to save. For the morning of 1 September he had arranged the biggest ever transport, to rescue 250 children. But Germany's invasion of Poland meant that the children at Prague railway station had to go home rather than travel to London. He said that nearly all of those children had died in the following six years.

Other people's resolute wish to salute him eventually made an impression. He accepted a knighthood from Elizabeth II in 2003 and the Order of the White Lion, the Czech Republic's highest honour, in 2014. The Czech government sent a plane to collect him for the ceremony. Supreme humility allied to supreme achievement was the distinguishing feature of the jolly old man I met in Ramat Gan.

II

In 1940, the British tried to help the French resist Nazi Germany. As France was falling, the British Expeditionary Force was pinned against the Channel coast in northern France, ripe for capture. Churchill ordered their evacuation. It was immediately clear that the Royal Navy had insufficient capacity to complete the evacuation by itself. Nautically minded Brits spontaneously decided to lend a hand.

Lambert 'Bush' Shepherd – a graduate of Jesus College, Cambridge, and a journalist – asked his editor at the *Evening Standard* for leave. The archive at Jesus picks up the story: 'When he returned, it was discovered that he had spent his leave evacuating troops from Dunkirk by means of a rowing boat.'[48] Shepherd had rowed single-handedly across the Channel, calm as a mill pond. At Dunkirk, he picked up two soldiers, who took turns rowing the boat back to Dover. Shepherd then returned to France alone to rescue two more. He rowed over eighty nautical miles to save four lives. Later that year, he joined the Royal Navy. Prior to sitting his final examinations for commissioned rank, he was posted to HMS *Hood* for probationary service. On 24 May 1941, in the Denmark Strait, the German battleship *Bismarck* fired a shell at *Hood* which triggered a magazine explosion that destroyed the aft part of the ship. With her back broken, she sank in less than three minutes with 1,418 men aboard. Shepherd was not one of the three survivors. Jesus College acknowledges his heroism with a scholarship, established by his father in his memory.

III

The UK (in its opinion) gave the world sitcoms on television. The Second World War inspired the series which is still the most repeated on British television: *Dad's Army*, a story about the Home Guard's improbable attempts to protect the local population against the Nazis in the fictional town of Walmington-on-Sea on the south coast. The platoon is a motley crew, under the testy supervision of Captain Mainwaring, a bank manager in civilian life. The largely predictable plot lines are quirkily scripted and beautifully acted. According to regular surveys, the programme gave the UK its funniest TV joke, in an episode featuring a group of German sailors who have been captured after their U-boat has sunk in the Channel. Mainwaring and his men must look after them until they are carted off for interrogation. Their leader objects to his crew's treatment and begins to compile a list of men whom he will seek out for retribution after Germany has won the war. The youngest member of Mainwaring's platoon, a milksop with a rare blood type, goads the Germans by singing a popular song which lambasts Hitler as a 'twerp'. When the German asks the man his name, Captain Mainwaring, trying to stiffen the resolve of his weakest link, barks, 'Don't tell him, Pike!'[49]

IV

In 1992, Great Britain had one of the best men's 4 × 400 metres relay teams in the world, hoping to add the Olympic title to the world championship they had won the previous year. British expectations for victory in Barcelona were high. Derek Redmond, a twenty-seven-year-old from Bletchley, was the squad's fastest runner. But before he could anchor the British quartet to glory, he had to take part in the individual competition. Having clocked the fastest time in the first round and won his quarter-final, Redmond settled confidently into his blocks for the semi-final. The event had been his main focus since taking up running as a teenager.

Redmond had a good start and was into his stride when

suddenly the BBC commentator reported something was wrong. On the back straight, Redmond had pulled up; his face was contorted in agony. He had pulled a hamstring, a devastating injury for an athlete. His whole Olympic Games ended in one second. That fact was clear to 65,000 spectators in the stadium and millions watching on television. And yet the young man whose dreams had just been crushed could not accept it. In tears, he rejected the stretcher proffered by officials.

Suddenly, a burly figure bustled from the stands. He brushed past trackside security and made his way to the side of the injured athlete. Redmond collapsed, sobbing, on to his father's shoulder. Jim Redmond briefly tried to persuade his son to throw in the towel ('You have nothing to prove'), but Redmond junior was determined to finish the race. The two made their way around the bend. Officials tried half-heartedly to shoo them from the track but recognised that their schedule was making way for something more important. Of course, a competitor who is helped is disqualified. But that was not the point. A father wanted to help his son. As the pair crossed the finishing line, the whole crowd rose to its feet, roaring its support. Not more than a dozen spectators could have known either man, but a father's love for his son was instantly recognisable. Redmond was listed as Did Not Finish, but he provided the Olympics with one of its most enduring images.

V

Queen Elizabeth II died on 8 September 2022. Plans for her funeral had been finalised years before. For the reign of Charles III, Lord Carrington is lord great chamberlain; a hereditary office whose duties include a prominent role in a monarch's funeral. Because he was seven years older than the queen, Peter (6th Lord Carrington) deputed his son to take part in London Bridge (funeral planning) meetings for more than thirty years before Elizabeth II's death.

Before the funeral on 19 September, her coffin was brought to the Great Hall at Westminster, where – like her father's, grandfather's and great-grandfather's before her – it rested on a purple catafalque, covered by the Royal Standard, topped by the imperial state crown, orb, and sceptre, and protected by a regularly changing guard of cavalrymen. For eight days, the British public filed by.

The Queue became an international phenomenon, its name reified with a capital Q. Planners had organised a route that stretched 16 km to its starting point in Southwark Park. Everyone who joined the Queue was able to view the coffin, in a setting that justified the wait. Some people queued twice. Planners ensured that bottles of water and thermal blankets were available, as the maximum wait extended beyond twenty-four hours. Celebrities joined the line in the same way as everyone else. David Beckham improved his already high public standing by queuing alone with a cap pulled over his eyes, which prevented his neighbours from recognising him until everyone was bunched up in Victoria Gardens, near their final destination.

The Queue was orderly, patient, enormous: everyman's and, particularly, everywoman's tribute to the late monarch. Caitlin Moran in her *Times* column admitted to watching the Queue on the BBC's parliamentary channel for hours, mesmerised by the 'innumerable women [who] on reaching their moment, at the end of The Queue, some having waited up to 24 hours, often with very small children ... blew a kiss to the Queen, and mouthed "thank you" before smiling and then bursting into tears.'[50] Dabbing their eyes, they emerged through Carriage Gates ready to tell any journalist who asked that it had all been worthwhile.

While writing this book, I looked for a statistic that best summed up the UK. I found my favourite in an article about birdseed. Apparently, Britons buy more than twice as much bird food as the rest of Europe combined. Brits define themselves as animal lovers; most people do. Across the world, people own pets and donate to the World Wide Fund for Nature. They contribute to donkey sanctuaries. But Brits also lend a hand to wildlife close to home. Of course, birds are wild and know how to fend for themselves – but why not help, if you can? A bird feeder may attract nothing more exotic than a bullfinch, but the procession of blue tits, great tits, and dunnocks gladdens the heart.

Most nationalities would confidently self-identify as humble, practical, funny, family-oriented, polite, and nature-loving; a few would claim additionally to be undaunted when the odds against successfully completing a task are ludicrously high; and very few would doggedly complete small tasks of an unfathomable importance to those who do not undertake those tasks. It is my contention that only Brits manage the full cocktail.

But a key part of Britishness is acid self-criticism. We pick at our failings publicly. We resist P. G. Wodehouse's advice never to apologise (in his opinion, 'the right sort of people do not want apologies and the wrong sort take a mean advantage of them').[51]

The fact that Brits are good chaps who know that they are not perfect might make us feel better about ourselves, and might inspire affection or respect elsewhere, but it does not amount to 'soft power': national characteristics by themselves have no power of attraction. But, as the UK recognises that the days of exercising hard power by itself are over, one thing generally agreed is that we still wish to play a role on the world stage. The only available option is soft power. What, then, constitutes the UK's soft-power offer? I believe it has seven components, the Magnificent Seven: British ways of doing important things which other countries want to engage with directly or might even want to copy.

The judiciary

The biggest jewel in the UK's soft-power crown, its Cullinan Diamond, is its judiciary. Every country claims to respect the rule of law. Every country emphasises the independence of its judiciary, with varying degrees of plausibility. The acid proof of independence is whether outsiders trust a given judiciary to arrive at objective decisions, grounded in laws which are transparent and evenly applied, in cases which affect them. The ultimate accolade is being a jurisdiction where international players resolve their legal disputes. The world comes to London for binding arbitration.

Even diamonds shatter when pressure is misapplied. Joseph Asscher took weeks to plan the cutting of the Cullinan Diamond; legend has it that he fainted when he finally cleaved the 3,106-carat stone in two in one blow. In 2023, the British government is showing rather less care than Asscher for its most precious jewel. The United Nations High Commissioner for Refugees has said the Illegal Migration Act, which received Royal assent on 20 July 2023, is a clear breach of the Refugee Convention. It expressly misapplies domestic legal protections against modern slavery and makes it more difficult for asylum claimants to challenge decisions or enforce their rights in UK courts. But, despite the evident wishes of its drafters, it cannot misapply the UK's obligations under international law.

The law exists beyond a short-term political agenda; it imposes restraints when ministers are not interested in being restrained. The forty-six countries that are party to the European Convention on Human Rights (ECHR) have committed themselves to high, binding standards in the knowledge that the effects of that commitment will not always be politically convenient; maintaining that commitment protects democracy.

In the 2020s, elements of the Conservative Party have begun to argue, increasingly stridently, that the ECHR is an unnecessary encumbrance, that the UK does not need an international guarantor of its freedoms and legal system, that ultimately sovereignty trumps fundamental rights. These elements may succeed in inserting an undertaking to leave the ECHR into the Conservative manifesto at the next general election.

Even the aspiration to leave damages the UK's international reputation. British lawyers helped draft the convention; they put the essence of British legal traditions into the document. And yet, because the convention may make it more difficult for a particular government to implement controversial policies, some would prefer to ditch a precious commitment rather than reshape a specific policy.

If the UK did this, the UK would be choosing the company of Russia and Belarus over Europe's democracies. If the UK did this, opponents of governments with a wavering commitment to fundamental rights would feel more vulnerable. If the UK did this, what government would be deterred from unilateral action by the fear of international condemnation? Whatever the (disputed) merits domestically of leaving the ECHR, the move would be seen as wholly negative in all parts of international opinion the UK cares about.

Bad bills are often amended into better acts, but a concerted government effort to pass a bad bill damages the UK's reputation as a place that respects the rule of law, abides by its international obligations, and enables people to enforce their rights before independent courts.

Over centuries, the key to the high reputation of the UK's judicial system has been the excellence of its judges: they are incorruptible; they reach their judgments without fear or favour; nobody brings a case to an English court confident of the result simply because of who they are – they, or their lawyers, have to make the best case under the law. By contrast, in China and Russia, the courts respond predictably to the express wishes of the government. Nobody other than a fool would voluntarily take on the government. Courts know how they are supposed to behave, even in the absence of explicit direction from above.

In all legal systems there is a process of appeal, which ends with some high authority with the power to exercise clemency. In some jurisdictions (I am most familiar with Sharia systems in the Islamic world), all junior levels and all participants in legal processes are aware of that possible late and decisive intervention; they are aware of it because it is frequently exercised and is often the moment when political or diplomatic considerations come into play.

Some legal systems have a reputation for integrity but a relatively narrow span of experience. Few litigants would fear caprice or political interference in a Nordic court, but complicated cases involving billions of dollars are rare in the courtrooms of Copenhagen, Helsinki, Oslo, Reykjavik, and Stockholm.

A key to London's reputation is how judges are trained, selected, and promoted. At all points, the process is independent, even if in the end every judge is nominated by the minister for justice and appointed by the king. The system relies on the judgement of the people at the top. Until the Constitutional Reform Act 2005, the apex was the lord chancellor, always a politician sitting in the cabinet, often as its second most senior member after the prime minister. But the lord chancellor was also always eminent in their profession; their professional qualifications were more important than their politics.

Lord Mackay was the last of the great traditional lord

chancellors, respected by his cabinet colleagues but not really part of their club, because his job was different. He did not campaign, never made a media appearance, and did not aspire to another job in politics. He had unimpeachable integrity, encyclopaedic knowledge of the law, and profound care for practitioners of his profession, yet even he sometimes found it difficult to get agreement for key appointments. In our last conversation, he told me that his greatest battle had been to secure the appointment of Tom Bingham as master of the rolls. In office, Bingham proved to be the defining jurist of his generation, and in retirement he wrote the definitive primer on the rule of law. But, even in the law, high quality can be threatening to the less gifted.

For centuries, English judges were a self-perpetuating elite. Judged by their performance, they continued to advance by traditional processes well into the era when closed and obscure practices were no longer acceptable for making senior appointments (in the UK, only ministers are now appointed without process, as the personal patronage of the prime minister). Since 2006, the Judicial Appointments Commission has recommended all judicial appointments. Its chair is one of the most important and yet low-profile jobs in public service.

In 2023, the Supreme Court of Israel became the most divisive issue in Israeli politics. The newly elected government (commonly described as the most right-wing in Israel's history) took office with 64 out of 120 seats in the Knesset. The election, which produced a six-party coalition government, was Israel's fifth in four years. The result was the first clear-cut victory, but clarity was achieved because of a shift of just 30,000 votes. Nevertheless, the new government considered its mandate decisive and chose to rule as if it had won by a landslide – that is, it chose to push controversial policies.

Israeli elections are often marked by the sudden emergence

of a new party or boosting of a previously marginal party. The leaders of two such parties quickly established themselves as the centre of gravity in the new coalition, setting the agenda. Bezalel Smotrich, leader of the Religious Zionist Party, and Itamar Ben-Gvir, leader of the Jewish Strength party, took aim at the Supreme Court. They anticipated judicial unhappiness with some of their key policies; their supporters talk of the court failing to respect 'parliamentary sovereignty', as if any parliamentary majority has the unfettered right to do whatever it likes with a country's constitution. Their agenda is overtly discriminatory: they want not merely a Jewish state but an exclusively Jewish state, in which Arab citizens can have either a lesser place or, eventually, no place at all. The truth (as ascribed to them by their opponents) is that they have been unhappy with the court's role in upholding equal treatment for Israel's citizens, Arab as well as Jewish.

The initial line of attack taken by Smotrich and Ben-Gvir was indirect; they focused on what they saw as the 'unrepresentative' nature of the court. The fifteen judges are overwhelmingly Ashkenazi; the Mizrahi (Jews originally from North Africa and the Middle East) who form the bedrock of support for the parties forming the coalition are underrepresented – if you believe that, in order to be legitimate, a judicial system needs to mirror precisely the composition of the society over which it sits in judgment.

In Israel, until now, and in England, judges have been selected only because of their qualities as lawyers. I once asked a member of the Supreme Court of the UK whether his court had a diversity problem. He answered swiftly: 'Oh, no, we have a very good mix of Oxford and Cambridge.' Action is clearly needed to expand the pool of possible candidates, but the fundamental point in an effective and respected judiciary is that excellence in the law rather than political affiliation or ethnic or religious sympathy is the only criterion determining who becomes a judge.

Some states in the US have taken a different path. In New Mexico and seven other states, voters elect judges for their state supreme courts in partisan elections. In 1994, when a judge in New Mexico awarded millions of dollars in punitive damages for injuries sustained by spilling piping-hot coffee from McDonald's, big corporations took a closer interest in elections to the bench there. In the following election cycle, judges' races were some of the most expensive in the country.

Although Scotland and Northern Ireland have separate laws and judicial systems, I label the system as British; the British legal system has the highest reputation of any in the world. Foreign countries cite British judgment more often than any other outside their own jurisdiction. Judges come to the UK for training and informal advice as new challenges in and to their own systems emerge. Judicial diplomacy is low in profile, but it is still the first plank in the platform of the UK's soft power.

Universities

In the late Middle Ages, across Europe, princes and bishops began to found universities as places for the teaching of divinity, the law, and medicine. Bologna was first in 1088, followed by Oxford (1096), Paris (1150), Cambridge (1209), Salamanca (1218), and Padua (1222). Charles University in Prague was the first German-speaking university (1347). The exact foundation dates of Oxford and Cambridge are disputed, but it is generally accepted that Oxford was first, and that Cambridge was founded by dons migrating from Oxford. By the middle of the fourteenth century, the collegiate structure of both universities was firmly established; by 1400 Oxford had eight colleges, which survive today, and Cambridge six.

The motivations of the founders of colleges were spiritual as much as educational. Christ's College, Cambridge, started life as God's House in 1437, founded by William Byngham to teach grammar to bright but impoverished boys from the North of England. In 1505, at the urging of her confessor John Fisher, Lady Margaret Beaufort refounded the college on its present site (King's College Chapel now stands where its original building once did). As an aged (in her sixties), rich (the richest in England, thrice widowed to her financial advantage), and well-connected (the mother of the king) woman, she had multiple objectives. The two clearest were the salvation of her immortal soul (as a good Catholic, she believed that a group of priests saying mass every day in perpetuity would speed her entrance into heaven) and the advancement of bright young men from the nine counties of the North. The difference in prosperity between the North and South of England was already stark in the early sixteenth century. The statutes are not completely clear about which nine counties she meant; they are most plausibly the nine north of the Trent, with Richmond (one of her titles) counting separately from the rest of Yorkshire.

In the late sixteenth century, Cambridge became the training ground of Puritans, and in the seventeenth century it identified with Parliament in the Civil War; Oxford was generally royalist. The divide was not absolute. In Christ's, the fellowship mildly favoured the king and the undergraduates Parliament (Oliver Cromwell studied at Cambridge's neighbour, Sidney Sussex College). Legend has it that the students showed their displeasure by refusing to rise when the fellows entered Hall for the evening meal, a practice that persists to this day.

Most colleges were small at their foundation, typically with a dozen fellows (usually priests or monks) and about forty commoners (students). In the late seventeenth and eighteenth centuries, they shrank. Their reputation was maintained by a few outstanding scholars: John Milton was an undergraduate at Christ's (where, according to provably false legend, he wrote *Paradise Lost* under the ancient mulberry tree which bears his name). Isaac Newton spent most of his adult life at Trinity College, Cambridge, discovering gravity, his three laws of motion, and calculus.

When I arrived in Cambridge as an undergraduate, I was told that Newton's achievements included the mathematical bridge over the Cam between the two halves of Queens' College; his design was not merely elegant but clever enough not to require a single nail or rivet. Curious admirers later deconstructed it in order to understand the design better, but were then unable to reconstruct it without adding rivets. Returning as a master, I discovered the legend was nonsense: William Etheridge designed the original bridge and James Essex built it, twenty-two years after Newton died in 1727.

In the eighteenth century, Oxbridge by and large lost its mission for academic excellence, becoming finishing schools for young aristocrats and well-to-do merchants before embarking on the careers chosen for them by their fathers (the Church and the military were most popular for sons who were not the heir). This parlous state of affairs continued into the nineteenth century. As late as 1850, only 22 of the 542 fellowships at Oxford were open to any (male) candidate, the rest being tied to specific schools or parishes.

Three factors turned things around: Prince Albert, science, and women. The prince was the moving spirit behind the Royal Commission for Enquiry into Oxford and Cambridge in 1850–52, which reorganised the two universities, introducing the idea of meritocratic entry to replace entry by patronage. Charles Darwin was an undergraduate at Christ's in the late 1820s, returning to Cambridge in 1836 to sort out the specimens he had amassed during the voyage aboard the HMS *Beagle*.

Lord Kelvin was a student and then fellow at Peterhouse in the 1840s. In order to support the study of science, the university built laboratories for the use of fellows and undergraduates from all colleges. The Cavendish Laboratory in Cambridge opened in 1874.

The first women's colleges appeared at about the same time: Girton College, two miles outside Cambridge, and Lady Margaret Hall (named in honour of Christ's founder) in Oxford. Since then, the size and academic reputation of the two oldest English universities have climbed steadily. Of almost 1,000 people awarded Nobel Prizes since 1901, a total of 121 have been affiliates of Cambridge; Trinity boasts more Nobel laureates (34) than any country outside the US, UK, Germany, and France.

Scotland started slightly later but overtook England for its number of universities by the end of the fifteenth century: St Andrew's (1410) was followed by Glasgow (1451), Aberdeen (1495), and Edinburgh (1583). The six original 'red-brick universities' (nicknamed after the principal material of their construction) gained their royal charters in the first decade of the twentieth century.

Tertiary education did not just encompass the universities: local technical colleges became world leaders in their specialisms, notably the School of Mines at Treforest in Wales (now part of the University of South Wales), which in its heyday had the reputation of being the best place in the world to learn about mining. Latterly, new universities have become world leaders in new disciplines: more than fifty people among the special-effects team that worked on the film *Avatar* trained at Bournemouth University.

While most medieval universities have been outstripped by more modern foundations in their vicinity (Heidelberg and Göttingen are pretty but average), in the UK, the old universities in England and Scotland have maintained their pre-eminence. In the annual tables ranking the world's universities, Oxford and Cambridge always feature in the top five, with Oxford regularly coming out on top (Harvard presenting the stiffest competition).

From the start, the Oxbridge institutions were international, and they have kept that outward-looking approach. At the height of the British Empire, promising young scholars from the colonies were despatched to Oxbridge, some staying but others returning to establish universities in their own countries. In the 1940s, Lee Kuan Yew – who would go on to become Singapore's prime minister – was an undergraduate at Fitzwilliam College, gaining the top first-class degree in law; bright young Singaporeans still head for Cambridge.

In the last twenty years, the number of postgraduate students has effloresced around the world, and Oxbridge has taken more than its fair share. Higher degrees (apart from the medievally originated 'doctor of divinity' degree) began to appear after the First World War; Oxford awarded its first DPhil in 1919. As demand for further research-based qualifications grew after the Second World War, Oxbridge colleges were at first as reluctant to accept these students alongside their male undergraduates as they were to accept women. Both universities set up colleges solely for postgraduates in the 1960s. Fifty years later, most of these colleges have become indistinguishable from older colleges (apart from generally being poorer), taking men and women, undergraduates and postgraduates, British and international students.

Every country which aspires to greater prosperity sees the advantage to itself of attracting talent from elsewhere. Countries with the greatest means have succeeded most at creaming off the best of other countries' students. The US is the most generous. In 2022, nearly 900 undergraduate institutions reported to the *US News* annual survey how much financial aid they gave a typical international student during the 2021–22 academic year. The average amount was roughly $22,000. Among the ten schools where financial aid for international students was highest, average scholarship money was almost $74,000 (with tuition fees of about $56,000). In 2022, 1,321 overseas students were studying at these ten universities. The not-so-difficult-to-follow plan is to give these students such a good American experience that they decide to stay. And they do. The positive results of this poaching for the poacher are evident in the number of American Nobel laureates who are hyphenated citizens: of over 400 American laureates, some 113 were born somewhere other than the US.

For over thirty years, the EU's Erasmus programme was the main way the UK attracted overseas students. The inability or reluctance of the British government to negotiate an extension to or replacement of Erasmus since Brexit has seen the number of EU students at British universities plunge. Demand from students from other parts of the world, particularly China, remains high. But the UK is milking its reputation: overseas students have to pay three times as much as British students for the privilege of a British-university education. Because excellence is international, British universities will remain excellent only if they remain open and attractive to the best international talent. The universities are jewels in the soft-power crown, but government policy may dull their glitter.

Science and technology

Britons have always been good at inventing and building things. Engineers Thomas Telford and Isambard Kingdom Brunel remain heroes, celebrated over 150 years after their deaths, the former with a new town named in his honour in

1963, the latter with a university founded in 1966. At the eleventh General Conference on Weights and Measures, in 1960, the international community agreed an International System of Units (abbreviated to SI in all languages) consisting of seven base units and twenty-two derived units. In naming all twenty-nine, conference participants sought to honour major figures in the history of science; their final list included more scientists from Britain than from any other nation.

The kelvin is one of two base units named after a person: Henry Thomson was the first scientist to become a peer in the UK, taking the title Baron Kelvin (Kelvin being the name of the river that flowed near his laboratory at the University of Glasgow). In 1848, Lord Kelvin identified absolute zero, so kelvin is the basic unit of thermodynamic temperature. Zero kelvin is -273 °C. In 1952, John Cage composed one of the most notorious pieces of modern music: 4'33", for any instrument or combination of instruments. The score instructs performers not to play their instruments during the entire performance. The piece consists of the ambient sounds of the concert hall where it is performed, but at its premiere was perceived as silence. Four minutes and thirty-three seconds is 273 seconds in total; Cage's piece at least unconsciously honours Kelvin.

Five of the derived units are also named after British scientists: the newton (for Isaac Newton) measures force/weight, the joule (for James Prescott Joule) energy, the watt (for James Watt) power, the farad (for Michael Faraday) electrical capacitance, and the gray (for Louis Harold Gray) the absorbed dose of ionising radiation.

British scientists and engineers have always risen to practical challenges. My grandfather used to tell a story about his early days at the UK Atomic Energy Authority. At some point in the 1950s, his laboratory received a parcel from the US containing a smart presentation box which announced on its lid that it contained the world's smallest tube. Some months later, the Americans were slightly affronted to receive the box and its contents back in the post without a note of explanation. They made tentative enquiries of their British colleagues and were directed to look inside their tube, where they found an even smaller one.

In the twenty-first century, the US leads the world in science and technology, and in the commercialisation of what their scientists and computer programmers invent. All the world's biggest tech companies are American: Apple, Alphabet, Meta, Microsoft, Amazon, and Tesla. In the West, only Germany's SAP SE gets close. The founders of these firms have become the richest men in the world and are international celebrities. When Mark Zuckerberg visited Germany in 2013, the state secretary at the foreign ministry marvelled at his reception: for three days, he was treated like a head of government, visiting from a particularly powerful state, with newspapers reporting his itinerary and even his most casual asides: 'Big tech bosses are the new princes.'[52]

The US has the capital to turn bright ideas into billion-dollar companies. At some point, science entrepreneurs in other countries find it easier to sell out to an American company than take their invention to the next commercial level. In 2014, Google acquired DeepMind, an AI company founded in the UK in 2010; Google later forecast that much of its profit over the next decade would be derived from technology bought in the UK.

The UK cannot take on the US, but it can be a next-tier player. In Europe, British business generates more 'unicorns' – business ideas that attract over $1 billion of investment when they come to market – than the rest of the continent combined. Across the UK there are inventors and entrepreneurs, developing ideas that might one day break out and grab the world's attention.

The excellence of British universities is directly linked to foreign interest in incubating these ideas. Telecoms at the beginning of the century was dominated by two Nordic companies, Ericsson and Nokia. Through Huawei, the Chinese successfully muscled into the sector; at a crucial stage in the development of the world market, they were able to undercut their European competitors by down-prioritising the security features in their systems. By the time the world woke up to Chinese methods to gain market share, Huawei was the world's biggest telecoms company, dominating 5G rollout and best poised to develop and market 6G and subsequent generations.

Ericsson and Nokia looked to their governments for regulatory help in Brussels. They were disappointed. In desperation, they turned to Margaret Beckett, at the time the UK's secretary of state for trade and industry. She helped them ward off the immediate danger of China moving in and taking over without Europe putting up a fight. Partly as thanks for her help, the companies located part of their research infrastructure at the University of Surrey. As a result, the world will have more than a Chinese Hobson's choice when deciding who is to provide the infrastructure supporting the next generations of telecommunications.

Nordic–British cooperation extends to pharmaceuticals. As the world was extolling the development of the Oxford–AstraZeneca Covid-19 vaccine (apart from Nicola Sturgeon, who invariably referred to the AstraZeneca vaccine), AstraZeneca (a British–Swedish company) was finishing its new $1.3 billion research-and-development facility in Cambridge, which was opened by the then Prince of Wales on 23 November 2021. Oxford, Cambridge, and London form a triangle of excellence in science; excellence attracts excellence. In Cambridge right now, more than 5,000 postdoctoral researchers are working in university and private laboratories. St John's

College, Oxford has just announced plans to build a science park in north Oxford to rival the one already being built by Magdalen College.

Scientists working in the UK are as international as their rivals and collaborators at Harvard or Stanford, and must remain international if the UK is to maintain its place at science's top table. Rejoining the EU's Horizon programme as an associate member in September 2023 was unalloyed good news for UK science and research. Although the UK will never be able to match the financial rewards of top American universities, its total lifestyle package attracts the best in the world to Britain. In 2023 at Christ's, the fellowship includes academics from Canada, Croatia, Hungary, Israel, Italy, Lebanon, Peru, Romania, Russia, Spain, the US, and Uruguay. For many academics the lower teaching burden gives Oxbridge an edge over the US, but foreign academics are increasingly irked by new difficulties in navigating British bureaucracy. Officialdom makes them feel that foreigners are not as welcome as they used to be, and that is becoming a problem. To maintain its edge in science and technology, the UK has to remain open to international students and researchers.

Culture

Human beings have more leisure time since the Agricultural and Industrial Revolutions. In England, before the eighteenth century, over 85 per cent of workers were working on the land six days a week with the help of horses or oxen (if they were lucky); having handed over most of what they produced to their landlord, they were just about able to keep themselves and their families alive with the balance. Cities were small, and industries, such as they were, were labour-intensive. People got their cultural fix from church; from travelling players, who performed at local fairs; and from stories handed down from one generation to the next and told by the evening fire.

Over the course of two centuries in the UK, all of that changed. Only 2 per cent of workers remained on the land; what they did there was as important as ever, sustaining a population that grew to ten times its pre-Industrial Revolution number. Towns and cities were more numerous and much larger, in 2021 playing home to 84 per cent of the expanded population.

People have always wanted beauty and culture in their lives; one way the Catholic Church was able to keep its grip on Europeans was by the loveliness of its architecture and music. Artists have always needed an audience to pay for what they do. Strolling players lived on the edge economically. Easier by far to set up a theatre and let the audience come to you. With more people living in cities, it was easier for providers of culture to make a living.

London had permanent theatres from the sixteenth century. Shakespeare's Globe was recreated in the 1990s, as small and wooden as the original, with verisimilitude in everything apart from the price of admission (one penny in 1600). In the 2020s, only Paris and New York rival London for quantity of theatres and concert halls; Paris has somewhat more and New York somewhat less than London's 204.

In the twenty-first century, people have more time to travel and more money to spend. Culture has been a massive beneficiary. Most of London's tourists take in a show; almost none of London's theatres or concert halls could survive without their foreign audience. One reason why *The Mousetrap* is still playing to big-enough audiences after seventy years (with a coronavirus-enforced break) is that it is the London production most foreigners have heard of. Foreign culture vultures inject $10 billion into London's economy every year.

The invention of the printing press transformed popular consumption of culture. Within a few decades, popular fiction rivalled the Bible as the most reproduced title. New art forms appeared in order to take advantage of the new technology: Samuel Richardson's *Pamela* is acknowledged as the first 'true' novel in the English language; within a century, Jane Austen, William Thackeray, and Charles Dickens had developed the novel into one of the most popular and most profitable art forms.

Books led the way. Photography, gramophones, radio, moving pictures, television, and online streaming were equally momentous inventions in the nineteenth, twentieth, and twenty-first centuries. More people have quick, easy, and cheap access to culture than ever before. And the UK is well placed to take advantage of that fact.

Norman Foster revolutionised the design of airports at Stansted and of skyscrapers in Hong Kong, both in the 1980s. I remember gazing across Victoria Harbour on my first visit in 1986 and seeing the Hongkong and Shanghai Banking Corporation (HSBC) building dominating the shoreline, then revisiting the city in 2019 and being unable initially to spot it among the forest of still-taller buildings. Richard Rogers gave Paris its most iconic building of the twentieth century when he put services in colourful pipes on the outside of the Pompidou Centre. Where their lordships led, Zaha Hadid and David Chipperfield followed this century. In art, David Hockney commands the highest prices at auction of any living artist (rivalled by Jeff Koons); Tacita Dean leads the challenge of the next generation, the only artist ever to have three exhibitions running simultaneously in London art galleries. In museum design, Neil MacGregor and Nicholas Serota showed the world how to change, maintain standards, and pull in larger numbers of visitors with their work at the British Museum and Tate Modern.

In all the visual arts, the UK can claim to rival the US as the leading player.

Music is humankind's most beautiful invention. These days, music accompanies every aspect of our lives. Classical music is available everywhere. So, too, is Mongolian throat music, if that's your preference. But by far the music most widely listened to is American and British rock and pop. Although the internet breaks new artists every day, only half a dozen young artists match the reach of singers and bands performing half a century ago. Adele, Harry Styles, and Ed Sheeran go toe to toe with Taylor Swift, Drake, and the Weeknd for the earbuds of listeners under the age of thirty. But the old timers do best. With nearly sixty years of stadium tours under their belt, the Rolling Stones are reckoned to be the human beings seen in the flesh by the most other human beings. The back catalogues of Freddie Mercury, Elton John, David Bowie, George Michael, and Bryan Ferry are worth hundreds of millions of dollars. But the most influential, bought, and played music of all is by the Beatles.

John, Paul, George, and Ringo arrived at JFK on 7 February 1964, to an America desperate to be cheered up after President Kennedy's assassination eleven weeks earlier. Their clothes, hair, and attitude were different; their music was more hummable, more exuberant, and more danceable than anything else around. Two days later they provided Ed Sullivan with his most memorable live show, and within weeks they had conquered US airwaves, their songs occupying all five of the top spots in the Billboard singles chart (a feat surpassed by Taylor Swift when she took the top ten spots in 2022). The whole world succumbed to Beatlemania. More than half a century later, Paul McCartney and the estates of John Lennon and George Harrison continue to rake in the royalties, and every band and songwriter continues to work in the Beatles' shadow.

The English language helps. Although English is the first language of less than 5 per cent of the world's population, it is by far the most popular second language. In the 2020s, about 1.5 billion people speak English. Books written by British writers do well internationally. The UK exports more books than any other country. When I worked in Israel (2003–06) the biggest-selling books each year were instalments in the *Harry Potter* series. All eventually appeared in Hebrew translation, but young Israelis were so impatient to keep up to date with the lives of Harry, Hermione, and Ron that they bought them in the original English. In descending order of sales, Agatha Christie, Barbara Cartland, J. K. Rowling, Enid Blyton, Jackie Collins, Jeffrey Archer, Edgar Wallace, Roald Dahl, J. R. R. Tolkien, C. S. Lewis, Alistair MacLean, Beatrix Potter, and Ian Fleming have each sold more than 100 million copies of their books worldwide.

Hollywood has also helped. Working in their mother tongue, British writers, actors, and technicians have done well in the country that produces the most commercially successful movies in the world. British studios co-produce many of the top grossing movie franchises, notably *Star Wars*. Television and streaming services have added to British success: *Game of Thrones* was made mostly in Northern Ireland and, since 2020, Netflix has invested £4.8 billion in the UK, with annual spending increasing by 50 per cent each year between 2020 and 2023 on productions such as *Bridgerton* and *The Crown*.

The UK's cultural offer is supported by the British Council. Conservative governments are ambivalent about the Council's contribution, arguing that James Bond, Paddington Bear, and Peter Pan have made their way into the cultural choices of other countries without official assistance. But the Council has persuaded policymakers in other countries to choose to teach British English rather than American English (notably in China) and profitably provides validation of prowess in English through International English Language Testing System (IELTS) language tests. In many countries, the Council is a person's first contact with British culture, helping to set a lifelong affinity.

The British cultural brand does not need much official tending, but officialdom needs to bear in mind that other countries can profitably piggyback on the UK. New Zealand stood in for Middle Earth for the filming of J. R. R. Tolkien's *Lord of the Rings* and *Hobbit* trilogies. Ireland, Canada, and some US states tailor their tax systems to appeal to the needs of English-language movie and television producers. In other words, the UK brand can thrive without the UK benefiting as much as it might financially.

Sport

One of the things the British think they gave the world is team sports. In fact, the Chinese and Mesopotamians take that honour. But eight of the ten most popular team sports in the world were codified in the UK. In order of global popularity, they are: football, cricket, hockey, tennis, baseball, table tennis, golf, and rugby. Football tops the table by any metric. Even though the Fédération Internationale de Football Association (FIFA) controls football's World Cup from Zurich, the Football Association (FA) in London still rules the game. Whether it is changing the points awarded for a win in a league from two to three, or how goal-line technology is used, the FA rules the roost.

England's role in organising and popularising the sport misguidedly led to the slogan 'Football's coming home' being used in each failed British campaign to secure the right to host the World Cup, and then in England's campaign at the competition when it has been staged elsewhere. To others, pride looks like hubris. Despite England's lack of success in the men's global tournament since 1966, the Premier League leads the way. Cable and satellite television popularised themselves by transmitting sport, and 'soccer' is the most popular sport in the world. In the last three decades, television rights have sold at auction for ever-higher amounts. In 2021, the Premier League renewed its deal with broadcasters for three years for a reported £5.1 billion. That money is (ahem – largely) invested in the sport, improving stadiums and raising the salaries of everyone connected with football, starting with the best players on the field.

The Premier League is the most competitive in the world. Germany's Bundesliga is dominated by one club, Bayern Munich; by drawing their final match of the 2022–23 season, Dortmund handed Bayern their eleventh successive title on goal difference. In France, Paris Saint-Germain have been Ligue 1 champions in nine of the last eleven seasons. In Spain, Real Madrid, Barcelona, and Atlético Madrid have shared the last nineteen La Liga titles. And in Italy in 2022–23, Napoli became the first team to break the twenty-year dominance of Juventus, Inter Milan, and AC Milan in Serie A. By contrast, seven teams have won the Premier League in England since it was set up in 1992: Manchester United, Manchester City, Arsenal, Chelsea, Liverpool, Blackburn Rovers, and Leicester (true, City have won the Premier League in five of the last six seasons). Leicester's victory was the least probable. At the start of the 2015–16 season, a fan could have got odds of 5,000–1 against Leicester winning that year (superfans placed the bet and cost the bookies about £25 million). The point is that, because the Premier League is the most competitive, its spectators are more likely to see a good match than those watching matches in any other league. It helps that clubs can afford to employ the best players: 133 Premier League players were members of their national squad at the FIFA World Cup finals in Qatar.

Some English clubs have history that appeals more widely than to fans within walking distance of their stadium. In the early 1950s, the manager Matt Busby built up Manchester United using mostly young local talent. The team that won the First Division in 1956 and 1957 was known as the Busby Babes. It was the first English team to compete in the European Cup, which the Union of European Football Associations (UEFA) established in the 1955–6 season. Returning on 6 February 1958 from the away leg of a quarter-final against Red Star Belgrade, their plane, carrying forty-four passengers and crew, refuelled at Munich. Conditions were icy, with slush accumulating on the runway. The plane made two abortive attempts to take off.

Despite the fact that snow then began falling even more heavily, the pilots tried a third time to get the Airspeed Ambassador off the ground. They informed the control tower that the plane had made 'V1', the velocity at which it was no longer safe to abort take-off, but they never announced 'V2', the velocity needed to leave the ground. Slowed by the slush, the plane overran the runway, ploughed through a fence, and broke apart. The tail section hit a barn; a fuel tanker parked inside burst into flames. Having saved himself, Harry Gregg, the goalkeeper, went back twice into the burning wreckage to rescue his teammates Bobby Charlton and Dennis Viollet. But seven players were among the twenty passengers who perished that afternoon. More than half the Busby Babes were dead or dying.

One who survived the day was twenty-one-year-old Duncan Edwards, widely considered the best player of his generation. In hospital his condition improved for a week, giving family and fans reason to hope. But doctors could not reverse the damage to his kidneys. During his second week in hospital, his condition gradually deteriorated until his death on 21 February.

More than 5,000 people lined the streets of his hometown for his funeral.

The world followed the drama in newsreels and newspapers. In Israel, Ehud Olmert (who would later become prime minister) won a school essay competition for his account. Along with countless other young people around the globe, he became a lifelong Man U fan.

Busby added to the club legend by rebuilding the team. Bobby Charlton (later to become only the second football player to be knighted) was joined in the United attack by a young player from Northern Ireland. George Best at his best was even better than Duncan Edwards. United continued to take part in European competitions and in 1968 lifted the European Cup, the second British team after Celtic to manage that achievement.

Busby's final retirement in 1971 was followed by fifteen years in the doldrums (the only period I ever went to Old Trafford, a bus ride from home in Eccles). Redemption came in the form of a Glaswegian with a good playing record, and an early management record which promised better: Aberdeen won three league titles, four Scottish Cups, one Scottish League Cup, and one UEFA Cup Winners' Cup with him in charge. After a faltering start in 1986 at Old Trafford, Alex Ferguson led United to thirty-eight trophies, including two European Cups, thirteen Premier League titles, and five FA Cups. Under his stewardship, the club became the most famous and the most valuable in the world.

Other English clubs were always nipping at United's heels. Being able to mount a serious challenge to United's dominance was usually associated with a significant injection of foreign cash. Roman Abramovich led the way, buying Chelsea for £60 million in 2003. I saw them beat Bayern Munich on penalties in the final of the European Cup in 2012 in Munich (and was impressed when the owner of the city's most famous nightclub refused €1 million to allow Chelsea players to party the rest of the night in private). After the UK imposed sanctions on Russia in the wake of the invasion of Ukraine, Abramovich announced that he was writing off over £1 billion the club owed him and putting it up for sale; an American-led consortium paid £4.25 billion in May 2022. Middle Eastern and Asian money followed Russian money into English football: Manchester City and Pep Guardiola climbed to the top with Emirati dirham, and Leicester and Claudio Ranieri with Thai baht.

The Premier League not only pulls money into the UK, it also plays a big part in shaping – usually positively – the rest of the world's opinion of the UK. For years, clubs have nurtured their fan bases overseas. When travelling in East Asia as PUS, I found my opposite numbers were invariably fans of an English club, generally the one that had been top of the league when they were ten years old; Liverpool, Manchester United, and Arsenal were especially popular. The single most surefire way to make progress in a territory is to buy a player from that territory and field him regularly in the first team. Tottenham have a strong following in Korea, courtesy of Son Heung-min. All clubs are on the lookout for Chinese talent.

Formula 1 is the world's most popular motor sport. In the 2021 season, its cumulative television audience exceeded 1.5 billion; 445 million viewers tuned into at least one race, with each race generating about $100 million in revenue. Seven of the ten teams racing in the 2023 season have bases in the UK: Red Bull, Mercedes (which between them have won every championship since 2010), Aston Martin, McLaren, Williams, Haas, and Alpine.

The British also have a reputation for organising sporting events well and for welcoming fans from around the world. The apotheosis was the London Olympics and Paralympics of

2012. Every event sold out. Every crowd was enthusiastic and respectful. The television pictures I saw in Germany where I was living at the time were joyous. Afterwards, the embassy organised a party in Berlin for returning paralympians. Some were veterans of five or more games. They were ecstatic about the London crowds. Until Sydney, they had been used to competing in empty stadiums. In Beijing, they competed in front of Chinese soldiers, resentful at being made to 'paper the house'. But in London, every session had an enthusiastic capacity crowd. The German minister for the disabled told me that he had to pinch himself at the sight of 70,000 people on a Saturday morning watching qualifying rounds with sympathetic interest, shushing themselves to ensure a blind competitor was given his best chance to perform well.

The UK's reputation for staging events has been on a rollercoaster since then, hitting a low point with the UEFA Euro final in 2021, when ticketless fans stormed past police into Wembley Stadium to watch England play Italy (and lose on penalties). One unruly, drug-addled hoodlum provided the match with its most abiding image – of him with a lighted flare up his bum. The following year, supporters of the women's game did much to restore the fans' reputation when England beat Germany in the Women's Euro competition; tens of thousands of mothers took their daughters to revel in the party atmosphere.

Britain also organises grand-slam events in other sports, notably tennis (Wimbledon) and golf (the Open). Even though Americans, Australians, and the French might hesitate to endorse the idea that these British events are the best, they do not dispute their high quality. Sport, codifying sport, popularising sport, and organising sport significantly boost the UK's soft power.

Media

Since the arrival of social media, young people access news from more sources. According to the regulator Ofcom, British teenagers these days get most of their news from Instagram, TikTok, and YouTube, turning away from traditional news on television and rarely opening a newspaper. Social influencers are news sources as trusted as established investigative journalists. People can now choose the source most congenial to them rather than accept the editorial priorities of the BBC or other national broadcasters.

Around the world, consumers of news have become more sceptical of traditional news sources, especially ones close to government. As part of his purported drive towards greater transparency, Elon Musk has labelled ever more accounts on Twitter as 'government' or 'official' or 'government-funded'. The label is a flag for readers to beware: the source might be more interested in plugging its line than telling the truth.

Musk's policy led to a spat with the BBC early in 2023: he decreed that BBC Twitter accounts should all be labelled 'government-funded'. The BBC fought back, pointing out the difference between 'government' and 'public'. The government provides no money these days for the BBC and exercises no editorial direction; everything comes from the licence fee (outside Musk's experience) and commercial sales (mostly selling programmes to other countries, but also including advertising on BBC World).

After summoning the BBC's North America technology correspondent to an impromptu ninety-minute interview (streamed live on Twitter before the BBC could edit it for its own channels), Musk changed his mind. From April 2023, BBC accounts were labelled 'publicly funded'. The BBC made its point, but the wrangle left me feeling uneasy. Parts of the BBC have traditionally been government-funded, notably the World

Service. In a cost-cutting exercise, the government withdrew that funding and included the World Service among the services funded by the licence fee in the budget of 2015, but the BBC has argued for reverting to previous practice ever since, and it achieved a partial restoration of FCDO funding in 2021, when the FCDO announced the provision of £94.4 million to the World Service from official development assistance. As importantly, the row about the source of funding is a proxy for a row over its editorial independence.

It is an article of faith that the BBC is editorially independent from the government. And yet practice is not the same as faith. The government appoints the chair of the BBC Board, approves all new Board members, and agrees extensions to their Board membership when they come up for renewal. This gives the secretary of state for culture, media, and sport (and the prime minister standing behind them) considerable power. Observed practice is that the BBC is unable to protect itself from appointments it dislikes. Controversy dogged the appointment as chair of Richard Sharp, who resigned after the barrister Adam Heppinstall found that he had breached the governance code for public appointments. It turned out that failing to mention his role in introducing Boris Johnson to the businessman Sam Blyth (subsequently guarantor on a large commercial loan to the prime minister) while running to be BBC chair amounted to a 'potential perceived conflict of interest'[53] (Sharp's words).

Secondly, to the vociferous complaints of the opposition, the BBC toes the government line, not everywhere or every day (the shortcomings of parts of government are grist to its news mill), but regarding policies of particular importance to the government, particularly Brexit. Ministers who were Brexiteers from the beginning complain that the BBC harbours 'remoaners'. Its coverage of the consequences of Brexit fails to satisfy either camp, studiously purveying the notion that 'the jury's still out' rather than declaring 'political nirvana' or 'unmitigated disaster'.

Despite the fact that it is not everything it aspires to be, the BBC is the UK's single most important media player internationally; in 2021 the World Service's audience was at a record high of 351 million per week, listening in 42 languages, with the BBC's global news services reaching 438 million every week. Even as he detected an over-large government role, Musk added that the BBC's website was one of the first he checked each day because he found it was one of the most objective and truthful. The BBC gets the facts right and, on the rare occasions when it does not, it corrects itself quickly.

Its reputation for integrity has been hard won over decades, and it stretches into the remote nooks and crannies of the world. When Michael Palin was filming an episode of *Himalaya* in the tribal areas of Pakistan, notoriously the most lawless areas in an unruly country, he reported that his producers were nervous. But his employer gave him a cloak of protection: 'Ah, you're from the BBC!' exclaimed a tribesman. 'Step this way!'

As the news landscape fragments, people are increasingly aware of two things. First, in an era when you can say whatever you like in public, rumour and malice can be presented as fact. The controls that editors previously exercised are obviously absent. And second, it is not only blowhard individuals who take advantage of a world without editorial standards; news organisations are less rigorous themselves. After the US presidential election in 2020, the losing candidate claimed to have been deprived of victory by tampered-with voter machines programmed to record votes for himself as votes for his opponent. President Trump provided no evidence for his oft-repeated claim. Fox News chose to report the claim uncritically, misleading the electorate and damaging the reputation of Dominion, the company that made the machines. In early 2023, a claim by Dominion against Fox was settled out of court for in excess of $787.5 million.

News consumers know from the reporting of outlets they favour that other organisations are capable of lying or misleading. So they will (I hope and expect) be increasingly sceptical of the output of all news organisations. Over time, news organisations with a record of truth-telling will reassert their pre-eminence in the world of news.

Three British newspapers are among the world's most trusted news sources: *The Economist*, the *Financial Times*, and *The Guardian*. Their reputation for probity means that the people they want to talk to when getting to the bottom of a story are more willing to open up to them. In every capital where I've worked, the sources of the *Financial Times* and *Economist* have been at least as good as the British Embassy's: senior officials and ministers have been happy to talk to their journalists, confident that they will not be misrepresented and that the resulting story will be accurate and read by people they want to inform.

The ownership structure of the *Financial Times* and *The Economist* has become more complicated since Pearson sold its stake in both in 2015. Nikkei, a Japanese holding company, now owns the *Financial Times*; the shares in the Economist Group previously held by Pearson are now owned by the Agnelli family (Fiat's major shareholders). Only a curmudgeon would question the editorial independence of either newspaper (and plenty of folk are monitoring); their reputation is for pursuing the stories they want without fear or favour.

The Guardian is owned by the Scott Trust, whose core purpose since it was set up in 1936 has been to ensure the financial and editorial independence of *The Guardian*. It does not charge for use of its website, but every time a reader views an article they are reminded of how many they have read that year and invited to make a financial contribution. The business model – relying for funding on readers' better nature – appears to be flourishing.

One other British title is among the most successful online newspapers worldwide: it helped that the *Daily Mail* entered the lists early. The content of its online edition is different from the paper edition; more stories are driven by good photographs. The algorithm that search engines use to recommend news stories prioritises articles with many pictures, so the *Mail* does well. *Tortoise* news defines itself by the animal that inspired its name, slow, not breaking news. It is not chasing that day's headline. It is aiming to dig deeper and set out facts at the length they require rather than the length permitted in a standard newspaper column. The BBC is also dipping its toe into new ways to convey the news. One of its correspondents, Ros Atkins, has pioneered the extended news clip, taking up to ten minutes to dig into a complicated story rather than confining himself to the usual ninety seconds allowed on a news bulletin. As well as appearing on the News Channel, Atkins's team uploads the clips to YouTube, where many have been viewed hundreds of thousands of times.

In its soft-power future, the British government needs to help protect the reputation of its media. Politics and media have a relationship of unequal symbiosis. Owners and editors need politicians to take up the causes and make the changes (including to the law) they rail about on behalf of their readers – but in the end they are more powerful than politicians, because they can make or break politicians. From the moment he announced his candidacy for the mayoralty of London, Boris Johnson has consistently been supported by the *Evening Standard*, bought in 2009 by the Lebedev family. Mr Johnson gave Evgeny Lebedev the ultimate prime ministerial thank you for that support; three years after Lord Lebedev took his seat, Johnson's gratitude is the only plausible explanation for Lebedev's presence in the House of Lords, where he has never voted and has spoken only once (but not about Russia, the subject on which he might be expected to have something interesting to say).

The great thing about owning a newspaper in the UK is that other newspapers will not be nasty to you: the Murdochs, Rothermeres, and Lebedevs have strikingly underexamined public lives; the Barclay family had to come apart at the seams before it became a news story. Just because other newspapers are not interested does not mean proprietors should be given a free ride. Media ownership excites relatively little public debate in the UK, and yet the political preferences of newspaper and satellite-television channels exert a powerful (and sometimes decisive) influence on British politics. Two of the great media dynasties are not British, and their main business interests are outside the UK. In the effort to maintain the quality of the output of its media, perhaps the UK needs to pay closer attention to media ownership.

Old institutions

In the six weeks between the announcement of my appointment as PUS and the day I started the job, I read the Gormenghast trilogy. A friend at the Bank of England said it best encapsulated the spirit of what I was about to undertake. Mervyn Peake started writing the quasi-medieval fantasy during the Second World War and published the third volume in 1959. The story is set in the vast castle of Gormenghast, presided over by the melancholy Lord Sepulchrave, seventy-sixth earl of Groan. It starts with two arrivals – a new heir and a new kitchen boy – and chronicles their lives. I enjoyed the first two books, and over the following five years found myself reflecting on Titus Groan and Steerpike. Their world is unfathomably large, complicated, and old; it hardly makes sense to the people in charge, even though the task of their lives is to be in charge; it makes no sense to outsiders but an interloper can make his way to its heart with energy, guile, and apparent respect for the status quo; it demands change but exudes menace to anyone trying to change it; everyone in the system understands instinctively that any change would imperil its time-honoured rituals, which, on balance, work well enough. When change comes, it is devastating.

If Brexit were a character, it would be Steerpike the kitchen boy, but so far the UK as Gormenghast has proved stronger. The old institutions hold firm. Three in particular – the monarchy, the City of London, and the civil service – are key to the UK's soft power. The monarchy is the foundation of the British state on which everything else rests; the fact that most Britons do not know that and might dispute the fact is part of its strength. The king is not a constant presence in national life. No one swears allegiance to him in a classroom; his picture does not habitually adorn even government buildings (although, in 2023, the government announced an £8 million programme to change that). Essentially, he is a background figure but also the country's backbone.

The king as an institution embodies what the UK cares about: duty, constancy, continuity, common sense, and the promise of bravery if required. He is the head of the armed forces and the fount of honour. He speaks for the nation at times of rejoicing, of tragedy, and of remembrance. He exists above politics, which means that when he speaks he speaks for and to everyone.

The British require some grandeur from their head of state. Before the eyes of the world, the person must look serious and be treated seriously. Despite sporadic efforts to whip up outrage

over the expense of the coronation, the UK enjoyed the specta-
cle and the public holiday. The human connection to a thousand
years of history was comforting: a man sat on a wooden throne
made for Edward I, over the Stone of Scone, a damaged medieval relic binding Scotland to the ceremony. He was anointed
with oil consecrated at the Holy Sepulchre in Jerusalem. He
was crowned twice, once by the archbishop of Canterbury
with the huge but impossibly unwieldy St Edward's Crown,
and later in the privacy of the Chapel of St Edward with the
more manageable but also more magnificently glittering Imperial State Crown, which includes the Black Prince's ruby and
Elizabeth I's four large pearls. Music accompanied the whole
ceremony, the most stirring piece composed by Handel in the
1720s for the coronation of Charles's seven-times-great-grand-
father, George II. And he arrived and departed in horse-drawn
carriages, one made in Australia, commemorating Elizabeth
II's diamond jubilee, with air conditioning and hydraulic sus-
pension, the other lumbering and notoriously uncomfortable
but unavoidable because of its antiquity.

King Charles is developing British ideas about kingship. Like
Edward VII, he has succeeded a long-reigning monarch, who
got away with some anachronisms and extravagance because
she was so beloved. Under Charles III, the monarchy will be
smaller and less remote. He is a conspicuously good and flawed
man, who espoused important causes decades before they
became fashionable: youth unemployment, human-scale architecture, and – supremely – the importance of protecting the
environment. He reuses and recycles. When Extinction Rebellion gummed up the streets of London with their protests in
2019, their leaders wrote to Clarence House apologising for
the noise and inconvenience they were about to cause a man
they admired, who was then the Prince of Wales. King Charles
embodies a humble, median, relatable leadership.

The British have been lucky with their run of monarchs for the last 200 years. Each generation of the royal family has had its wild and unsuitable characters, but the crown has always found its way to the right head. In an episode of *The Crown*, Prince Philip (Tobias Menzies) tells the queen (Olivia Colman) that Tommy Lascelles (George VI's private secretary) once compared the House of Windsor to a Reichsadler, a heraldic eagle with two heads, each generation having a 'dutiful, reliable, and heroic' head and a 'dazzling, individualistic, and dangerous'[54] head. The analogy holds good as far back as the children of Victoria: Vicky was steady and Bertie was wild but redeemed by accession; among Edward VII's children, George was steady and Eddy wild; among George V's children, George VI was steady and Edward VIII wild. As a shot of Princess Margaret (Helena Bonham Carter) fills the screen, Prince Philip continues that in the subsequent generation Lilibet is steady and Margaret wild. The analogy can be extended further, with Andrew and Harry playing 'wild princes' to the 'steady princes' Charles and William.

King Edward VII might be said to prove (but equally Edward VIII might be said to disprove) the idea that doing the job helps the monarch to do the right thing: everyone treats you respectfully, everyone around you is trying to help, life is comfortable, and your duties are clear. Looking ahead, preparation of the heirs is key; once the succession is secure, the 'spares' should be released from titles and public duties; they can enjoy family holidays in implausibly gracious surroundings but for the rest they make their lives as private citizens. The children of Princess Anne are the model. So, the laser-like focus is on the Prince of Wales and Prince George. Until George has children Princess Charlotte cannot do precisely as she likes, but the Waleses can already plan a 'normal' life for Louis. He need never give a television interview nor be the subject of a newspaper story;

he can be a private citizen with the same right to privacy and anonymity as any British citizen. The media genie is one of the most difficult to stuff back into the lamp, but a line might be drawn now for Prince Andrew and Prince Harry; they are private citizens who will never again play a public role.

A small royal family would continue to fulfil the duties expected of it: the king would broadcast on Christmas Day, open Parliament, troop the colour, lead national remembrance in November, and distribute Maundy money before Easter. He would receive foreign visitors his government wanted him to receive and make overseas visits to countries his government wanted him to visit. Honours would be given in his name and he would award some of them in person.

For the rest, he would be a benign and inscrutable presence at the top of the system. The palaces, castles, and spectacles associated with him would continue to draw domestic and foreign visitors. Occasionally he would feature in political life, being snapped receiving a new prime minister, but these appearances would be formal, with all political drama having been resolved before his involvement, because that is what the rest of the system owes him: the defusing of controversy before the king has a part to play.

The king is essential to the UK, and he is essentially British. But he is also head of state in fourteen other realms. This is an anomaly which is impossible to justify from the UK's point of view, and increasingly difficult to understand from the point of view of those realms. The strongest tie of sentiment – which caused countries, at the moment of their independence, a moment of excitement but also uncertainty, to ask a familiar figure to continue in an office which she had filled with grace – broke with the death of the queen. King Charles's advisers in realm capitals can do themselves and him a service by address-ing the anomaly and repatriating the job of head of state before crisis hits. Because one day crisis will hit; its timing and precise content are unforeseen, but a key component of that crisis will be a head of state who is an outsider and whose role is complicated or made impossible by that fact. The sacking of Gough Whitlam by the governor-general of Australia in 1975 was a foretaste, not an aberration.

Although no country that does not already have a monarch is likely to choose one as head of state, the king is a model for other ceremonial heads of state; the role of the president of Germany or president of Israel is similar in their systems; indeed, the framers of the German and Israeli constitution-like basic laws had the House of Windsor's example before them as they set out the duties and responsibilities of their head of state. For the publicity it generates and the example it sets, for its convening power, the House of Windsor is a key component of UK soft power.

The City of London is the second oldest of my three old institutions. Medieval kings were always strapped for cash, and the merchants who ran the City became adept at extracting permanent privileges in exchange for temporary lines of credit. In the same year the barons required King John to grant the Magna Carta, the City persuaded him to allow London aldermen to choose their own lord mayor rather than accept a royal nominee. In the following centuries, the City enhanced its self-regulation.

Post-Brexit, the City remains Europe's pre-eminent financial centre. Its advantages are entrenched: the common law is more flexible and quicker to accommodate change than Napoleonic Code jurisdictions. Its lawyers are forward-thinking, for example, Geoffrey Vos's ground-breaking work on regulating cryptocurrencies. Its spirit is free market, not unfettered but significantly freer than dense continental oversight. It is simultaneously traditional and capable of breath-taking innovation, for example, the Big Bang deregulation of the London Stock Exchange in 1986. It boasts an agglomeration of expertise which it augments with overseas talent, generally encouraging British governments to maintain an open immigration policy. The fact that London is a satisfying place to live explains why the City is then able to retain so much international talent.

The civil service is the newest of my three old institutions. The idea that ministers should be able to draw on the expertise of impartial officials before they take decisions started in the UK. The Northcote–Trevelyan reforms (1854) ensured that civil servants were appointed and promoted on merit and were politically neutral (therefore able to serve any government returned to office by the electorate); the reformers also encouraged the idea that civil servants should have deep experience in the policy field on which they were advising.

All countries with public services that are admired externally have an independent civil service. In league tables (such as they are), the UK vies with Canada, Denmark, Singapore, Australia, and New Zealand for top spot; the main thing their public services have in common is an independent civil service. Despite external admiration, the British system is under pressure. Two recent prime ministers, one egged on by his chief of staff, behaved as if the civil service was a problem they had to overcome.

If a prime minister's objective is to break the law, the civil service is a problem. In more-or-less his final act as cabinet secretary, Mark Sedwill deemed that civil servants could work on the Internal Market Bill because the attorney-general, Suella Braverman, had opined that it was lawful. To Braverman's annoyance, he did not endorse her view that seeking the power to break international law was different from breaking international law. The attorney-general's view of what is lawful guides the British system but it can be challenged. Shortly afterwards, clearly disagreeing with his boss' assessment, Jonathan Jones, permanent secretary of the Government Legal Department, resigned after the secretary of state for Northern Ireland said in the House of Commons that the draft legislation would break international law in a 'very specific and limited way'.[55]

Reading about the government's plans to break international agreements which the same government had signed within the previous twelve months, I was completely dismayed. I hope I would have treated the matter as a resignation issue if I had still been on the books. Six months later, when choosing a motto to go with my new coat of arms, I selected *Pacta sunt servanda* (agreements must be kept), the most basic principle in international law.

Johnson's successor behaved in the same way towards the civil service. Despite being in office for just forty-five days before announcing her resignation, Liz Truss managed to sack the permanent secretary at the Treasury and sideline the national security adviser. Until the markets made plain their unhappiness, her chancellor came close to appointing a civil servant with not one day's experience of working in the Treasury as its new civil servant head.

As the retired civil servant who tweeted that Number 10 under Johnson 'keep changing their story and are still not telling the truth' two days before he was forced to resign, I am not the most popular spokesperson for my profession among his supporters. But all I did was ask Number 10 to come clean when it had repeatedly failed to tell the truth. The team led by Johnson seemed to me to be exploiting the fact that serving civil servants can neither contradict their ministerial bosses nor defend themselves in public. After retirement, I felt my continuing obligations: not to make the professional lives of former colleagues more difficult, and to remain loyal to my former political bosses. But in the end I felt a greater obligation to the truth. It seemed that Number 10 was deliberately concealing an important fact, which only I could put authoritatively into the public domain. The lesson for Johnson's successors is not that civil servants are disloyal; it is that civil servants are there to do a particular job. They advise ministers in private; their advice is based on the best evidence and their considered judgement, grounded in experience. As long as ministers uphold their side of the bargain, civil servants must uphold theirs: they must not leak or even brief journalists unless it is their job (in comms) or at the express instruction of a minister.

Civil servants are not there to deceive for ministers or cover up ministerial mistakes or accept ministers' bad behaviour. That said, it feels wrong to me for parliamentary select committees to quiz civil servants when they suspect ministers have done something wrong; they should put their questions direct to the minister concerned. MPs will neither increase their knowledge of what happens in departments nor improve accountability by setting ministers and civil servants against each other.

Prime ministers up to and including David Cameron understood all that. The not-so-old ways were lost for a time but can be restored quickly; indeed, Prime Minister Rishi Sunak has started as if that is his explicit intention.

11

Policies

Niche hard power

Yoav Biran was right: in the twenty-first century, most countries (not just EU countries) do not need a foreign policy. They need to choose between the US and China (with Russia in its wake) and then slipstream the policies of Washington or Beijing.

To its discomfort, the EU remains the junior partner in geopolitics to the US. President Macron hates the reality, but cannot do more than talk about greater autonomy without imperilling the essential advantages in defence and security that Europe derives from the US, especially with war raging in the East of the continent.

The UK also works out its foreign policy in the American slipstream; like the EU it has the ability to influence (at least occasionally) American choices and to nuance its position, never fundamentally disagreeing but not always tied wholly to Washington.

Within the EU, France wants to lead and even to dominate foreign policy debate (and is not much bothered about being seen to make that effort); Germany wants to be seen not to dominate European debate (even when it is increasingly irked when it fails to get its way); Italy wants to be seen at the same table as those who dominate European debate; and the EEAS demands a seat at that table. Other countries debate foreign affairs in parliament and take part in Foreign Affairs Council discussions in Brussels, but essentially they are trying to influence Berlin, Paris, and the EEAS and go along with whatever emerges from that three-cornered process.

The UK can be a factor when Washington and Brussels are debating an issue, but the UK is no longer a sovereign foreign-policy player. The change crept up on London over half a century. After a magnificent performance in the Second World War, one vital to the Allies' victory, the UK secured a permanent seat at the top table (not surprisingly, given that its officials had helped to design the post-war order), but it failed to notice that the substance required to justify that place was almost immediately lacking. The British liquidated their empire, partly in response to demands for independence but also because they could no longer afford to run it. Suez was the proof that should not have been ignored, but the evidence of the fall was so disagreeable that collectively the country quietly ignored it.

And the fall was not continuous or always precipitate; sometimes the UK's international fortunes ticked up. The Falklands War was a close-run thing, but in the end it was supremely and undeniably a victory. Interventions in Sierra Leone and Kosovo were small but decisive. But the bigger story was the UK making an appearance increasingly as the US's junior partner and chief cheerleader. In the 1960s, Harold Wilson's signal foreign policy achievement was keeping the UK out of the US's war in Vietnam. Nearly forty years later, Tony Blair took the UK into a US war that was equally unpopular with the British people; he thought it was a just war and he thought the UK's presence would influence American conduct of the war. Events proved him wrong on both counts.

After the deployments in Iraq and Afghanistan, only the boldest military planners now foresee the possibility in the short term of the UK being involved in aggressive military action beyond its borders (peacekeeping is a different matter). That era is over. Military action is a relatively rare feature of international policy. But the British role in the rest of foreign-policy action is also smaller. Leaving the EU was the most recent significant development to reduce the British role. Boris Johnson's government chose to leave without agreeing new arrangements for foreign, security, and defence policy cooperation (evidently making the choice because the Europeans wanted such arrangements). Three years later, Brussels finds that its foreign-policy making proceeds just fine without constant input from London.

The exceptions are the biggest issues, when the Americans and other G7 partners are engaged; the most important example right now is policy towards Ukraine. Because the UK is, for the time being, the largest European contributor to NATO's capabilities, the UK is a full participant these days in debates about Ukraine.

I do not argue that the UK should retreat more than it has done, or that we cannot be effective hard-power foreign-policy players when acting in company. But in future we will be niche hard-power players, and we should have policies and structures which recognise that reality. The UK can be an effective international player, even as it accepts that its role will be smaller and more targeted than it was when Churchill was alive.

For centuries, the UK's armed forces had global reach and a global role; territory was acquired in order to help the Royal Navy work everywhere. India was the jewel in the crown; Britain felt the need to dominate sea routes between Britain and India, first via the Cape of Good Hope and, after the opening of the Suez Canal in 1869, via the Mediterranean, Red, and Arabian Seas. The retrenchment after India's independence in 1947 was slow and reluctant, almost as if the original rationale for capabilities on the other side of the world had been forgotten.

In the 2020s, the role of all British armed forces needs to be more tightly focused on the UK, where their work remains vital. The first duty of any government is to ensure the safety and security of its citizens. There can be no downgrade in the importance of the navy, army, and air force. But their tasking and capabilities need to change.

The nuclear deterrent

My biggest idea is that the UK should put its nuclear deterrent on the negotiating table. Nuclear disarmament has been snarled up since Putin decided that the possession and threatened use of nuclear weapons was the best route to being seen and treated as a world power. Traditionally, British governments have argued that their nuclear armament was so small compared with the US's and USSR/Russia's that it would come into consideration only when the two traditional superpowers had made savage cuts in their inventory.

Logically, that is true: the number of British warheads is dwarfed by American and Russian holdings, being less than 10 per cent of either. Other things being equal, we can (and have) camped on our traditional arguments. Indeed, new Russian belligerence is an argument for maintaining the status quo. But other things are not equal.

First, the nuclear deterrent is vastly expensive, although the costs are incurred over so many years that, big though they are, they can disappear in the detail of the defence budget. The 2015 Strategic Defence and Security Review (SDSR) confirmed the UK's commitment to maintaining an independent minimum credible nuclear deterrent. At the time, costs for four new Dreadnought-class submarines were estimated at £35 billion, including inflation, over the thirty-five years of the programme, plus a contingency of £10 billion. In 2020, the government announced its intention to replace the UK's sovereign nuclear warhead; the replacement will be 'sovereign' yet 'integrated'[56] with US systems. The Ministry of Defence has not yet estimated the total cost of this key element of the programme.

In defence procurement, accurately estimating costs and delivery times is notoriously difficult. For example – admittedly a particularly bad example – the Ajax programme to supply armoured fighting vehicles passed its Preliminary Design Review in 2012. By 2017, General Dynamics was supposed to supply 589 Ajax vehicles at a total cost of around £5.5 billion. By the spring of 2023, only twenty-six vehicles had been delivered and none was operational, at a cost of £3.5 billion and counting. The only thing certain about renewing the nuclear deterrent is that it will be more expensive than initially announced. Unless you are the Pentagon, these costs, running into tens of billions of pounds, are huge; at the very least, the opportunity cost – other programmes, including in defence, foregone – should be debated.

Second, the British government has always made much of the fact that its nuclear deterrent is 'independent'. But it is not. It is wholly dependent on the US. Nothing whose existence depends on someone else's continuing goodwill can claim to be independent.

Third, the UK will never use a nuclear weapon. Never. Period. British nuclear doctrine has always been framed in terms of a last resort when all other options are exhausted and when only a nuclear strike could save us. Extreme and exceptionally rare circumstances are generally understood. Recent public pronouncements (perhaps unintentionally) muddied the water. In the Iraq War, Geoff Hoon (defence secretary) said that British nuclear weapons might be deployed to protect British troop formations (he was spitballing, and wrong). In

the Integrated Review of 2021, the government took a step
away from disarmament (increasing the ceiling of the nuclear-
warhead stockpile from 180, as announced in the 2010 SDSR,
to 260); it also appeared to expand the circumstances in which
the use of nuclear weapons would be contemplated away from
the existential. For some reason, reviewers believed that introducing greater ambiguity would confuse potential enemies in
a way helpful to UK defence.

In the twenty-first century, there is only one signal advantage
to possessing nuclear weapons: it guarantees invulnerability at
home. No one will invade a state possessing nuclear weapons. It
is generally understood that an external threat to the continued
existence of the state is the only circumstance in which the use
of nuclear weapons might be contemplated. The lesson that
North Korea and Iran drew from the fall of Saddam Hussein
and Muammar Gaddafi was that a regime is left vulnerable by
losing or giving up its nuclear programme. As a man with his
finger on a nuclear button, Kim Jong Un was courted by President Trump; despite their protestations that Iranian nuclear
power would be exclusively civilian, the ayatollahs authorise
the spinning of ever more gyroscopes and the enrichment of
uranium to ever higher percentages, producing a quantity and
quality of fissile material compatible only with the manufacture of a nuclear device.

But most countries do not need nuclear weapons to be invul-
nerable at home. Germany and Japan do not fear for their
independence because they lack nuclear weapons. Right now,
some commentators point out that Ukraine once had nuclear
weapons; giving them up made Ukraine not merely vulnerable
but also a target of attack. But the government in Kyiv never
controlled the nuclear weapons on its territory; the Kremlin
always had ultimate control. After the break-up of the Soviet
Union, Ukraine was housing dangerous and possibly unstable

weapons over which it had zero control; it was in its interest to negotiate their removal.

The UK feels vaguely that possessing a nuclear deterrent is the price a country pays in order to remain a permanent member of the UN Security Council. It is true that all the P5 are acknowledged as nuclear-weapons states under the Nuclear Non-Proliferation Treaty, but that treaty post-dates the formation of the Security Council. The P5 are the P5 because that is what the UN Charter stipulates. None of them would lose their seat if they gave up their nuclear arsenal.

Ministers, especially Conservative ones, fetishise the nuclear deterrent: their argument appears to be that, although the UK no longer calls the shots, at least it still has nuclear weapons, because it belongs to the most exclusive of clubs and can never be pushed around. But the UK was pushed around – in the Falkland Islands, Iraq, and Afghanistan – and the option of using nuclear weapons was never seriously considered. I am not saying that no one in the system fleetingly floated the possibility (clearly Hoon said something), but I am saying that in the conduct of every single conflict in which the UK has been involved during my professional life, British nuclear weapons were not a factor.

My analysis – profoundly different from the UK government's assessment – is that the UK's opponents have concluded that there are no plausibly imaginable circumstances in which the UK might strike them with a nuclear weapon. That conclusion renders the nuclear deterrent functionally useless: an enormously expensive and ultimately pointless white elephant.

Realising that had we not acquired a nuclear deterrent we would not try to acquire one is different from recognising that we would be better off without the one we have. In diplomacy, you never give up something for nothing. I would start by changing the UK's position on global nuclear disarmament by offering to bring the UK deterrent into the negotiation earlier. In typing that sentence, I see how little it means: Russia has reminded the world of its nuclear arsenal repeatedly since invading Ukraine in February 2022; right now no one seriously thinks that any form of nuclear disarmament negotiation might get off the ground. The UK changing its position might be a formal event, but it would not make a difference.

I would not advocate a unilateral move, but I would urgently re-examine the programme to renew the UK's nuclear deterrent. The continuous at sea deterrent (CASD) served its purpose during the Cold War, but its rationale thirty years after the Cold War ended should be scrutinised anew. If the explicit overall aim of British policy is nuclear disarmament, then the UK does not need to continue its present state of nuclear readiness. Removing the option of the UK being able to kill millions of people, getting rid of the deadliest weapons ever invented, is in the end the right thing to do. All the arguments I make above are ancillary.

The Royal Navy

Ever since CASD was launched in 1969, it has been the main business of the Royal Navy. One nuclear submarine armed with nuclear missiles is always at sea; one boat typically spends three months patrolling the North Atlantic. If that were to end, the Royal Navy would again be seeking a raison d'être. The launch in the past decade of two new aircraft carriers could perhaps provide a new mission. Yet, as HMS *Queen Elizabeth* and HMS *Prince of Wales* await aircraft of a type that can use them, their early deployments have not been promising. Sailing through the South China Sea demonstrably annoys the Chinese, yet all the Chinese have to do is protest and wait a week for the flotilla to leave. There is no prospect of and nothing to be gained by attempting a permanent stationing of ships on the other side of the planet. And the fact that they are conventionally rather than nuclear-fuelled complicates their deployment, because they require constant refuelling.

Building the aircraft carriers provided temporary employment in a deprived part of the UK (Rosyth, next to Gordon Brown's constituency), but they do not enhance either the UK's reputation or its defence capabilities. No orders have followed from other parts of the world, and the relevance to the defence of the UK in the North Atlantic is unproven. Pinprick annoyance to potential adversaries which leads nowhere is no justification; they could and should be sold.

The Royal Navy lost its place at the apex of British defence with the invention of aircraft that can transport thousands of soldiers around the world in a matter of hours. Strategically, there is no case for a blue-water navy for a medium-sized power in our neighbourhood. We still need to defend our shores, but we need smaller ships rather than aircraft carriers for that purpose.

Our armed forces are steeped in tradition, but the UK is close to the point where tradition is driving the need for them to maintain separate identities. When Jeremy Heywood was its head, the civil service successfully pressed for the amalgamation of ancillary services. That programme could be advanced further. Beyond the defence of the UK, the task of the armed forces would be twofold. First, they would continue to fulfil their obligations to allies in NATO. (The diplomatic term most misused by politicians is 'ally'; the truth is that the UK's defence obligations are confined to NATO countries; other arrangements – such as AUKUS with Australia and the US and the Five Power Defence Arrangements with Australia, Malaysia, New Zealand, and Singapore – are consultative.)

The subordinate task would be military training and

peacekeeping. The UK already does this; help for Ukraine's army before February 2022 was the UK's main contribution to ensuring that Russia's initial assault failed in its objectives. When Zelenskyy addressed the Houses of Parliament in January 2023, his most widely reported request was for fighter planes. But he also asked for more training. We use official development assistance (ODA) to help partners who qualify under the rules of the Organisation for Economic Cooperation and Development (OECD). But the fields in which we can give ODA are severely constrained: humanitarian assistance primarily, but also help in developing healthcare, education, and governance. Defence and security are specifically excluded, and yet these are precisely the sectors where partner governments need most help, according to their own analysis. We should accept Zelenskyy's challenge and, if unable to carry the day at the OECD in Paris, be prepared to spend ODA on the areas we want rather than on what the OECD requires.

The United States

Any change in the UK's defence and nuclear posture highlights the UK's dependence on the US. No one likes acknowledging dependency, but when it comes to deciding the fundamentals of a foreign policy it needs to be acknowledged. The relationship with the US challenges (or even turns on its head) Palmerston's contention that Britain had 'no eternal allies' or 'perpetual enemies'; only British interests 'are eternal and perpetual, and those interests it is our duty to follow'.[57] He made the observation while serving as foreign minister of his era's hegemon. A hegemon has more choices; it can abandon friends and break commitments with fewer negative consequences for itself. No longer being in that position, the UK has for some time (without always fully acknowledging the fact) behaved as if the relationship with Washington were so important that the UK would sometimes do things only because the US asked, or even because we anticipated an American request. The instructions of Tony Blair's chief of staff to Christopher Meyer before he started a six-year stint as British ambassador at Washington could not have been clearer: 'We want you to get up the arse of the White House and stay there.'[58]

The brutal truth is that sovereignty is not what it used to be. In the end, sovereignty is about control of decisions that affect you; someone or something that controls its environment is sovereign. Membership of the EU was not the main reason the UK was losing sovereignty. Six decades of losing position in the world and of rising globalisation, which the UK could not resist, were the main reasons people (especially older people) felt that the UK was not as sovereign as it used to be. Once, we could stand alone or cooperate on our terms. No more.

The even more brutal truth is that the UK has already rejected the most promising way of achieving economic prosperity and making its way in the world outside the EU. Freed of EU restrictions, the UK could have embraced hyper-globalisation, being open to any country or company that wanted to work here; the UK could have become 'Singapore on Thames'. But total openness involves an unacceptable level of vulnerability: China would have been able to dig in deeper. Rather than pushing hyper-globalisation, the post-pandemic UK government has instead joined other governments in focusing more on domestic resilience; higher prices are worth paying in order to guarantee more resilient supply chains. Even if globalisation cannot be reversed, it can be slowed down.

Having left the EU and rejected the idea of a closer relationship with this era's rising hegemon, the UK has only one choice: an even closer relationship with Uncle Sam. The relationship will work more smoothly, with fewer opportunities for misunderstandings, if both sides are honest. We won't always do what they want, but when we don't, we'll explain why; they won't always listen, but when they don't, we'll hope they'll explain why.

Despite the fact that the US became an independent state only in defiance of Britain, the political relationship has been close since the second half of the nineteenth century. It is true that problems persisted longer than contemporary politicians admit in speeches: in 1847 Michigan moved its state capital to Lansing because Michiganders felt Detroit was uncomfortably close to British troops in Windsor, Ontario. But by the turn of the twentieth century, the alliance was solid. In both world wars, it was the UK's strategic objective from the outset to bring the US into the conflict on the British side; securing that objective meant that victory followed inexorably. Since doing the lion's share in defeating Nazi Germany, the US has been the single most powerful international player in the world.

Images characterising the partnership have always been uncomfortable, showing the UK as – in the words of one anonymous US administration official in July 2023 – 'just so needy'.[59] The special relationship was never exclusive; every country has a tailored relationship with the US, and the relationships with Israel and Ireland are at least as special (in terms of taking the president's time and US money) as the relationship with the UK. Macmillan's conceit that the UK played Greece to the US's Rome never caught on: it was as patronising as it was inaccurate.

The UK is a valuable ally to the US. In the last twenty years, the UK has stood beside the US more staunchly than any other country, sacrificing its own young people in armed conflicts that were more important to the US than the UK. But as the UK now adjusts to a different position on the world stage, that will not happen again. The UK will not in future wholly identify its interests with the US in the way Tony Blair did. The UK will have no closer ally, will never stray into the camp of an alternative hegemon (including Europe, if a future French president ever gets Macron's way), but it will not be as militarily active outside its home area as it was in the late 1990s and early 2000s.

Of course, the UK would be taking some risk. The so-called 'Greatest Generation', which fought the Second World War and felt most passionately about the transatlantic relationship, has died out. The US these days is as much a Pacific as Atlantic power; a growing number of Americans speak Spanish as a first or only language. Americans increasingly resent the money they spend on being the world's police. One of President Trump's achievements was to get European allies in NATO to recognise that they had to contribute more to their own defence. But an American expectation that the UK and other Europeans must do more is reasonable; it does not change the UK's fundamental alignment with the US.

More problematic is the US's increasingly hostile relationship with China. On the basics of the ideological conflict – our preference for democracies with free and fair elections, for human rights, for free trade, for the rule of law – the UK will always line up with the US. But it is the UK's strategic objective to ensure that China never becomes our enemy. So, I can imagine a point where China policy diverges. The fact that the UK might not fight if the US chooses to go to war over Taiwan might lessen our clout in Washington, but so be it. The US is our major ally, but dependence, even in the closest relationship, has its limits. We choose Uncle Sam, and as long as we remain semi-detached from our continent, we will never choose anyone else – but we do not want to be the fifty-first state of the Union.

France

Post-Brexit, the UK needs a new relationship with its main neighbours, starting with France – through history until the start of the twentieth century, the UK's longest-standing adversary but, by most measures, the country which most resembles the UK. We are a similar size (in 2021, France had a population of sixty-eight million, the UK sixty-seven million). We have the largest two colonial empires of the nineteenth and twentieth centuries, which we liquidated at more or less the same time and pace. We maintain close links with former colonies (France through the Francophonie, the UK through the Commonwealth). We are the two Western European nuclear-weapons states and permanent members of the UN Security Council. Our armed forces are the two largest, most capable, and most regularly deployed in Europe.

Despite the similarities and a tendency to sentimentalise the past and the future possibilities of our bilateral relationship (see every speech made by either head of state at a state banquet), we disagree constantly and consequentially. France is still not a fully integrated member of NATO; successive presidents hold out hope for the EU replacing NATO as the focal point of Europe's defence. In the Brexit negotiation, France consistently took the hardest line on protecting the integrity of the single market. At times it felt like Paris wanted the closest possible defence and security relationship at the same time as the most distant economic relationship with London (to have their gâteau and eat it, you might say). I am a Brit; my list of British transgressions is shorter, but I know the UK passes up no opportunity to prove to Washington that it is the better ally, and I suspect that a French colleague would be able to compile a list of British faults as long and glaring as mine of French shortcomings.

But the bottom line is that France and the UK are close in

every possible way. There is no possibility of being on different sides on any global issue of significance. Each side needs
irrevocably and enthusiastically to embrace the other. And we
need to do that despite Brexit, because that is in the interest of
both countries.

Germany

Germany is simply the biggest country in Western Europe.
It always has been. The 'German question' in the nineteenth
century was basically the rest of the continent acknowledging
that they had no idea of how to contain or relate to Germany
once it unified, a development that after the Congress of Vienna
(which awarded the coal-rich Ruhr to Prussia) came inevitably
closer with each passing decade.

In the twenty-first century, Germany does its best to disguise
its pre-eminence, and France lends a hand by noisily behaving as though Germany plays second fiddle, but Germany is
Europe's top nation. The difference from the mid-twentieth
century is that Germany does not want to exploit that fact
– quite the contrary, Germany is happy to follow the advice
that the writer Thomas Mann gave an audience of students
in Hamburg in 1953 and work towards a European Germany
rather than a German Europe. The issue is no longer contain-
ment or competition but rather how to achieve maximum
cooperation.

Ireland

British policymakers think too little about Ireland. Yet of all
our neighbours Ireland knows the UK best and in past centuries
suffered most from London's policies. Any new British ambassador at Dublin knows that they have to study bilateral history

back to Henry II in the twelfth century; in all eras, the Brits generated the problems, some of which (the Great Famine, the War of Independence) are keenly remembered today, others of which continue to have everyday political consequences (the Plantation of Ulster in the seventeenth century). In the nineteenth century, the Irish migrated not only westwards to the US and Canada but also to the rest of the British Isles in droves (including some ancestral branches of my family tree); their citizens continue to enjoy more rights in the UK than the citizens of any other country.

The relationship with Dublin should be handled out of Number 10 (as it was until David Cameron became prime minister), not left to one of the most junior ministers in the cabinet. The Taoiseach and prime minister should meet with their ministerial teams at least once a year. In a world where the UK thinks first of its neighbourhood, the only country with which the UK shares a border needs to feature more prominently in British policymaking.

The importance of balance

Even with a more focused foreign policy, the UK has a role further afield, for historical reasons. From Arab–Israel to India–Pakistan, the British were central players at the inception of disputes which remain unresolved. The UK has usually pursued a balanced approach: one reason why these disputes started was that both sides had legitimate but incompatible claims. The work of diplomacy is to help them pick through the possible resolutions short of war. This is principally the task of the diplomats of the countries directly involved, but others – knowledgeable, sympathetic to, and credible with both sides – have a role.

One old dispute in which the UK has lately unapologetically

taken sides is the rivalry across the Persian Gulf. British commercial interests in the region are dominated by Saudi Arabia these days, and Iran makes trouble in every way it can; the choice has been easy to make. But short-term factors should not blind us to the fundamentals of the dispute or where our longer-term interests lie. In the end, outsiders favouring one side over the other (no matter how reprehensible the behaviour of their favoured side) is exacerbating regional problems. Helping the two sides achieve a stable equilibrium that respects each side's interests would better serve British interests.

Commercial interests should not trump strategic interests: they are part of the picture, not the whole picture. The UK has allowed itself to be dazzled by Saudi Arabia's commercial prospects. For example, in 2017, Crown Prince Mohammed bin Salman announced plans to build Neom, a city on the Red Sea coast. Over the past six years, his ambition has grown to encompass five distinct projects: a ski resort (Trojena, already awarded the 2029 Asian Winter Games), an industrial complex (Oxagon), a port and airport (Neom Bay), a luxury resort (Sindalah), and, dwarfing all else, a linear city. The Line is planned to be 170 km long, 500 m high, and 200 m wide; by comparison, the Shard (London's tallest building) is 'just' 310 m tall. When it is finished, the Line will house nine million people at a population density of 260,000 per km² (compared with 74,000 per km² in Manila, the world's most densely populated city in 2020). The project is mad, a proof of the dictatorial power of one man. The opportunity cost boggles the mind: there must be at least a billion better ways to spend $1 trillion. Any partner who truly wanted to help Saudi Arabia would try to dissuade the crown prince, and yet Western (including British) firms prefer to pocket consultancy fees already running into tens of millions of dollars.

Overseas Territories

The OTs are scraps of empire still ruled by the UK. Typically, they receive scant attention in London. Whenever policy is reviewed, the reviewers conclude that it's all rather complicated and difficult, and so it's probably best to stick with the status quo. The OTs are like a diamond necklace encircling the globe: precious, beautiful, and so expensive that only an owner careless of money could afford to keep them. I urge the next government to rethink.

The OTs have striking features in common: they are all small, all remote from the UK, mostly isolated, mostly islands, and mostly reliant on the provision of elaborate financial services to keep their economies afloat. They also benefit from active lobbyists in London who make the case (supported by *The Telegraph* and the *Daily Express*) that the wishes of their citizens are paramount. All OTs benefit from the policy consequences of the Falklands War, which enshrined self-determination as a fundamental right for the citizens of all OTs.

Yet self-determination is not absolute. The international community has to agree the units entitled to determine their status. Small units cannot successfully pursue a claim for self-determination without outside support. One of my favourite Ealing comedies is *Passport to Pimlico*, whose plot is driven by the discovery of an ancient document ceding a small section of central London to the French duke Charles the Bold; Pimlico (briefly) declares self-rule. The screenwriter's choice of a Burgundian conceit for his story is cunning: Burgundy thrived at a time when units of government could be minuscule, with the views of their residents counting for almost nothing in deciding who should rule them. The dukes of Burgundy, whose main title was French, ruled a patchwork of territories, mostly in the Low Countries. By marriage, inheritance, conquest, purchase, and swapsies, they united Benelux.

In reality, many small countries are able to maintain their independence despite their inability to defend themselves. What these have in common is antiquity (think Vatican City, Liechtenstein, or Monaco) and the agreement of more powerful neighbours that their interests can be served by allowing a patch of territory independence rather than seeing it absorbed by a neighbour. Napoleon III wanted to buy Luxembourg from the Netherlands; the Germans objected and the grand duchy remained in Dutch hands until Wilhelmina became queen of the Netherlands in 1890; at the time, Luxembourg's adherence to the Salic law prevented a woman from becoming grand duchess.

Small units exercise self-determination only when their big neighbours allow them or when a more distant guarantor requires their neighbours to respect their choice. Argentina claims the Falkland Islands; only action by British armed forces prevented them from exercising that claim in 1982. What was most objectionable, even at the time, was the unilateral nature of action by Buenos Aires. Territories have regularly been transferred by negotiation (the transfer of Hong Kong island, held according to treaty in perpetuity, was just over the horizon at the time of the Falklands War). The only scheme to make the Falkland Islanders more self-supporting financially has been selling licences for fishing illex squid (beloved of Spaniards). Though much trumpeted, oil is a dead end. The world may need new sources of oil during the energy transition, but it does not need to extract that oil from any of the few pristine environments left on the planet. A Falklands oil industry should be ruled out on environmental grounds (the fact that extraction costs are exorbitantly high merely reinforces the case). Forty years after the war and ten years after Lady Thatcher's death, it is time to look again.

In the end, 3,000 people cannot tell sixty-seven million what to do. Their choice costs British taxpayers several hundred million pounds every year. The UK defends the islands as if the threat of invasion continues to be imminent. It is not. Everyone involved seems to have forgotten that Falkland Islanders are not entitled to make demands which they cannot meet themselves; their wishes are a factor, but not the decisive one. Other possible forms of relationship need to be re-examined, models which acknowledge the islands' proximity to Argentina, the lack of contemporary British strategic interests in the South Atlantic, and the fact that resupply of the islands is prohibitively expensive if Argentina is cut out of their supply lines.

Before the Falklands displaced it in 1982, Gibraltar was the OT which excited the most passionate interest among Conservative MPs. At school in the 1970s, my classmates chuckled over a map of the world 'as seen by a Tory MP'; the whole of the Iberian Peninsula was labelled 'Gib'. Gibraltar ceased to be a strategic asset for the UK after the Royal Navy withdrew east of Suez in 1971. Again, 34,000 people cannot dictate to sixty-seven million; they can whip up their friends in Parliament and the press, but everyone else is entitled to look at what the UK gets out of the present arrangement. In the 2020s, supporters of the status quo still confidently make their case. On 27 June 2023, the governor was quoted in *The Times*: 'The importance of Gibraltar is now greater than it has been for forty years, since the end of the Cold War. With a resurgent Russia and an assertive China, its strategic significance as an entry point for the Atlantic and Mediterranean is obvious.' Indeed, but it is significant for the US Sixth Fleet rather than the Royal Navy, which no longer has the assets to respond to Gibraltar's renewed strategic significance.

When the cartographers cracked their joke, Spain was still a fascist dictatorship under General Francisco Franco. But democratic Spain has been the UK's ally since 1982. Gibraltarians no longer need the same protection against their neighbour as they did in the 1970s. Their fear of change has caused Gibraltarians to doubt the helpfulness to them of anyone who might precipitate that change, principally Spaniards and the British Foreign Office. But, in thirty-eight years at the FCO, every official I saw working on Gibraltar embraced Gibraltar's understanding of its own interests; I was a lonely voice. I urge the next British government to consider the case for no longer allowing its Gibraltar policy to be determined on the Rock.

The Sovereign Base Areas are also an anachronism, negotiated between unequal parties at the moment of Cyprus's independence. Sixty-odd years later, the benefit to Cypriots of 2.5 per cent of their territory falling under British sovereignty in perpetuity is unclear. A British offer of negotiations might help unlock talks with the Turks in the North. Years ago, I made a similar suggestion, which sent the Ministry of Defence into a fury. Of course the benefit to them of the status quo is a factor, but it is not the only factor. And in diplomacy it is generally better to deal with a problem when it is still a dot on the horizon rather than wait to be forced to the negotiating table.

In the problematic case of the British Indian Ocean Territory (BIOT), policymakers rely on the lack of public outcry to maintain an unjustified status quo. That status quo is not merely unjustified but has been found to be illegal by the International Court of Justice in The Hague. Of course, you might dislike the judgement (I do), but the UK is a country of law and fulfils legal obligations even when disagreeable. During the period of empire, the UK administered its far-flung territories in the Indian Ocean as one administrative unit. One of the sins against the Fourth Committee at the UN (which deals with decolonisation) is slicing and dicing colonies at the moment of independence. In the 1960s, the UK reckoned that the lack of historical and population links between Mauritius and the

Chagos Archipelago justified their separation. It also separated (a split which has never been challenged) and recognised the independence of the Seychelles and Maldives. Chagos, and more particularly its principal island, Diego Garcia, is valuable real estate. It is almost the antipode of the continental US; from Diego Garcia, the US military can survey all the world it cannot survey from home territory. Americans regularly describe it as their most important overseas base. The US is the UK's tenant there on always renewed long leases. As a matter of urgency (the court ruling is now four years old), Mauritius, the US, and UK need to reach a new agreement.

That process is complicated by the plight of the Chagossians – the islanders, who were forcibly expatriated in the 1950s and 1960s – and their descendants. Most of them settled in Mauritius or Crawley (Sussex), with a smaller community in the Seychelles. They need to be given a stable present (Parliament has only recently given citizenship to those living in the UK) and the basis for a more certain future. It seems to me that the older people among them remember their childhoods with more affection than accuracy; the islands are unlikely to see the significant resettlement that some of their supporters demand. The infrastructure required to sustain twenty-first-century life on tiny atolls thousands of kilometres from the nearest landmass is simply too expensive. The errors of the past cannot bankrupt the present.

All the OTs outside the Mediterranean are suddenly of increased environmental importance. Years ago, policymakers considered pouring concrete to create (in effect) fixed aircraft carriers in strategically important parts of the world. These days, the OTs fit more into the planetary agenda: MPAs already surround Pitcairn, Saint Helena, South Georgia, and the South Sandwich Islands. Extending those MPAs and helping the locals make money out of high-end environmental tourism looks like the most promising future strategy for most OTs. They will not like – but, to repeat, their wishes are not the only factor – a demand from London to move away from some of the financial services their economies have relied upon. Yet the financial services offered in the Cayman Islands, British Virgin Islands, Bermuda, and elsewhere now threaten to damage London's reputation. As the government gets to grips with economic crime, the consequences will unavoidably affect the OTs (the same is true of the Crown Dependencies – the Channel Islands and the Isle of Man).

The OTs cannot remain in the policy pending tray, with only supporters of the status quo speaking up whenever they hit the headlines. Their reluctance to contemplate new constitutional arrangements cannot remain their trump card. In 1967, Anguilla objected to being lumped with Saint Kitts and Nevis as a third island in an associated state prior to independence; the other two islands were remote from it and somewhat larger than it, and Anguillans feared being swamped. But their remaining a part of the UK is increasingly difficult to explain to the people of the UK. The three options that need to be dusted down are: (a) independence, (b) accepting greater guidance from London, and (c) negotiating a closer relationship with the preponderant power in their vicinity.

Official development assistance

The UK has one of the strongest reputations worldwide for providing humanitarian assistance. I saw for myself the pre-positioning of basic provisions and equipment in Kathmandu which had allowed the Department for International Development (DFID) to respond swiftly after the devastating earthquake in Nepal in 2015. However, the decision by Boris Johnson's government in November 2020 to cut ODA from o.7 per cent to o.5 per cent of gross national income has dented the UK's reputation. Spending ever larger amounts of ODA inside the UK is damaging that reputation further. It is not only that ODA is being used to pay for refugee programmes (the Canadians do that), it is how the money is spent – on prison ships and schemes to expel refugees to Rwanda. Only the minister who initiated the policy could claim with a straight face that the spending of ODA is making the lives of refugees better or easier (which is the perception of how money is spent in Canada). The spending of ODA should be a jewel in the overseas-policy crown. It needs to be restored to o.7 per cent.

Human rights

In sharpening the focus of our overseas effort, we should not lose sight of the issues Britons care about. Respect for human rights defines the UK (another spur to looking again at BIOT). I once got into trouble as PUS by saying that the FCO was moving resource away from human rights (we were – ministers had set other priorities which required resourcing). But my point then and now is that human rights is part of core FCO/FCDO work; every officer should have human rights on their mind and in their objectives. Human rights are a network priority, not an issue siloed for a few people to work on full time.

The UK has many human-rights priorities: ministers add to them without rationalising or subtracting. The Preventing Sexual Violence in Conflict Initiative, protecting the freedom of religion or belief, championing twelve years of quality education for girls, campaigning for LGBTQ+ rights, opposing modern slavery, promoting Holocaust awareness and education – all are good and worthy objectives. But running so many campaigns simultaneously dilutes their impact.

That said, I have a proposal for one more, not so much a

campaign but a tool to promote awareness of what makes democracies better than dictatorships. Every year, the FCDO might publish a 'killing index'. From time to time, every state kills its citizens. Some do it deliberately, by executing prisoners or mowing down demonstrators with machine-gun fire. And all states kill people by accident, most often via police officers, prison warders, or others in law enforcement and security. But how many die, and what happens next? Are those responsible held accountable? Are lessons learned? The countries that do most to protect their citizens from accidental or deliberate death at the hands of agents of the state are, I submit, likely to have the best overall human-rights record. Nobody monitors those deaths; I believe that having that information would be good for policymaking.

12

Organisation

Internal

Machinery of government (MoG) changes are massively disruptive to Whitehall; prime ministers know that, and yet none (in office for more than six weeks) can resist them. Despite the stakes, a prime minister is not obliged to listen to their cabinet, even when members get a whiff of what's afoot before it happens. MoG changes are never completely thought-out in advance; even issues as basic as the name of a new department can prove problematic. Tony Blair almost saddled Alan Johnson with a revamped Department for Productivity, Energy, Industry, and Science, which produced the unfortunate acronym 'PEnIS'. Once launched, MoG changes always take longer to bed in than everyone involved hopes.

When Boris Johnson was foreign secretary, he and I discussed how the UK might reorganise its overseas effort. As notionally the government's top diplomat, he was disagreeably aware when travelling that substantial parts of foreign policy were not his responsibility, or even susceptible to his influence. We considered in particular DFID, the Department for International Trade (DIT), and the Department for Exiting the European Union. The existence of the latter was an annoyance to someone who wanted to lead the Brexit negotiation, but it was clearly temporary. DIT also had a time-limited feel, having been created to negotiate as quickly as possible replacement trade deals to kick in as soon as the UK stopped benefiting from EU deals. He focused on DFID and bided his time.

As prime minister, Johnson returned to the issue. In the reshuffle of February 2020, he signalled the direction of travel when all seven junior ministers working for foreign and development secretaries became joint ministers working for both departments. The following June, he announced the departments' merger; the Foreign, Commonwealth and Development Office started business on 2 September 2020. Because preparatory work had been conducted by such a small team (composed entirely of FCO officials), the announcement came as a disagreeable surprise to many officials in DFID.

A few years later, the new department still suffers teething problems, but it is recognisably a new department. Because the overseas effort is merged, the UK has been able to deal swiftly with some of the highest-profile new challenges. Ukraine is the most obvious example: under an ambassador in Kyiv with an extensive aid background, political, security, and development teams and policies are working in harmony. The response to the devastating earthquake in Turkey in February 2023 is another example. But success does not protect the new department. Much of the development community (NGOs, think tanks and charities) remains unhappy with the merger and is working hard to extract a promise from Keir Starmer to de-merge the department if Labour wins the next general election.

I hope (surprise – former FCO PUS writing) that he does not. The merger seeks to increase the coherence and impact of the UK's overseas policy. Too many times between 1997 and 2020, the FCO and DFID had different policies, visible to overseas partners. From the start, the prickly personal relationship between Clare Short (secretary of state for international development, 1997–2003) and Robin Cook (foreign secretary, 1997–2001) set the tone for everyone working for them. Chances to cooperate were consciously avoided. In the early 2000s, the UK rebuilt the High Commission compound in Kampala. Instead of one new building, the two departments ended up with two, their separate approaches solidified in brick.

Development assistance is a vital component of British overseas policy, but, as with any other government spending, it is taxpayers' money; it is not charitable money, subject to different rules. It is legitimate (and I would say necessary) for it to be spent according to British interests. The International Development Act 2002 requires ODA to be spent on the elimination of poverty. Even were that ODA's only use, political judgement would be required to decide exactly which projects in which countries to support (clearly the UK is not going to achieve the epochal objective by itself). But the rules allow other objectives and, as President Zelenskyy has argued, the UK might – in pursuit of its interests – consider expanding those purposes still further.

The importance of ODA could have been better acknowledged in FCDO structures at the start; the explicit objective then was a merger at the genetic level, a total integration, but the skills of diplomatic and development officers are not wholly overlapping circles on a Venn diagram, and they do not need to be. In July 2023, the appointment of a second permanent secretary focused on development went a long way to address the distinctive contribution point.

A country as large as the US can afford (or get away with) sixteen separate agencies working in the overseas policy space. The UK cannot. Even if a new Labour government wanted some detailed changes, I hope it would recognise the basic rationale for the merger, see that it is beginning to pay dividends, and preserve the idea that overseas policy needs to fall under the direction of one cabinet minister (let's call that person the foreign secretary). If, instead, it chose to de-merge, some individuals may be gruntled, but the system would take the whole of a new administration's first term to sort itself out; the UK's effectiveness overseas would suffer as a result.

Trade is the other aspect of overseas policy often combined in other countries with diplomacy and/or development assistance. Under Rishi Sunak, it has found its place in an expanded business department. Let the Department for Business and Trade run for the length of the next Parliament, if not longer; it is at least a configuration that is familiar from the days of the old Department of Trade and Industry to many of the officials working there.

Scotland

I include Scotland under internal organisation because I hope that Scotland will remain part of the UK (but a book with, I hope, a shelf-life of five years must consider other possibilities). Every independence-supporting Scot makes the point that Scotland would be a viable country on the international stage. Indeed. Size is not the critical consideration for whether a country is recognised, but rather legitimacy. If Scotland achieved independence by legally negotiated means, then every member of the UN would welcome Scotland as the UN's 194th member state, starting with the UK (which would retain all the privileges as the successor state because of its overwhelmingly larger size: think Russia and the fourteen other ex-Soviet republics in 1991).

Scots would unarguably be citizens of a smaller country, and although smaller countries exist and even flourish, none is a major international player. Just because it is possible to be a small country does not mean that the status is desirable for its citizens. In a peaceful present, people easily forget the disadvantages of being small. Whether it is desirable to be part of a smaller country should also be part of the debate.

No doubt an independent Scotland would swiftly apply for membership of the EU. First, the Scots would have to overcome resistance to the EU27 accepting an application. Neither Spain nor Slovakia has recognised the independence of Kosovo, which means that Kosovo is highly unlikely to change its relationship with the EU from 'applicant' for membership to officially recognised 'candidate'. The Spaniards and Slovaks dislike, for domestic reasons, the idea of regions benefiting from breaking away from their countries. For Madrid, this is an existential issue: Catalonia is by far the richest province of Spain; if it were no longer contributing to the Spanish exchequer, Spain would be much poorer. By demonstrating that a newly independent status would not include membership of the EU, Madrid sends a strong signal to Barcelona.

Even if Scotland were one day to become a member of the EU, its status would be different from when it was a member as part of the UK. It would have to accept all those parts of the *acquis* – the common rights and obligations of EU member states – from which the UK had negotiated exemptions. It would have to adopt the euro. It would have to be a full member of the Schengen area, and accept all parts of EU justice and home-affairs policies. It would have no rebate on its budgetary contribution. And, with a population of five million, it would be one of the smaller member states.

When I was ambassador at Berlin, I was in the office of the chancellor's foreign-policy adviser when the Chancellery's switchboard called him and asked if he wanted to listen in to Merkel's phone call with an EU leader. I got up to go. He waved me back into my seat, and was evidently embarrassed by his gesture by the end of the call. Before the foreign prime minister came on the line, Merkel asked her advisers why she had to take the call, wondering just what business there was to discuss. Her advisers pointed out that the country was about to take up the rotating presidency of the EU and added that one call would probably suffice for her new colleague's entire period in office. Scotland would be joining the club of such small and less influential states.

Some may not mind that. But in every international negotiation size matters. Whether in Brussels or New York, Scots would overnight go from being citizens of one of the half-dozen main players to one of the bottom-half players. Leaders of such countries find it difficult to defend their national interests – not impossible, just significantly more difficult, and this would be a self-inflicted difficulty.

Most countries, apart from the US and China, are substantially dependent on other countries. The Scots can choose their dependency: either on London (where their voice is loud and influential) or Brussels (where their voice would be neither loud nor influential).

Five final points: first, what is the magic about the administrative unit of Scotland? Scots would be seeking a new arrangement, so it would be legitimate for distinct sub-units to consider their futures separately. Why should the Orkneys and Shetland Islands (with all that oil) automatically prefer rule from Edinburgh (560 km from Lerwick) to rule from London (slightly less than twice the distance)? Why shouldn't London consider offering the Shetland Islanders or Orcadians inducements to remain part of the UK?

Second, who is the electorate? During the 2014 Scottish independence referendum, only people living in Scotland who were in Scotland on referendum day were allowed to vote. But what about people born and raised in Scotland but living (a) elsewhere in the UK (that is, living in another part of the country of their birth) or (b) elsewhere in the world? Moving to a different part of the country does not amount to emigration; it does not seem to me a choice punishable by disenfranchisement.

Brits living overseas, even for decades, have recently been enfranchised in national elections in the UK; surely Scotland moving in the opposite direction needs at least to be debated.

Third, how long a residency in Scotland is required to vote? Should the franchise start at eighteen or sixteen years old, or younger? Should people who are resident but not (yet) citizens be allowed to vote?

Fourth, given that the vote determines Scotland's fundamental place in the world, should a simple majority of those turning up to vote be enough, or a supermajority, or a majority of the entire electorate? Just because a certain set of rules applied in 2014 does not mean the same rules need apply in future.

And fifth, what attitude should the people of the rump UK take should the Scots choose to leave? In the 2014 referendum, Alex Salmond constantly assured 'yes' voters that the rest of the UK would be generous. He cited no evidence to support his assessment. I love my country, all of my country, of which Scotland is an integral part. Some of my ancestors left the Highlands in the middle of the eighteenth century to settle in a different part of the same country. Scotland is part of my identity (though I would play no part in a referendum, just like last time). But if Scots rejected my country, I would feel aggrieved. I would feel similarly to how nationals of the EU27 felt when the UK rejected the EU in 2016.

The vote for independence would be a one-day phenomenon, but the process of separation would not be. If the vote were for independence, that new status could happen only after a protracted negotiation. The Scots should not expect the rest of the UK to do them any favours (and they would want many), and they should not expect a 'quickie divorce'. A union that has been growing and intensifying for over 300 years would take many decades to disentangle. The UK's negotiation to leave the EU would be a model (an unhappy one).

External

Most basically, the UK should maintain its global network of posts. The UK has interests (notably, consular interests) in every part of the globe. Every time we have closed a sovereign post, we have regretted it; when we have returned the locals have been less grateful than we would like (the insult of departure takes time to forget). Presence does not need to mean large presence. The excellence of the head of mission and the adequacy of the resources at their disposal count most. Good ambassadors benefit from a house where they can respectably entertain local dignitaries and a car (preferably of British manufacture) that looks the part. Increasingly, with small teams, they can work out of part of their residence.

The UK is good at preparing its ambassadors for their work. I would propose three tweaks. First, the general fluency of ambassadors in the languages of the countries where they work is higher than in 2015. But it could be better still, which requires more training with an emphasis on media work. These days, nearly all diplomatic negotiations are conducted in English; there is no downside to doing detailed technical work in your mother tongue. But most people consume their news in their own language. Ambassadors will always do better in local media markets if they can speak the local language well enough to respond to the local Jeremy Paxman. A high bar. But UK representatives need to clear that high bar.

Second, having made the investment in training, ambassadors generally need to be left in post for longer than other officers in their mission. Three years is too short; four should be the standard and five should be easily negotiated with the administration in London (the presumption should be that a request for an extension will be accepted). I would not rule out six years, but that is probably long enough. There comes a point where the danger that people forget who they are working for outweighs the benefit of their experience and contacts.

Third, I would allow ambassadors greater discretion in deciding local priorities. Of course, overall direction comes from ministers in London, but ambassadors should have leeway and some resource to develop areas which, in their judgement, look promising locally. I used to say to every new departing head of mission, 'You have the whole bilateral relationship in your hands – don't limit yourself to politics, defence, or commerce.'

On this minimal resource, we can build where necessary. Some posts will always be large. And some will need reinforcing. After the Brexit vote, every sovereign post in Europe was reinforced because bilateral relations everywhere became more important; the tendency to do ever more business through the EU Commission in Brussels was reversed. The FCDO needs to be able to shift resources at the margin, but when there is a secular shift (viz. 2016) more resource from the Treasury will sometimes be necessary.

Since 2016, the FCO/FCDO has re-examined its main networks. Three are promising. First, middle powers that are close to bigger powers – Canada (US); India, Japan, and Australia (China); Turkey (EU). Second, the most like-minded in our neighbourhood: at its smallest, the non-EU North of Europe (Norway and Iceland), plus the rest of the Nordic countries (Denmark, Sweden, and Finland), plus the North Sea and Baltic Sea countries (the Netherlands, Germany, Poland, Lithuania, Latvia, and Estonia). Third, the larger Commonwealth: India, Pakistan, Bangladesh, Australia, New Zealand, Canada, Nigeria, South Africa, and Kenya.

Some of these groups already have structures: the UK is part of Northern Lights meetings (essentially the second grouping). Some have structures of which we are not part, but with which we might become associated: the Quad of Australia, India,

Japan, and the US. Within the Commonwealth, an explicit grouping of the dozen largest member states would be resented by the other forty; the third grouping probably requires a series of more intensive bilateral engagements.

If the UK focuses more on its soft power, the Commonwealth immediately becomes both more interesting and more problematic: more interesting because cultural, educational, legal, and publishing links are already strong across the Commonwealth; more problematic because the imperial legacy might lead partners to think that the UK's objective is 'back to the future', with the UK looking too energetic or wishing to be too dominant. The suspicion that Global Britain was Empire 2.0 did not help its brand acceptance.

13

Conclusions

This book tries to answer one question prompted by two overlapping historical processes: what should the UK do in the world (a) after eighty years of decline and (b) having left the regional organisation that had increasingly become the focus of its overseas efforts in the forty-five years of membership? Nostalgia is a flimsy foundation for policymaking: it may comfort the nostalgic, but it never convinces anyone else. Nostalgic readers will reject the notion of British decline. They make the question more difficult to answer for the UK as a whole: as anyone starting a twelve-step programme knows, the essential first step is acknowledging you have a problem. But their refusal to acknowledge the problem does not make it go away.

In the 1960s, Macmillan concluded that Europe was the answer to Acheson's jibe: having lost its empire, the UK's best chance of continuing to play the role it still wanted to play in the wider world was through the EEC. Many of his compatriots (particularly in his party) were never happy with that answer. In 2016, that unhappy group came to power on the back of the UK's vote to leave the EU (the EEC's successor from 1993). After a fraught negotiation that could never have achieved what the government wanted (preserving the benefits of membership, which they liked, without paying the price, which they did not), the UK left the EU on 31 January 2020.

Changing the UK's relationship with its neighbourhood makes the challenge of dealing with the decline in hard power even more difficult. The next British government will face that challenge. It will not be obliged to tackle it; no inside or outside force will oblige the UK to come up with a convincing answer. Inertia, drift, and complacency are the default options for any foreign policymaker. The world is not demanding a British role. The chair of the House of Commons Foreign Affairs Committee might ask where the British plan for peace in the Middle East is, but no one in the Middle East will. The world does not need a British initiative on anything at all any more. The same can be said about almost all players (including the EU and Russia); the only unarguable exception is the US, still the world's mightiest single power. The absence of interest or action from Washington can be a material factor.

The two key questions for the UK are: does the UK still seek a role in the world? And is the world better off if the UK plays an active role? The first gets relatively little attention, the assumption across centuries being 'yes'. The evidence is that the UK continues to be willing to devote significant resource to acting on the international stage; the most obvious example is the number of military deployments undertaken by British armed forces since the Second World War. With thirty-two such deployments, the UK has been more active militarily than any other European country.

The world is the UK's oyster. A. C. Benson wrote the lyrics to 'Land of Hope and Glory' in 1902, but its sentiments still seem valid: 'Wider still and wider shall thy bounds be set.' To be a force for good in the world is the UK's insatiable appetite. The Treaty of Paris, which ended the Seven Years' War, gave Britain an empire on which the sun never set, and in the twenty-first century (courtesy of OTs in the Atlantic, Pacific, and Indian Oceans) that remains the case. British territory beyond the British Isles on which the sun is always shining has diminished (to an area slightly smaller than Wales), but the UK's view of the importance of its role has not.

I assume that the UK will want to continue to play a global role. So, what is the best content of that role for the answer to the second question also to be 'yes'? The answer is soft power, the power of persuasion and attraction. Some politicians dislike the notion of soft power because much of it is not controlled by ministers; indeed, ministerial decisions are as likely to hinder as help its effectiveness. Soft power often works best when the government gets out of the way.

British soft power is a blend of principles, practice, and aspiration. Elements are shared with many countries but, because the UK is globally networked, the British blend is uniquely effective. Lack of domestic appreciation of the British blend partly explains why it is under threat. Traditionally, British politicians have treated their opponents with respect and seen them socially. The fact that two red lines still feature on the floor of the chamber of the House of Commons is a reminder that that was not always the case: opponents had to be kept more than two sword-lengths apart. In times past, in both the House of Commons and the House of Lords, the dining room had a long table at which any member wanting to eat would simply take the next vacant seat. Meeting over a meal, you see someone at their best advantage; you understand them better and respect them more. The Commons has abandoned the tradition; these days MPs eat in their party groups, and they are worse off as a consequence.

Opponents also used to deal with each other regularly during general-election campaigns. Candidates were grilled at hustings. They held events together in school and village halls, where voters could ask questions. The rise of social media has put paid to most such events. I hope we cling to what remains.

I was in Washington in 1997 when Labour won its landslide victory. The embassy threw a party; the time difference with London meant that most guests were still around when the most exciting results came through (Enfield!). One Massachusetts congressman was intrigued by the phenomenon of acting returning officers announcing the breakdown of votes cast with all candidates ranged behind them, generally on a stage that was slightly too small for the purpose. When the result was declared, the winner shook hands warmly with everyone else. The congressman remarked that in twenty years in federal politics he had still to meet any of his opponents.

Those at the top of the British system also used not to behave as if 'winner takes all'. They were conscious of being custodians, knowledgeable about what went before, and respectful of their successors' room for manoeuvre. They recognised the lack of wisdom in changing the system in ways they would not want their opponents to exploit, should they replace them in government. Now the feeling is that ministers must do as much as possible in as short a time as possible, and it must be so thoroughgoing that opponents (if ever returned to power) would find it impossible to unpick later. Moderation, proceeding in stages, going the whole hog only after concept is proven, are all out of fashion.

Although the British blend is under threat, it is resilient and coming through a time of turbulence. In 2022, the House of Commons disposed of two prime ministers in short order. Parliament had not seen such political drama in living memory. A friend's uncle came up with the insight (known in his family as Sweet's Law) that whenever you think you have hit rock bottom, things inevitably get worse. But the system proved comfortably up to the task of removing leaders who had shown, for different reasons, that they were incapable of fulfilling the duties of head of government.

I know some commentators argue that 'soft power without

hard power is, frankly, no power at all';[60] I heard Lord Hintze make that point in his maiden speech in the House of Lords. I disagree. Ireland, for example, has massive soft power – just ask President Biden to explain the influences that shaped him, or visit Chicago, New York, Scranton, San Francisco, or Washington on St Patrick's Day – but it has no hard power. Meeting Hintze partway, it is true that the UK has more soft power because it also has hard power.

Hard power, like sovereignty, is not what it used to be. At bottom, hard power is about coercion, about making people do or accept what they do not want to do or accept. Amassing an empire is the ultimate expression of hard power. But these days ordinary people have more agency. Until the majority of their populations lived in cities, rulers could rely on their subjects doing as they were told. Religion helped: a force for conservatism, its priests taught their followers to respect established rulers. Peasants did not always knuckle down and accept the role assigned to them, but the Pastoureaux (1251 and 1320), Peasants' Revolt (1381), and German Peasants' War (1524–5) were all short-lived: the rural poor ran riot for a time, killing some of and spooking all of their overlords, but the revolts burned out as quickly as they had begun.

The disparity between rulers and ruled continued in the early colonies: the outsiders had access to more advanced technology, and the diseases they imported proved more fatal to the locals than the diseases the locals exported to Europe (although syphilis took over 400 years to treat effectively). Greater knowledge, better organisation, and, supremely, more lethal weaponry gave colonialists the edge. The number of Britons in India never exceeded 150,000, yet they were able to control 300 million locals. The Sepoy Rebellion in 1857 warned the outsiders that this could not last, yet independence was not achieved for another ninety years.

The US, the most powerful country to see itself as a former colony, led demands for self-determination as it framed its peace demands, having joined the First World War. Nine of President Woodrow Wilson's Fourteen Points were about the evacuation of territory, the changing of borders, independence for peoples previously part of empires, and the adjustment of colonial claims, 'based upon a strict observance of the principle that in determining all such questions of sovereignty the interests of the populations concerned must have equal weight with the equitable claims of the government whose title is to be determined'.[61]

Since the Second World War, all of Europe's overseas empires have been dismantled, except for a score of British-, Dutch-, and French-controlled islands (plus French Guiana, on the mainland of South America), whose populations are too small, too vulnerable, and/or too reluctant to contemplate independence. President Putin may think he can reverse the phenomenon, but eighty years of history suggests he cannot: once it has established its sense of separate identity, a population will not willingly submit to renewed outside control. As long as external help is forthcoming, that willingness has so far proved more durable than the will of would-be conquerors.

The Americans led huge coalitions in the conflicts in Iraq and Afghanistan, and yet the international forces were not able to impose their will. For most countries, no cause outside their borders is worth sending their young to die for. In my most optimistic scenario, the war in Ukraine is the last gasp of one country trying to absorb another against its will. Everywhere, the locals are the key actors determining their own fate. At the same time, the world has not suddenly become peaceful; unresolved border disputes can still flare into open conflict in Africa, Asia, and Europe. And varieties of civil war rage or fester in a dozen countries: most armed conflict these days is internal.

The UK can be a significant player in the issues it cares about – the three mega-challenges – principally as a wielder of soft power, acting in partnership. It is a common human failing to downplay the importance of our strengths. For some British traditionalists, soft power is too pallid or inchoate to count. If they looked more closely, they would see the benefits of the power of attraction, of setting an example that others want to adopt or adapt for themselves; they would also see the link between soft and hard power. To generate more than a fuzzy friendly feeling in onlookers, the most effective soft power must be underpinned by hard power. Hard power is an essential ingredient, one that doesn't overwhelm others but whose absence makes all the difference – like yeast in a loaf of bread.

These days, Beijing is interested in the UK as much for the soft power that still eludes China as for the UK's residual hard power. The Chinese are fascinated by the 'Magnificent Seven', even though some British ministers would prefer the UK to be less attractive to outsiders. One proof of British soft power is the desperation of some refugees to come to the UK. Ignoring the expensive nastiness of present government policy, potential immigrants focus on a longer tradition of openness to help people in dire need. Merely by standing up to speak, Alf Dubs – one of the children rescued by Nicholas Winton in 1939 – reminds us that there is a better way. Fundamental to reaching a better, more effective policy will be greater cooperation with our EU neighbours. They face similar problems; common problems are generally best tackled together.

I once worked for a boss who would disappear into his private bathroom each morning to arrange his remaining hair over his bald pate. Clearly the view in the mirror satisfied him that he looked as if he had a full head of hair. The UK military has had a 'comb-over' approach to its capabilities for decades. From a certain angle, military leaders hope to convince the world that they have a full complement of kit; despite the capacity of middle-aged men to convince themselves of things they know not to be true, they must know that the people they care about (the UK's main allies and main opponents) know different. It is time to face up to the more threadbare truth.

Maintaining defence spending is vital: the world is a dangerous place. But that money need not be thinly spread, as it is now. A UK restructuring its military away from nuclear, away from aircraft carriers, away from expeditionary forces would be a different international player, unfamiliar to itself at first. But it would be a UK that could concentrate on what it does best, on the defence of the homeland and NATO allies against the threats they are most likely to face, and on areas where it has most to offer the rest of the world – the Magnificent Seven, discussed in Chapter 10.

Historically, previously great powers have found it difficult to sustain a role commanding wide attention when a different power has displaced them. The UK would be trying something new, a military and diplomatic evolution. Such an evolution eluded Spain after 17 September 1665, but natural history offers hope. For many years, four blocks of sediment donated by a local amateur palaeontologist lay undisturbed in the Dutch museum to which he had donated them. In late 2018, Daniel Field of Christ's College detected a skull within one block. Less than two years later, his resulting research paper described a key link between dinosaurs and birds; he named the 'wonder-chicken' *Asteriornis*, after the Titan Asteria. To escape Zeus's unwelcome advances, Asteria transformed herself first into a quail and then into an island, where Apollo was born.

Reinvention can lead to even greater things. *Asteriornis* gave dinosaurs an afterlife. Soft power can give imperial Britain a diplomatic afterlife. As a model for how a country in the twenty-first century can order itself, acknowledging its imperfections, striving always to address them, and so being a better global citizen, the UK can persuasively answer Acheson.

Part of the model might be a new attitude to economic growth. In common with most Western countries, the UK has striven to maximise economic growth for as long as anyone can remember. Economists in the 1970s flirted with the idea that there might be limits to growth, but new inventions and new discoveries of raw materials allayed that fear for a time. But, in the end, the Earth is a closed system. With eight billion people on the planet striving for greater material prosperity (and the prospect of an extra three billion joining them before the end of the century), we might look more seriously at our economic priorities.

I wrote the second half of this book in Cuba, in the middle of an energy crisis. At the petrol stations that had fuel, long lines of cars (latter-day Ladas and American old-timers) stretched for over a kilometre (in queues with gaps – so no one could capture the disarray in a single photo). My wife Olivia and I were driven from Havana to Varadero and back, along a quiet dual carriageway with almost as many pony-and-traps as buses. Cubans are poor, bored, and politically oppressed; the young and ambitious leave in droves. And yet social solidarity is high, crime low, drugs almost non-existent, the streets safe, and the education system strong. It is easy to understand why collectively they resist America, just ninety kilometres to the north. Would a highway clogged with traffic, white goods that are habitually replaced rather than repaired, and drug lords exploiting rising material prosperity really be progress? Cuba can teach as well as be taught. Other economic models that do not rely on financial services and attracting dodgy foreign cash must be studied, especially as we get serious about the planetary agenda.

Reaching the end of my only book about foreign policy, I

return to the importance of partnership. These days the UK can do almost nothing of consequence to others by itself (only the US and China can). I have argued that, logically and realistically, the only short-term option the UK has, having left the EU, is to double down on the relationship with the US. And yet that does not feel like a robust medium-term option: the disparity in size will not shift in the UK's favour; the US is changing in ways that will make it more difficult for the UK quickly or automatically to rally to its new causes. If at some point American hostility towards China becomes aggression, the UK must retain the room for manoeuvre to go its separate way. We can try out creative new groupings; the middle powers look promising. And yet, ineluctably, our neighbourhood once again presents itself as the best long-term option. History matters most, and geography matters almost as much: if they audit their own interests, the countries that share our continent, our values, and our interest in tackling the megachallenges will, before my children are my age, want us back. If they are wise, they will give us the same membership terms we had before we left.

For four years, I led a team of civil servants in the FCO that contributed to a Whitehall-wide effort to get the best possible deal from Brussels. Two years after the full provisions of that deal kicked in, it is clear that it is not functioning well from the UK's point of view. The UK is not a big enough player to set its own standards with the rest of the world happy to trade with us on that basis. Trade with the EU is more difficult, and trade with everywhere else has not become appreciably easier. But still for many the possibility that Brexit is bad for the British economy is an unthinkable thought.

The UK has complicated its relationship with its neighbourhood but will survive well enough. To flourish, the UK will need, even in the short term, a more constructive relationship with Brussels. Under Prime Minister Sunak, the UK has begun this process. In the next decade, I predict that those in power discover that even Sunak's Windsor Framework – which replaced Johnson's Northern Ireland Protocol for dealing with goods moving between the European single market and Northern Ireland – does not work well enough from the UK's point of view. To do everything we want to do, to give ourselves the best chance to lick the three mega-challenges, we need a much closer relationship with the EU.

All parties may agree that talk of rejoining remains premature, but the idea should not be dismissed. Brexit supporters believe leaving was right in principle; they contend that the problem was with its execution, and they do not recognise the possibility that Brexit could never be satisfactorily negotiated. That attitude will take time to change. The UK can, no doubt, flourish well enough outside the EU but, as Macmillan recognised, Europe is the UK's best option if it wants to maximise prosperity and influence. Whether the EU would want us back is an unanswered question. But, in the longer term, our mutual interest may lead both sides to conclude that the UK and Europe would be better off with the UK inside the EU.

Experts' reputation has taken a public pasting in the UK in recent years, and I am setting myself up, as a former PUS at the FCO, as an expert. All I ask is that readers take a look at the case I make before rejecting it. I hope they follow the advice offered by the only Nobel Prize winner for medicine I have ever entertained for dinner. The main guest at one of the first big meals I presided over at Christ's was Martin Evans, laureate in 2007. Unfairly (without warning him), I drew heavily on his example in my after-dinner speech. He demanded the right of reply, and gave the students a single ringing piece of advice: 'Don't believe anything anyone tells you until you have checked its truth for yourself.'[62] Precisely.

Abbreviations

AI	Artificial intelligence
APEC	Asia-Pacific Economic Cooperation
BIOT	British Indian Ocean Territory
CASD	Continuous at sea deterrent
CCP	Chinese Communist Party
COP	Conference of the Parties (to the UN Framework Convention on Climate Change)
DFID	Department for International Development
DG	Director general (the second most senior civil-service rank after permanent secretary)
DIT	Department for International Trade
ECOWAS	Economic Community of West African States
EEAS	European External Action Service
EEC	European Economic Community (Common Market)
EP	European Parliament
FCDO	Foreign, Commonwealth and Development Office (which replaced the FCO in September 2020)
FCO	Foreign and Commonwealth Office
G7	Group of 7 (Canada, France, Germany, Italy, Japan, UK, US plus EU)
G8	Group of 8 (G7 members, plus Russia)
G20	Group of 20 (G8 members, plus Argentina, Australia, Brazil, China, India, Indonesia, Mexico, Saudi Arabia, South Africa, South Korea, and Turkey)

GPT	Generative pre-trained transformer
LLM	Large language model
MoG	Machinery of government
MPA	Marine protected area
NATO	North Atlantic Treaty Organization
NGO	Non-governmental organisation
NSC	National Security Council
NSS	National Security Strategy
ODA	Official development assistance
OT	Overseas Territory (one of the last fourteen remnants of the British Empire)
P5	The five permanent members of the UN Security Council
PUS	Permanent under-secretary of state
SCO	Shanghai Cooperation Organisation
UEFA	Union of European Football Associations
UN	United Nations
USSR	Union of Soviet Socialist Republics

Notes

1   Lynch, J, *Spain under the Habsburgs* (1981), vol. 2, page 14

2   Trevor-Roper, H. R., *Spain and Europe 1598–1621*, The New Cambridge Modern History, vol. IV, p. 269

3   British and Foreign State Papers 1849 – 1850, Vol. XXXIX, pp 333 – 334

4   Asey, E. *The Life of John Temple, Viscount Palmerston 1846–1865* (1876), vol. 1, pp 183 – 184

5   Hansard CXII [3rd Ser.], 380–444

6   Ibid.

7   HC Deb 01 March 1848 vol 97 cc66-123

8   Peter Hennessy, *Winds of Change: Britain in the Early Sixties* (2019), 181.

9   Quoted in Douglas Brinkley, *Dean Acheson and the "Special Relationship": The West Point Speech of December 1962*, in The Historical Journal, 33:3 (Sept 1990). The letter is among Acheson's papers at Yale: Series 1, box 28, folder 359. In a letter of 31 January 1963, Acheson reacted to a clipping from the Sunday Telegraph, containing Selwyn Lloyd's commentary, sent to him by Schlesinger.

10 Catterall, Macmillan Diaries, 1957 – 1966, Vol. 2, p 523

11 Quoted from 'Hitler Made Same Error Says Mr Macmillan', Daily Telegraph 8 December 1962

12 Lord Hailsham quoted in The Daily Mirror, 13 December

1962, 'The Friends Who Stamp on Britain'
13 'New Power Rising', *The Spectator*, 14 December 1962.
14 'Acheson', *The Economist*, 15 December 1962.
15 I am quoting what Lord Renwick said in my presence when I worked for him in Washington.
16 Statement issued by Andrew Mitchell on the FCDO website, 26 July 2023.
17 HMS Swallow, ship's log
18 Proceedings of the National Academy of Sciences, reported by the BBC, 16 May 2017
19 Boris Johnson first mentioned 'Global Britain' to me the evening he became foreign secretary (13 July 2016)
20 Le Journal du Dimanche, 23 October 2022 (translation on Twitter)
21 Lewis Carroll, *Alice Through The Looking Glass*
22 Catherine Cookson took part in a pro-EEC broadcast on 30 May 1975
23 Reported in Financial Times, 3 June 2016
24 Relayed to me by Philip Hammond who was reporting reaction of foreign businessmen to the Brexit negotiations
25 Nestor the Chronicler's description of the travellers' reaction to Hagia Sophia
26 Lord Robertson of Port Ellen's speech in House of Lords, Hansard, vol. 819, 10.48am, 25 February 2022
27 Angela Merkel quoted in 'Merkel' (Netflix, 2023)
28 McCain quoted in an interview with Candy Crowley on 'State of the Union', CNN, 16 March 2014
29 President Zelenskyy speaking in Westminster Hall, 8 February 2023
30 Michael Howard, *Clausewitz: A Very Short Introduction*, p 76
31 Interview given by Putin to Megyn Kelly on CBS News' 'TODAY', March 2018

32 George Macartney, *An Account of Ireland in 1773 by a Late Chief Secretary of that Kingdom*, p55.; cited in Kevin Kenny's *Ireland and the British Empire*, p72

33 Alain Peyrefitte, *The Immobile Empire*, p 84

34 Stephen R. Platt, *Imperial Twilight*

35 Qianlong Letter to George III (1792), University of California, Santa Barbara

36 ibid

37 Quoted in Allen S. Whiting, Chinese Nationalism and Foreign Policy after Deng, The China Quarterly

38 From a speech by Xi Jinping at the National People's Congress in 2023

39 Barry O'Meara, *Napoleon in Exile or A Voice from St Helena*, 1822, vol. 1, 26 March 1817, p 472

40 ibid

41 'China signs 99-year lease on Sri Lanka's Hambantota port', Financial Times, 11 December 2017

42 2001: A Space Odyssey (1968), screenplay by Stanley Kubrick and Arthur C. Clarke

43 ibid

44 Gordon Moore was interviewed by Rachel Courtland for IEEE Spectrum: Special Report, 30 March 2015

45 See Eric Schmidt's interview with Ylli Bajraktari, CEO of the Special Competitive Studies Project, The Mystery Ahead of US for Mankind, scsp222.substack.com 6 April 2023

46 'On the Dangers of Stochastic Parrots: Can Language Models Be Too Big?', 2021

47 Schmidt, Interview with Ylli Bajraktari

48 Archive of Jesus College, Cambridge

49 Dad's Army, Series 6, Episode 1, 'The Deadly Attachment' written by Jimmy Perry and David Croft

50 *The Times*, Monday 19 September 2022

51 P G Wodehouse, *The Man Upstairs*, 1914
52 Observation made to me by the German diplomat Markus Ederer.
53 Richard Sharp's resignation statement, https://www.bbc.co.uk/news/uk-65421992
54 'The Crown', Season 3, Episode 2, 'Margaretology', 2019, written by Peter Morgan, Jonathan Wilson, Jon Brittain
55 Brandon Lewis, Hansard Volume 679, 8 September 2020, Northern Ireland Protocol: UK Legal Obligations
56 The United Kingdom's future nuclear deterrent: the 2021 update to Parliament, published 16 December 2021
57 Lord Palmerston, House of Commons, 1 March 1848
58 Christopher Meyer, *DC Confidential*, 2005
59 An anonymous US administration official quoted by Luke McGee, CNN, 9 July 2023
60 From the maiden speech of Lord Hintze, Hansard Volume 827, 26 January 2023
61 From point 5 of President Woodrow Wilson's Fourteen Points, 1918
62 A translation of the Royal Society's motto: 'Nullius in verba'.

Index